EXTRAORDINARY MEASURES

EXTRAORDINARY
MEASURES

Afrocentric Modernism
and Twentieth-Century
American Poetry

LORENZO THOMAS

THE UNIVERSITY OF ALABAMA PRESS   Tuscaloosa and London

2 3 4 5 6 7 8 9 . 07 06 05 04 03 02 01

Designer: Michele Myatt Quinn
Typeface: Stone Sans, Stone Serif

Cover illustration: Aaron Douglas, *Study for mural in Dallas, Texas* (1936). Courtesy the African American Museum, Dallas, Texas.

∞

The paper on which this book is printed meets the minimum requirements of American National Standard for Information Science–Permanence of Paper for Printed Library Materials, ANSI Z39.48-1984.

Library of Congress Cataloging-in-Publication Data

Thomas, Lorenzo, 1944–
     Extraordinary measures : Afrocentric modernism and twentieth-century American poetry / Lorenzo Thomas.
     p. cm. — (Modern and contemporary poetics)
Includes bibliographical references (p.) and index.
ISBN 0-8173-1014-2 (alk. paper)
ISBN 0-8173-1015-0 (pbk. : alk. paper)
1. American poetry—Afro-American authors—History and criticism. 2. American poetry—20th century—History and criticism. 3. Modernism (Literature)—United States. 4. American poetry—African influences. 5. Afro-Americans in literature.
I. Title. II. Series.
PS310.N4T48 2000
811'.509896073—dc21
                                                   99-6833

British Library Cataloguing-in-Publication Data available

To my mother, Luzmilda Gilling Thomas;
and for the future:
Joanna, Rhamis,
Rochelle and Roderick,
and Jamal.

Contents

Illustrations

Acknowledgments

"I dream a world / and then what," asks Harryette Mullen in her book-length poem *Muse and Drudge*. The fact is that dreams, and plans, need time and work before they come to anything. A work written as an ongoing project over several years accumulates a debt to others that can hardly be repaid simply by publishing the book. There are many people, therefore, who deserve my personal word of thanks for helping this project along at crucial moments. This work has profited from thought-provoking questions posed by Susan Stanford Friedman, Aldon Nielsen, and Eleanor Withington; constructive comments from Charles Bernstein and Hank Lazer; and a lively conversation with Jerry W. Ward, Jr., that has continued for two decades. The friendship, wisdom, and enthusiastic encouragement of Stephen Stepanchev must also be counted part of this book's genesis.

I have certainly enjoyed the intellectual encouragement and comity offered by my colleagues at University of Houston–Downtown, especially Susan Ahern, Barbara Bartholomew, B. Christiana Birchak, Michael Dressman, and William Gilbert, some of whom also helped assure that institutional support for travel was generously provided by my department. A grant from the university's Organized Research program was specifically useful in preparing the manuscript, and a fellowship from the National Endowment for the Arts several years ago facilitated research that is incorporated here.

Earlier versions of some chapters have been presented as papers to the Modern Language Association, the South Central Modern Language Association, the American Studies Association, and the Middle Atlantic Writers Association, and I deeply appreciate the generous, directive comments of many colleagues offered as a result of those occasions. Parts of this book have also appeared in print in *Callaloo: A Journal of African and African American Arts and Letters;* the special issue of *Nimrod* entitled "New Black Writing"; *Close Listening: Poetry and the Performed Word* (Oxford University Press), edited by Charles Bernstein; and *An Area of Act* (University of Illinois Press), edited by Aldon Lynn Nielsen. Grateful acknowledgment is given to these editors and publishers. The epilogue benefited greatly from responses to earlier versions from colleagues attending the Southern Conference in African American Studies and the "Black Liberation in the Americas" conference sponsored by the international Collegium for African American Research—held respectively in Houston and at Westfälische-Wilhelms Universität in Münster, Germany—in the spring of 1999.

My work has also benefited from the excellent collections and helpful staff members at the University of Houston libraries, the Fondren Library at Rice University, the Atlanta–Fulton County Public Library, the Columbia University Library, the magnificent Boston Public Library, the Harry Ransom Humanities Research Center at the University of Texas at Austin, the Heartman Collection of the Texas Southern University Library, and —from those late summer afternoons when Ernest Kaiser first opened its treasures to me until the present—the New York Public Library's peerless Schomburg Center for Research in Black Culture.

I am grateful also to Curtis Clark and the staff of The University of Alabama Press and to Jonathan Berry and Karen Luik for their enthusiastic and conscientious assistance in preparing the manuscript and index.

Some of the ideas in this book will, to those who know, certainly reveal my indebtedness to a quietly intellectual couple who met each other as members of a literary workshop: my father—a young man who avidly read the works of J. A. Rogers as they appeared—and my mother, a young woman raised in the UNIA who, she tells me now, went to the movies almost every day after school. No less do I owe thanks to my brother, Cecilio Thomas, an artist who carries an archive of cultural history in his head—and also knows how to put his hands on any specific book or piece of paper. Similarly, Doris Lang's support and patience could never be repaid. If this book fulfills the ambitions that I have for it, much of the credit belongs to all of these true friends; if there are shortcomings or errors, the blame is mine alone.

Permissions

Thanks are gratefully extended to the following publishers and individuals for permission to quote from copyrighted materials:

Works by Alvin Aubert quoted by permission of the author.

Works by Amiri Baraka quoted by permission of the author and Sterling Lord Literistic.

Works from *Joker, Joker, Deuce* by Paul Beatty, copyright © 1994 by Paul Beatty. Used by permission of Viking Penguin.

"Geography of the Brain" and "Sanctuary" by Donald Davidson from *Poems 1922–1961,* copyright © 1966. Used by permission of University of Minnesota Press.

Works by Tom Dent quoted by permission of Walter J. Dent, administrator of the Estate of Tom Dent.

"Starchild" by Thomas Sayers Ellis, copyright © 1999 by Thomas Sayers Ellis, quoted by permission of the author.

"A Dollar's Worth of Blood, Please" by Kenneth Fearing from *Complete Poems* edited by Robert M. Ryley, copyright © 1994. Quoted by permission of National Poetry Foundation.

Works by David Henderson from *De Mayor of Harlem,* copyright © 1970 by David Henderson; and *Neo-California,* copyright © 1998 by David Henderson, quoted by permission of the author.

Works by Calvin C. Hernton quoted by permission of the author.

Quotations from *Arcade* by Erica Hunt, copyright © 1996 by Kelsey Street Press. Used by permission.

Quotations from *The Weather That Kills* by Patricia Spears Jones, copyright © 1995 by Coffee House Press. Used by permission.

"Bob Kaufman Reading at Vesuvio's" by Kaye McDonough, from *Umbra/Latin Soul,* ed. David Henderson, copyright © 1974 by Society of Umbra. Used by permission.

Works by Harryette Mullen quoted by permission of the author and Singing Horse Press.

Quotations from *Where a Nickel Costs a Dime* by Willie Perdomo, copyright © 1997 by Willie Perdomo. Used by permission of W. W. Norton.

EXTRAORDINARY MEASURES

Introduction

The subtle analytical powers that enable a poet to comment on life seldom guide her ambition—which, presentation copy in hand, hastens toward any presumably literate being.

Thus Phillis Wheatley's *Poems on Various Subjects, Religious and Moral* (1773) reached Thomas Jefferson's desk. He did mention the book in his writings but not in a way that would have pleased the poet. When Jefferson assessed the intelligence of slaves in Query XIV of *Notes on the State of Virginia* (1787), he surely knew that the argument he felt required to make was untenable, yet he blundered along, presenting a catalogue of increasingly ridiculous illustrations intended to demonstrate the innate inferiority of Africans. Regarding the blacks' possibilities for intellectual development, Jefferson comments: "Most of them indeed have been confined to tillage, to their own homes, and their own society: yet many have been so situated, that they might have availed themselves of the conversation of their masters; many have been brought up to the handicraft arts, and from that circumstance have always been associated with whites" (Lauter and others I, 903).

The slaves, Jefferson suggests, should have benefited from such advantages. "But never yet," he reports, "could I find that a black had uttered a thought above the level of plain narration; never see even an elementary trait of painting or sculpture" (Lauter I, 903). The idea that cooks and butlers might find time to pursue the arts is not entirely fantastic, but the suggestion that they would be expected to contribute to the master's witty table talk does seem a bit disingenuous. Regarding Wheatley's work, Jefferson chose to be mischievously droll: "Misery is often the parent of the most affecting touches in poetry.—Among the blacks is misery enough, God knows, but no poetry." Wheatley's poems, he concludes, "are below the dignity of criticism" (Lauter and others I, 903–904).

Whether or not Jefferson was a sincere racist, it would have been surprising indeed if the militantly secularist sage of Monticello had endorsed Wheatley's "To the University at Cambridge":

> Students, to you 'tis giv'n to scan the heights
> Above, to traverse the ethereal space
> And mark the systems of revolving worlds.
> Still more, ye sons of science ye receive
> The blissful news by messengers from heav'n
> How *Jesus'* blood for your redemption flows.
> (Lauter and others I, 1060)

At the end of this address to the brilliant young men of Harvard, Wheatley transforms conventional neoclassical modesty with a switch. Providing moral instruction to her "betters," enjoining the scholars to avoid error, Wheatley arrogantly adds, "An *Ethiop* tells you," in a tone of officious mockery that has been used with stinging effectiveness by black women ever since.

Despite the cruel disdain of readers like Mr. Jefferson, Phillis Wheatley suffered no inferiority complex regarding either her status as a slave and devout Christian or her mastery of the neoclassical poetics of her time. As the very first serious American poet of African parentage, Wheatley can be compared quite favorably with Philip Freneau, and she was certainly a better poet than Timothy Dwight or Jefferson's protégé Joel Barlow. As Richard Wright noted with some sarcasm, Phillis Wheatley "was at one with her culture" (78). In the period of the American Revolution, Wright explained, "Slavery had not yet cast its black shadow completely over the American scene, and the minds of white people were not so warped at that time as they are now regarding the capacities of the Negro. Hence, the Wheatley family was quite free of inhibitions about educating Phyllis [*sic*]; they proceeded to educate her in the so-called classical manner; that is, she got the kind of education that the white girls of her time received" (*White Man, Listen!* 78). When Wright made these comments in 1957, he echoed Wheatley's best-known (and most controversial) poem and also employed Wheatley's own highly developed manner of ironic "signifyin'." The brilliant couplet that concludes "On Being Brought from Africa to America" (1773) convinces one that Wheatley, as James A. Levernier has pointed out, requires more than superficial readings. The usual interpretation, based on the poem's grammatical structure, is:

> Remember Christians // Negroes, black as Cain,
> May be refin'd and join th' angelic train.
> (Lauter and others I, 1058)

While this reading may be permissible, it may also be a mistake. Depending upon where you place the caesura, Wheatley may be not simply addressing her readers as Christians but rather making a list of all those who (according to John 3:16) may be saved:

> Remember [dear reader] // Christians
> Negroes
> [sinners such] as Cain

All of these individuals can be redeemed by Wheatley's Christ. The fact that the poem clearly suggests *both* readings makes a single reading inadequate.

Contemporary readers who feel comfortable seeking affinities of gender and color may be disposed to recognize kinship between Wheatley and the extraordinary linguistic magic of Harryette Mullen's *Muse and Drudge* (1995):

> stop running from the gift
> slow down to catch up with it
> knots mend the string quilt
> of kente stripped when kin split
> (Henning 10)

These lines acknowledge the African presence still felt by an African American poet of the 1990s. We may understand that Phillis Wheatley had mastered the ironic skills of the poetic style commanded by Alexander Pope (who also got short shrift from Thomas Jefferson), but we should not overlook the influence on Mullen's work of Gertrude Stein, Oulipo word games, and an African American vernacular that—for its own reasons—has carefully cultivated the same sort of double-coded understatement that Phillis Wheatley explored in formal eighteenth-century English. As Bob Perelman has noted in another context, sociology (which *is* necessary to the reading of African American literature) can sometimes "obliterate the complexities of the writing" (*Marginalization of Poetry* 127). And as I have suggested, sociology can also sometimes highlight these complexities.

In other words, understanding African American poetry of any era requires an ability to hear "the whole voice." This literature does more than merely provide a convenient database for sociologists (though at least one early anthology was conceived with such a purpose in mind). Besides the obvious demonstration of poetic competence, Phillis Wheatley's story offers at least two other important lessons. First, of course, is the fact that African American poetry is as old as the nation itself. Second, America's racial attitudes exhibit the same longevity.

Other African American poets have suffered the same sort of blatantly dismissive reception that Jefferson accorded Wheatley. In a recent article, David Jarraway notes that Langston Hughes was held in similarly low esteem by his own editors at Knopf. While the staff behaved like rock 'n' roll groupies when Wallace Stevens dropped in, one editor recalled: "Hardly anybody cared about Hughes. As far as I am concerned, he wrote baby poetry, poor stuff. If we had to go out to do lunch with him, say to a French restaurant in mid-town, it was kind of embarrassing. He was a nice enough guy, but you couldn't get around the race thing" (Jarraway 820). This anecdote is annoying for several reasons quite apart from any consideration of the language or manners that diners are required to display at New York City's French restaurants. Jarraway is understandably disgusted by the denigration of a poet who has occupied so much of his own intellectual activity, but even he seems to miss the point. If it had been possible—through some Wellsian tinkering with space and time—for the same editor to have been asked to lunch with the dauntingly intellectual Melvin B. Tolson, there would *still* have been the "problem" of the man's race.

Indeed, Tolson himself suffers from "the race thing" precisely because of his demanding intellectuality. As Michael Bérubé shows in *Marginal Forces/Cultural Centers* (1992), Tolson's aspiration to canonicity is often viewed as unnatural (165–167). Denying to Tolson what would be assumed for any white American poet who began publishing in the 1930s, critics have often viewed Tolson's employment (and mastery) of the Modernist idiom as an "appropriation" rather than an inheritance (189). While not necessarily isolated from the "mainstream" literary scene, African American writers have always faced the problem of how to join in a discourse that, like Mr. Jefferson's table talk, has usually ignored their presence on the scene.

But the truth, as Jefferson was well aware, is that African Americans are not aliens here but sharers and shapers of what has come to be American culture. African American individuals who have avoided the psychological dysfunction that Du Bois diagnosed as double consciousness have done so by understanding this truth and by knowing, as well, who they are.

From the moment of Phillis Wheatley's self-identification as an African to the present day, there has been a rich and energetic Afrocentric tradition in American poetry that attained a powerful and variegated expression in the twentieth century. I want my meaning to be clear, however. "Afrocentric" does not mean "African" anymore than "Eurocentric" means "European." Both words indicate a cultural frame of reference regarding history. Notwithstanding the polemical intentions of those who have made both words elements of political controversy, the coinages are closer in structure to the word "egocentric" than to "heliocentric." An Afrocentric perspective, natural to some Americans, remains a possible alternative for others; as Amiri Baraka put it in *Home: Social Essays* (1966), though we might be looking at the same thing, "the view from the top of the hill is different than the view from the bottom of the hill" (171).

American writers, since the appearance of de Crèvecoeur's *Letters from an American Farmer* in 1782, have tried to demolish Eurocentricity and to enlist us in the adventure of creating an American perspective. Afrocentricity, a corrective offered by those who suffered most from Eurocentrism, has a similarly early appearance in Wheatley and in David Walker's *Appeal* (1830), an African American journalist's rebuttal of the racial slurs included in Query XIV of Jefferson's *Notes on the State of Virginia*. Addressing "the colored citizens of the world," Walker declared, "You have to prove to the Americans and the world, that we are MEN, and not *brutes,* as we have been represented, and by millions treated" (50). To the extent that misrepresentation of Africa and Africans helped justify or rationalize slavery, and provided the foundation for subsequent social and economic oppression, the Afrocentric view balances the equation and discredits the assumptions that fuel racism. One could argue that Afrocentricity should yield in the face of the same quite reasonable arguments that have been aimed against the Eurocentric perspective. It is important for us to understand, however, that while we have all been quite thoroughly trained in Eurocentrism, the countervailing view has been just as carefully marginalized. Nevertheless, the debate has continued and attention to Afrocentricity's salient critique—most eloquently presented in African American art, music, and literature—can only be enlightening. It brings light out of darkness.

To appreciate properly the artistry of contemporary African American poets, we must trace the history of the themes, motifs, and poetic techniques that they employ—and we must relate these to a larger literary and social discourse.

The term "Modernism," a logical name for twentieth-century art and literature, also resonates with complex connotations. If nothing else, the emergence of communications increasingly dependent upon electricity—from high-speed newspaper printing presses to automobiles to motion pictures and radio—separated the culture of this century from that of earlier eras. But what was perceived as technological progress necessarily provoked a crisis of social and personal values, a sense that the gulf between this age and the past, while welcome, demanded a bridge.

At the risk of oversimplification, one might say that the major objective of Modernism was repeal of the nineteenth century. Steven Watts has usefully suggested that, in addition to attacking genteel bourgeois values, early Modernist art in the United States "sought to recombine the elements of human experience strictly separated by Victorianism" and did so by questioning the binarism that defined "civilized and savage, reason and emotion, intellect and instinct" (87). The younger African American artists of the Harlem Renaissance—two generations removed from any experience of slavery, most of them from a middle-class background—nevertheless understood that their investment in Modernism was rendered problematic by race as well as by class issues and by aesthetic theory.

When used today by the likes of Newt Gingrich, the word "civilization" is meaningless, but one need only reread Ezra Pound's "Hugh Selwyn Mauberley" (1920) and Countee Cullen's "Heritage" (1925) to see how central an issue civilization actually was—central to matters as diverse as international politics, efforts to manage or uplift the urban poor, the manners of a commercial society, and intellectuals' growing interest in Freudian psychoanalysis. In this context the Modernist interest in "primitive art" reveals some disturbing elements. A willingness to go to school to wisdom, wherever found, is admirable. But the idea that the art of the sophisticated metropolis might be revitalized by an infusion of energy from more instinctual (that is, less "civilized") peoples often comes uncomfortably close to replicating the exploitation of the same peoples by modern capitalism. On another level, the concerns expressed by Pound and Cullen are central to George Wells Parker's challenging essay "The African Origin of the Grecian Civilization." Published in the *Journal of Negro History* in 1917, Parker's work anticipates the stance taken by the prolific J. A. Rogers, George G. M. James's *Stolen Legacy* (1954), and Martin Bernal's *Black Athena* (1991) in questioning the Eurocentric version of world history. As Houston A. Baker, Jr., has pointed out, Modernism's "acceptance of radical uncertainty" must be measured against the extent to which ideas of white supremacy, anxious or complacent, constituted nineteenth-century authoritarianism (*Modernism and the Harlem Renaissance* 3–5).

At the turn of the century, Edmund C. Stedman, editor of *An American Anthology: 1787–1900,* found the state of the art so dismal that he characterized the last quarter of the nineteenth century as "the twilight era" of American poetry. A rising generation of poets, critics, and readers vociferously agreed. Louis Untermeyer's *The New Era in American Poetry* (1919) pronounced Stedman's anthology a "gargantuan collection of mediocrity and moralizing," finding fewer than 100 of the book's 900 pages worth reading (9). Untermeyer and his peers thought it was time for a new era. So, for the same and different reasons, did young African American intellectuals—the best educated of whom would create the vibrant Harlem Renaissance of the 1920s. This movement established an authentic presence in American literature as well as a sense of autonomy. The Harlem Renaissance artists were concerned with complex issues of politics and aesthetics, of presentation and representation. In his avant-garde manifesto "The Negro Artist and the Racial Mountain," Langston Hughes called for art that would "cause the smug Negro middle class to turn from their white, respectable, ordinary books and papers to catch a glimmer of their own beauty. We younger Negro artists who create now intend to express our individual dark-skinned selves without fear or shame. If white people are pleased we are glad. If they are not, it doesn't matter" (95). It is worth noting that this 1926 manifesto appeared in the *Nation*. The engine supplying the power for Hughes's manifesto, and for the Renaissance itself, was the political struggle for recognition of the black American's rights as a citizen and for an end to the system of social and economic segregation that denied these rights. If such a goal appears quixotic today, we should remember that the system of segregation was not institutionalized until the 1880s, with most of the local and state anti-Negro legislation being firmly established between 1905 and the beginning of the First World War.

Though the depression marked the end of the most active phase of the Harlem Renaissance, the campaign for social justice continued unabated throughout the 1930s and the years of World War II. This campaign found a voice in the works of poets such as Margaret Walker, Owen Dodson, and Melvin B. Tolson. The Black Arts movement of the 1960s paralleled the Harlem Renaissance and saw its role as completing the unfinished business of the 1920s. The movement was a self-conscious response to Hughes's question "What happens to a dream deferred?"

The answer was that it *does* explode—but like a star, not like a bomb—sending out pulsars of its galactic energy in all directions. As Aldon Lynn Nielsen has pointed out, the advent of the Black Arts movement in the mid-1960s revealed "a nationwide convergence of innovative poets whose formal accomplishments were a break from the conventions of their predecessors but whose breaks with convention must be read in the dynamic context of the writings that preceded theirs" (*Black Chant* 43). The present collection of essays seeks to reconstruct this context and to demonstrate that the African American poetry of our moment is fruit that took a century to develop.

The work of the writers studied here, American poets with a sensitive awareness of their African heritage, is informed by their personal and passionate confrontation with what critic Clyde Taylor has succinctly termed "the selective humanism and partial enlightenment of European expansion" (305). These poets are, in other words, variously involved in the currents of Modernism by both artistic inclination and historical necessity. Also important for understanding this rich vein of American literature is the realization that, even had black poets wished to create within the pristine seclusion of a "dark tower," their color made it impossible for them to avoid involvement in the turbulent racial politics of the United States. These writers, as Maria K. Mootry noted regarding Gwendolyn Brooks, maintained "a fundamental commitment to both the modernist aesthetics of art and the common ideal of social justice" (1). My discussion will concern itself in particular with how such a commitment could often be problematic. The creative activity of African American writers, of course, also paralleled, influenced, and responded to social and artistic developments in the national "mainstream" culture. This fact, largely ignored in "standard" American literary history (and in many myopic discussions of the African American community), affords a point of departure for *Extraordinary Measures: Afrocentric Modernism and Twentieth-Century American Poetry*.

PART ONE

The Matrix of Modernism

1

Fenton Johnson

The High Cost of Militance

At the dawn of the twentieth century, the most celebrated black writer in the United States was twenty-seven-year-old Paul
Laurence Dunbar. A best-selling poet, Dunbar had also written songs
for hit Broadway musicals and short stories that regularly appeared in
magazines such as *Harper's* and the *Atlantic Monthly*. He was as popular
with white Americans as Bill Cosby is today and just as beloved by the
African American community.

Dunbar's lyrics in the formal tradition were more than competent.
He understood—as some of his critics, then and now, did not—that the
huge popularity of his poems in Negro dialect resulted from his ability
to transmit slightly different messages to black readers and white readers simultaneously. Though the writers of the Harlem Renaissance in
the 1920s worked to diminish his reputation, Dunbar created the model
for twentieth-century African American poetry. Yet as race relations
continued to deteriorate after Dunbar's death in 1906, younger writers
understood that a much more militant race consciousness than his
would be required. They could not guess, however, what such militance
would cost.

The story of one of the era's most promising young intellectuals not
only offers a unique (and usually overlooked) perspective on the early
development of Modernism but also reveals how perilous is the path to
Parnassós for a black American poet.

Fenton Johnson (1888–1958), poet and editor, is recalled mostly, by
Arna Bontemps and others, as a tired old writer who settled into a
lonely desk at the Federal Writers Project in Chicago, where he may

have passed on some words of wisdom to a young and energetic Richard Wright. Between 1912 and 1925, however, Johnson was actively involved in both Harriet Monroe's New Poetry movement and the militant black nationalist network that preceded the Garvey movement.

Fenton Johnson's poem "Tired" (1919) profoundly disturbed editor James Weldon Johnson, who in *The Book of American Negro Poetry* (1931) noted its "disillusionment and bitterness" and the attitude that "there is nothing left to fight or even hope for." The lines of the poem are often quoted:

> I am tired of work: I am tired of building up
> somebody else's civilization.
> (*Others for 1919* 77)

Johnson's ironic statement, anticipating Aimé Césaire's *Cahier d'un retour au pays natal* (1939), is the expression of a constructive negativity shared by militant writers, such as Cyril Valentine Briggs, George Wells Parker, and J. A. Rogers, who were committed to exposing white supremacist distortions of world history—described, in Johnson's memorable words, as "somebody else's civilization." As Parker wrote in *The Children of the Sun* (1918), "Today there is not a single book printed in the English language that [shows] the African race as the real founder of human civilization" (4).

James P. Hutchinson, carefully reviewing Fenton Johnson's three published volumes of dialect and conventional lyrics, concluded that "Tired" and other poems that are frequently anthologized are "not typical of Johnson's body of poetry. The reason for their critical popularity seems to be both their divergence from the body of Johnson's insipid poetry and their true ring of emotion and theme" (15). In *Black American Writing from the Nadir* (1989), the insightful Dickson D. Bruce agrees that Johnson was "not really a radical poet, either stylistically or in terms of his main themes and images [but] nevertheless took pains to put his work in a black cultural context" (226). In fact, a close examination of Fenton Johnson's journalistic career between 1916 and 1921 places him squarely in the black cultural nationalist milieu and may help to illuminate the race consciousness that informs much of his poetry regardless of the poetic fashion he decided to employ.

"The choice of becoming a black intellectual," wrote Cornel West in 1985, "is an act of self-imposed marginality; it assures a peripheral status in and to the black community" (110). Seventy years earlier, however, such a view would have seemed unthinkable. In the early years of the century, black people had advanced from 90 percent illiteracy at the end of the Civil War to 80 percent literacy, and black intellectuals saw that they played a central role in guiding and informing the community. The new level of literacy suggested to a number of them, including Fenton Johnson, that the community needed a race-conscious press that would, as Johnson stated in the first issue of the *Champion Magazine,* "impress upon the world that it is not a disgrace to be a Negro, but a privilege" (5).

Robert E. Park commented on the unusually strong sense of solidarity in the black community during World War I and concluded that "race consciousness is the natural and inevitable reaction to race prejudice" (294). Sociologist W. O. Brown, however, offered an even more normative definition. Race consciousness was not an angry response, a social aberration, or deviant behavior, but "merely another form of group consciousness, serving the same purpose and playing the same role in the life of the individual that any other type of group consciousness does." Of course, for a group that perceived itself as oppressed, "race consciousness takes on a wider meaning and importance" than would other indexes of membership or allegiance (Brown 97). In *The Betrayal of the Negro* (1965), historian Rayford W. Logan described the decades before World War I as the nadir of American race relations, a period marked by a dramatic increase in lynchings and official government hostility toward black citizens. In Houston, Texas, for example, the first segregation ordinances were enacted in 1907 and incrementally expanded until 1922, and as Aldon Lynn Nielsen shows in his important book *Reading Race* (1988), even the avant-garde literary world in this era sometimes reflected not only a lack of sensitivity but also overt anti-Negro sentiment. Artists, like the majority of their fellow Americans, were locked into an unregenerate white supremacist worldview (Nielsen, *Reading* 31–39).

African American race consciousness found its proper calling in the correction of a version of world history that had been seriously and deliberately skewed to suit the purposes of white racism and European colonial expansion into Africa and Asia. An indication of the important—indeed central—place accorded such corrective literature among black intellectuals at that moment may be found in the January 1916 inaugural issue of the *Journal of Negro History.* Tuskegee professor Monroe N. Work contributed an essay documenting the achievements of Africans from the smelting of iron to ancient Egypt's dynasties, the medieval University of Sankore at Timbuktu, and modern accomplishments in the African diaspora. "Of these facts," he stated, "most modern historians know but little and Negroes in general almost nothing" (34; McMurry 90).

Work, of course, made it clear that such knowledge is crucial. "From it," he wrote, "we can draw inspiration" (41). As Work's essay suggests, African American race consciousness in this era had two major components. The theme of ancient African glory was a counterargument advanced to combat derogatory racist stereotypes, but it also supported a contemporary mission. The missionary impulse constituted a fundamental element of the Afrocentric position and was clearly expressed by Edward Wilmot Blyden in his essay "The African Problem and the Method of its Solution" (1890). Blyden praised the American Colonization Society—an organization instrumental in the establishment of Liberia as a refuge for emancipated slaves—as "first of all the associations in this country to have distinctly recognized the hand of God in the history of the Negro race in America—[the first] to have caught something of the Divine purpose in permitting their exile to and bondage in this land" (45). As Blyden saw it, God's purpose in submitting his people to epic trial was to prepare a generation of educated African Americans for service as "the chosen instrument" of the African continent's twentieth-century redemption and modernization (48). Blyden, born in St. Thomas in 1832, had emigrated to Liberia in 1850 and was an ordained minister, but by the time of his 1890 lecture tour in the United States, his concept of African redemption was intended to be understood as more political and anticolonial than mystical. The concept finds echoes in the writings of Frederick Douglass and W. E. B. Du Bois, among others. In the Sunday sermons of the black church, the same message was customarily interwoven with exhortations for local and personal efforts toward self-determination. This activist component of African American cultural nationalism envisioned great future contributions to world civilization (as if to balance those of antiquity) and, as David Levering Lewis has suggested, remained an engine of subsequent movements for civil rights and civic assimilation (Lewis, "Shortcuts" 96). Race consciousness, then, historically generated strategies ranging from assimilationist programs to projects advocating emigration. Above all else, however, it remained an attempt to define and maintain one's chosen identity.

Fenton Johnson's poetry explores the elements of identity in the way that we expect from the genre, but his activities as editor of the *Champion Magazine,* and later the *Favorite Magazine,* exemplify a type of

1. Fenton Johnson, ca. 1915.

race consciousness that sought to promote "brotherhood of the races" based on mutual respect (*Champion* 169). In spite of his recent obscurity, Johnson's sincere and sometimes desperate efforts toward this goal afford an instructive and fascinating glimpse into American literary history.

Born to middle-class parents in Chicago on 7 May 1888, Fenton Johnson was the nephew of John "Mushmouth" Johnson, a well-connected figure in the city's cabaret business. Perhaps as a result of this kinship, and in line with his own precocious self-assurance, Fenton enjoyed a range of associations that cut across lines of class. He attended the University of Chicago and Northwestern University and studied for a year at Columbia University's School of Journalism in New York. He also taught for a year at the Kentucky State University of Louisville, a college whose enrollment at the time was exclusively black. Johnson was attracted to a literary career quite early. He published his first poem in a Chicago newspaper at age twelve and by his college years was writing plays that were performed at Robert Mott's Pekin Theatre, a popular Chicago nightclub and concert hall.

Johnson's plays have apparently been lost, but the venue is interesting. In July 1905 Charles Marshall, the critic for the *Indianapolis Freeman,* described the Pekin Theatre as *the* place to go in Chicago. Marshall praised Joe Jordan's "superb orchestra" and noted "a well dressed audience, a beautiful, well-lighted, well-ventilated theatre," and a balcony for "those who wish to see and hear well" (Sampson, *The Ghost Walks* 346–347). Of the actors associated with the Pekin resident theater company between 1907 and 1909, the best remembered is Charles Gilpin, who achieved national acclaim in 1920 as the star of Eugene O'Neill's *Emperor Jones* (Wells 294; Brawley, *The Negro Genius* 287–288). Fenton Johnson's dramatic programs must have been ambitious productions, for according to the *Freeman's* critic, "there is never a dull act at the Pekin" (Sampson 346–347).

Although he was dour in his later years, Johnson seems to have been sociable in his youth. His parents were comfortable enough financially to own their home and gave Fenton a car when he was in college. Close associates included his cousin Henry Binga Dismond, also an aspiring poet and popular athlete, who—in 1918—was among the select few African American college graduates chosen for officer training with the army's Eighth Illinois Regiment at Camp Des Moines. Both Johnson and Dismond were active in the Alpha Phi Alpha fraternity (Major and Saunders 326, 330–335, 337). Johnson was the more intellectual of the two, more talented and more ambitious as a poet; but Dismond eventually became a prominent and wealthy dentist in Harlem.

The young pair's uncle, Jesse Binga, was known as a man who was strictly about business. He established the Binga State Bank in 1908, but his wealth did not gain him acceptance in the upper echelons of Chicago's African American society. In those rarefied genteel circles it was widely rumored that Binga's good fortune—and his bank's—depended on his brother-in-law's money. Worse, John "Mushmouth" Johnson's affluence and considerable political influence were alleged to derive from his position as head of the city's illegal "numbers" racket (Drake and

Cayton II, 465; Major and Saunders 304). While Jesse Binga earned a reputation as a shrewd businessman, his behavior as a banker also reflected race-conscious civic concern. As historian Christopher Robert Reed notes, Binga "invested heavily in his own community, especially in real estate mortgages, which enabled many blacks to become first-time homeowners" (60). When the depression forced the Binga State Bank to close in 1930, W. E. B. Du Bois pointed out that, as far as the white bankers and officials of the government's Federal Reserve System were concerned, "Binga was not the kind of man whom they wanted to [see] succeed [because] he represented the self-assertive Negro, and was even at times rough and dictatorial" ("Binga" 425).

If the tightening grip of segregation was making life for black folks more difficult in the South, during the first decade of the century a city like Chicago seemed full of bright promise—especially for a confident young man like Fenton Johnson. Proudly encouraging the ambitions of Johnson and his peers, Johnson's community declared that these young people were, in fact, something new under the sun. Though Johnson had been active as a poet, he did not begin his journalistic career until 1916. Pleased to shoulder his responsibilities as one of the race's college-educated youth, his first editorial stated his objectives in optimistic terms: "*The Champion Magazine* comes out of the wilderness with the aim to make racial life during this twentieth century a life worth living. America cannot accomplish her purpose so long as her peoples remain unassimilated. The Negro, due to a prejudice born of politics and the spirit of slavery, has remained alien, and will remain alien so long as his problems are placed in the hands of propagandists" ("The Champion Magazine" 5). In place of political propaganda, the *Champion Magazine* spoke of "reconciliation of the races," which would be achieved through an effort "to lift up the spirit of the Negro so that he may be able to realize that he is a force in world achievement" (5). The underlying reasoning, of course, was that if the black race could recognize its own true worth, others would be obliged to acknowledge it as well.

The *Champion Magazine,* which lasted for eight monthly issues in 1916 and 1917, was an energetic and intelligent journal that must be counted as an important expression of twentieth-century black nationalist race consciousness. Modeled in format and content on W. E. B. Du Bois's *Crisis,* Fenton Johnson's journal included contributions from such notables as the historian George W. Ellis, Alice Dunbar-Nelson,

2. *Champion Magazine*, January 1917. The design of
the magazine was modern, but the image of the Sphinx
alerted readers to the journal's place in an Afrocentric
tradition.

William Pickens, Joseph Seamon Cotter, Sr., Robert T. Greener, Georgia
Douglas Johnson, and Benjamin Brawley. Chicago contributors and staff
members included Binga Dismond (who edited a section on sports), poets
Eulalia Y. Osby and W. H. Hendrickson, and Hiram Holland. William H.
Ferris, later an editor of *Negro World,* the Universal Negro Improvement
Association (UNIA) newspaper, served for a time as associate editor.

Indeed, the tone of the journal was set by Johnson with a great deal
of guidance from Ferris. Through Johnson, relations with the *Crisis* were
cordial and reciprocal, while Sudanese journalist Duse Mohamed's Fleet

Street headquarters in London functioned (probably through Ferris's efforts) as the magazine's foreign office. Ferris supplied the magazine's contact with an international network of black nationalists, one result of which was Marcus Garvey's article "West Indies in the Mirror of Truth." This essay, published in the January 1917 issue of the *Champion Magazine,* was Garvey's first appearance in print in the United States.

Armed with degrees from both Harvard and Yale, the erudite Ferris was an effective and experienced networker. A member of Alexander Crummell's American Negro Academy, he also kept in close contact with militant journalist John Edward Bruce and bibliophile Arthur A. Schomburg. Ferris offered aggressive support to Du Bois in his turn-of-the-century debate with Booker T. Washington on the merits of liberal education, had attended the meetings of the Niagara movement, and wrote the two-volume work *The African Abroad* (1913), which—like the works of J. A. Rogers in more recent years—attempted, using history, to refute racist propaganda about black inferiority (Ferris II, 863–866; Hill I, 526 n. 75; Moss 127–128). How the *Champion Magazine* helped maintain and extend Ferris's network is evident from an article on Duse Mohamed's *African Times and Orient Review* (April 1917), from an interesting critical reevaluation of poet Phillis Wheatley that serves to boost Schomburg (February 1917), and from the contributions of Schomburg and Monroe N. Work (in April 1917 and October 1916, respectively). Though Ferris left Chicago to join Garvey's *Negro World*, *Champion Magazine* showed his influence throughout its life.

Champion Magazine was funded by Jesse Binga and established its offices in buildings he owned. In addition, there is evidence that Binga sometimes intervened in its management. Binga, who was viewed by some as "a man who always drives a hard bargain," regarded himself as a business partner rather than as a patron of the arts (Cantey 352). On 11 December 1916 the publishing company was incorporated, with Binga as president and his wife, Eudora Johnson Binga, as secretary-treasurer. By March 1917, possibly because of the magazine's fiscal sluggishness, Fenton Johnson no longer appeared as editor on the masthead, although he continued to be a major contributing writer.

By seeing how one major news event was handled in the *Champion* and other journals, we can better understand the ideological perspective of the militant black press. Militant race consciousness was not, for example, incompatible with Earl E. Thorpe's analysis that black Americans' "political and social faith has been the traditional faith in America and they speedily and unhesitatingly have risen to the colors when the nation was imperiled by war" (xix). In 1916 the United States was not yet involved in the great European war, but the president found work for his generals in small international firefights. In one case, things got seriously out of hand.

Carrizal is a little town about eighty miles south of El Paso. The Texas Rangers made a brief foray into the area in 1879 during the Tenth Cavalry's pursuit of the Apache leader Victorio. Not much else is recorded as having happened there until General John J. Pershing's 1916 Punitive Expedition, an exercise that sent the Tenth Cavalry's famed "Buffalo Soldiers" across the Rio Grande in an attempt to arrest Pancho Villa. Before it was over, President Woodrow Wilson had mobilized the National Guard and had massed 50,000 troops on the Texas border. An incident at Carrizal pushed the nation to the brink of war. Given the pervasiveness of white supremacist attitudes, the incident was all but inevitable. At the time "gringo" arrogance was common among white American officers in the field. One of them, Lieutenant George S. Patton, Jr., ordered a Villista officer who had been killed in action lashed to the bumper of his Dodge touring car, thereby treating the body as if it were a hunting trophy (Leckie 214; Braddy 58; Vanderwood and Samponaro 188).

The Carrizal disaster occurred on 20 June 1916 after Captain Charles T. Boyd, on a reconnaissance mission with his fifty-one black troopers and another thirty-six-man patrol, was denied passage through the town by Mexican General Félix U. Gomez, commander of a 400-man garrison force. Boyd defiantly dismounted his troopers and ordered them to advance across an open plain—straight into the Federales' machine gun fire.

"The 'little battle' of Carrizal," wrote Haldeen Braddy, "was in actuality the most humiliating defeat suffered in the entire course of the Punitive Expedition" (56). Of the ninety men and officers of Troops C and K of the Tenth Cavalry, half were killed, wounded, or taken prisoner (Vanderwood and Samponaro 191; Braddy 48–53).

The news of Carrizal exploded in the militant black press. The *Crisis*, for example, printed reports about the incident for four months. In August, it offered a sobering summation:

Carrizal was a glory for the Mexicans who dared to defend their country from invasion and for Negro troops who went singing to their death. And the greater glory was the glory of the black

men, for Mexicans died for a land they love, while Negroes sang
for a country that despises, cheats and lynches them.

Even across the sunlit desert as they died came the last shriek
of a human bon-fire in Texas where Southern "gentlemen" and
"ladies" capered in glee. ("Carrizal" 165)

The reference to the lynching in Waco, Texas, was supplemented by
details in another part of the magazine.

Fenton Johnson's editorial "Review of 1916" in the January 1917 issue of the *Champion Magazine* pursued the theme of glory and race redemption through individual self-sacrifice that can be found in many
of his poems and short stories: "The American Negro astonished his
public by displaying at Carrizal the most remarkable heroism since the
charge of the Light Brigade. The hearts of the North and the South
melted toward those who laid down their lives in the interest of their
fairer brother and an administration noted for its hostility to colored
races. The martyrdom of Carrizal was the happiest stroke in the calen-
dar of Negro achievement. The hour of racial reconciliation was brought
nearer" (237). Incongruous as it may appear, there is no irony lurking
here. In the December 1916 issue Johnson had run a cartoon by E. C.
Shelton titled "The Negro: 'Those Are My Achievements.'" It depicted
an Egyptian mason standing with mallet and chisel before a stele that
bears the usual expected list of African achievements. Here, however,
following TUSKEGEE and THE A. M. E. CHURCH, is the bold inscrip-
tion CARRIZAL (168).

A variant on the theme of bloody redemption appears in Johnson's
story "The Call of the Patriot," published in the *Crisis* in February
1917. The protagonist is a militant black professor at a southern college
who forms his male students into a self-defense militia to prevent
lynchings yet dies heroically at the hands of a white mob. Indeed, martyrdom is the point of the short story. As Professor Garrison Simpson
expires, a young southern white woman, who had been his classmate
at the University of Chicago, implores: "When you go before the God
of both races, entreat Him to remove this prejudice that is gnawing the
heart of society" (173). One can only be thankful, for the sake of the
race, that some black folks have always been able to talk with God without doing it face to face.

The theme of martial martyrdom actually appears even before Carrizal in an important poem included in Johnson's 1915 volume *Visions
of the Dusk*. "Soldiers of the Dusk" is an eloquent and perfectly control-

led poem commenting on the deployment of colonial African troops in the European War. Johnson salutes "Black men holding up the earth," fighting to help the colonizers survive each other, and notes the irony of this endeavor:

Zulu, robbed of land and home
For the robber bares his heart
(147)

The poem concludes with the assurance that the patent injustice of the situation cannot go unnoticed:

But the God of Calvary
Will in years unborn be just
To the men who died for men,
Victims of the war god's lust.
(148)

What remains interesting about this poem is that, while these soldiers are characterized as "victims" rather than "heroes," they have still gained a moral superiority as a result of their sacrifice. The poem documents a general consensus among race-conscious nationalists as early as the autumn of 1914, explicitly stated in the *Journal of Negro History* in 1918. A reviewer of Sir Harry Johnston's *The Black Man's Part in the War* wrote: "Taking into consideration that the United Kingdom now rules 50,000,000 of Africans who are well represented in the battle line by the thousands of Negroes fighting to make democracy safe in the world of the white man, from which they are excluded, this sympathetic writer here endeavors to give these soldiers of color credit for their unselfish services" (331).

The differences (or similarities) between the experiences of the African troops and the Buffalo Soldiers at Carrizal tested Johnson's faith in white Americans' ability to embrace the moral reconciliation that he believed to be the solution to race prejudice. Some daily newspapers, in fact, printed letters cruelly belittling the Tenth Cavalry's loyalty. Still, Johnson's deep concern about the incident is significant. Indeed, the search for a metaphor that would communicate his hopeful theme— despite so much evidence to the contrary in newspaper dispatches—informs Johnson's early poetry.

The volume entitled *A Little Dreaming* (1912), Johnson's first collection, shows him to be a gifted apprentice with a sensitive ear. There are poems in the dialect style of Paul Laurence Dunbar and in standard English traditional stanzas. The racial content of these poems, however, reflects the accepted stereotypes of the day. In "The Ethiopian's Song" there is the joyous abandon of a being free in nature:

> All the earth is slave to me
> All the orbs are merry chimes.
> White man longs to rule the world
> I am happy where I am,—
> I, the Lord of sweet content.
> (*A Little Dreaming* 37)

A companion poem, "The Mulatto's Song," strikes a predictably tragic note:

> I am like a prince of France,—
>> Like a prince whose noble sires
> Have been robbed of heritage;
> I am phantom derelict,
> Drifting on a flaming sea.
> (38)

A much more successful inquiry into the peculiarities of race in the United States is "To an Afro-American Maiden." Here Johnson calls upon "Proud America to nurture one / Who has robbed the ages of their store, / Races three within her bosom strive" and

> within the face of one whose race
> Dwells exiled throughout this western land,
> Comes in fancy all the days long dead
> As tho' painted by a master hand;
> Rich old Ethiop and Greece are there
> In the swarthy skin and dreamy eye,
> And the red man of the forest grants
> Raven hair and figure tow'ring high.
> (54)

The woman's beauty, then, is a gift of her multiracial ancestry. This is a simple fact, even if the "color-line" mentality of white Americans would make it a political issue. A similar, much less accomplished poem reinforces Johnson's point of view. In "My Love," the poet issues a challenge:

> Young gallant from the fairer race of men,
> > Have you a love as comely as the maid
> To whom I chant my lyre-strung passion songs?
> (*A Little Dreaming* 240)

He boasts that

> Her face is golden like the setting sun
> Her teeth as white as January's snow
> Her smile is like a gleam from Paradise
> ("My Love" 240)

What is noticeable in this poem, however, is the absence of any specifically African physiognomy among the lady's attributes.

As suggested earlier, poems included in *Visions of the Dusk* (1915) reveal a more developed race consciousness or political maturity. In his introduction to *Songs of the Soil* (1916), Johnson balances the usual Afrocentric view of precolonial African splendor with an ironic acknowledgment of cultural assimilation in the United States. Although the black man experienced slavery as his "epic hour," his history represents "a wealth of buried tradition": "Builder of empires that have crumbled and enslaved during the age of pirates and adventurers, he has taken his place in the greatest of republics as a peasant and menial. He has preserved none of his traditions, but has added to what we call Americanism his droll racial instincts" (*Songs of the Soil* i). The process of cultural assimilation, then, operates in two directions. For Johnson, poetry is a means both of exploring the buried African traditions and of understanding the American culture that has been created precisely *because* of the presence of Africans in America. Johnson set an ambitious goal for his poetry.

The best poems in *Songs of the Soil* are those that abandon dialect while attempting to explore the more authentic form of the Negro spiritual. As Johnson notes, "the barbaric splendor of those songs are lost in the dialect of the plantation. To clothe a Negro hymn with dialect is like writing the ancient Hebrew psalms in the Yiddish of the Ghetto" (iv). A poem such as "Song of the Whirlwind" does not imitate the vernacular language of the spirituals but instead quietly elevates the form and replicates the process by which the "black and unknown bards" of the antebellum era recast the Bible in their own lyrical vocabulary:

Oh, my God is in the whirlwind,
I am walking in the valley
Lift me up, O Shining Father
To the glory of the heavens,
I have seen a thousand troubles
On the journey men call living
(*Norton Anthology* 926)

Here Johnson echoes the beautiful "Soon I Will Be Done" without mocking its sincere simplicity: he captures the mood of the old spiritual in a vocabulary suited to his own era.

Similarly, "The Lonely Mother (A Negro Spiritual)" presents a stunningly beautiful lyric that speaks simultaneously of the Christian pietà and of any mother separated from her child. Most interestingly, the persona becomes the medium for the voice of one who shall bring comfort to all such women:

Row, O mighty Angel, down the twilight
Row until I find a lonely woman,
Swaying long beneath a tree of cypress,
Swaying for her son who walks in sorrow.
(*Songs of the Soil* 9)

In their precise and marvelous music these lines rival those of Ezra Pound, and it seems not at all farfetched to imagine that Johnson's poem—with its wonderful conflation of biblical passion and deep South landscape (cypress :: sorrow)—might have influenced Jean Toomer's songs in *Cane* (1923).

Among the volume's poems in standard English, "Harlem: The Black City" is interesting in the way it echoes Dunbar's novel *Sport of the Gods* (1902) and prefigures some of Claude McKay's sonnets. Although New York was then welcoming what Gilbert Osofsky called "the migration of the Talented Tenth"—gifted, ambitious, and educated people such as Fenton Johnson himself—the poet charges that the city offers a bad bargain:

We live and die, and what we reap
Is merely chaff from life's storehouse

Harlem, like the great cities of the Bible and ancient fable, can only distract and destroy its visitors and inhabitants:

We ask for life, men give us wine,
We ask for rest, men give us death
(6)

The contemporary critical response to these poems was gratifying to
Johnson and, for us, reveals much about the diverse cultural investiga-
tions and fascinations that would shape Modernist poetry in the United
States. Favorably commenting on *Songs of the Soil,* Alice Corbin Henderson suggested that the African American writer should move beyond
the conventions of literary dialect in order to

> invent a new and individual idiom based upon the characteristic
> speech of his people. And I would also recommend that all negro
> poets make a study of their folk-songs, collecting all they can, for
> it is through such songs that they will learn to know their own
> race. (159)

By the time this review appeared, in the June 1917 issue of *Poetry,*
Johnson had long ago been moving in that direction.

Perhaps *Songs of the Soil* can be understood as a necessary clearing of
the throat, a last glance at dialect verse that allows Johnson to proceed
with the experiments that would yield his best poetry. Until 1915
Johnson had been publishing poems in African American magazines
including the *Crisis* and Boston's *Citizen,* edited by Charles P. Lane with
George W. Ellis and William Stanley Braithwaite as associates. Johnson
did not, however, feel that the appeal of his work was limited to readers
of these journals. Indeed, the publication of *Songs of the Soil* seemed to
invigorate Johnson and to open a wide vista of opportunities. One of
the journals receptive to Johnson's efforts was Harriet Monroe's *Poetry:
A Magazine of Verse.*

So much critical attention is devoted to *Poetry's* place in the history
of high Modernism that we tend to overlook the magazine's role in promoting what Mary Austin called "the resident genius" of the American
continent, something that she and others believed could be found in
folk culture (Cronyn xxviii). The February 1917 issue of *Poetry,* for example, featured "interpretations" of Native American songs by Austin,
Constance Lindsay Skinner, and others. These poems, with excerpts
from Natalie Curtis Burlin's *The Indians' Book* (1907), formed the core
of an anthology edited by George W. Cronyn that was published a year
later by Boni and Liveright. Harriet Monroe approached the project

with a characteristic sense of urgency, noting the vividness of the songs and worrying that "the tribes, in the process of so-called civilization, will lose all trace of it; that their beautiful primitive poetry will perish among the ruins of obliterated states" ("Aboriginal Poetry" 251). Interest in Native American traditional poetry was not new, of course. Henry Rowe Schoolcraft's translations, first published in the 1840s, had provided material to Longfellow for *The Song of Hiawatha* (1855). What was perhaps new was the similarity that Carl Sandburg perceived between Native American poems and "the modern imagists and vorticists" ("Aboriginal Poetry" 255).

The New Poetry movement's infatuation with noncanonical sources ranged from Witter Bynner's popularization of Chinese poetry and Pound's explorations of the Provençal troubadours to Austin's own idiosyncratic theory regarding connections between Native American songs and Imagism (Gish 42, 157 n. 7; Howard 106). Bynner's interest in the imaginative works of what he called "declining races" was even more problematic; as Brenda Maddox perceptively notes, "Silk neckerchiefs and silver jewelry notwithstanding, Bynner was first and foremost a Harvard man" ("Desert Harvest" 494; Maddox 314). Though he was happily ensconced in an adobe house in Santa Fe, New Mexico, Bynner's attitude of cultural imperialism differed little from that displayed, in significantly varying degrees, by fellow Harvard alumni such as T. S. Eliot and Alain Locke. A much more sensitive investigator of folk culture was Natalie Curtis Burlin, a musicologist and protégé of Franz Boas, who was also part of the *Poetry* magazine circle during this period (Clements 282–284). Best remembered for her collection of Native American songs, Burlin also collected African American folksongs at Hampton Institute and compiled a volume of African folklore. Her interest in African lore developed, says William M. Clements, "because of her belief that the distinctive qualities of the music of Black Americans emerged from the racial heritage they shared with their eastern hemisphere ancestors" (294). Though Boas cautioned Burlin lest she make oversimplified generalizations about cultural retentions, she expressed a viewpoint shared by many of the period's artists and writers who explored non-Western art (Clements 293–295). Fenton Johnson's poetic experiments with the spirituals—though inspired by very different ideas—complemented the interests of the *Poetry* magazine group, particularly the enthusiastic Alice Corbin Henderson.

In poems written in the 1930s, Johnson was still searching for ways to capture the vernacular spirit on paper. "A Negro Peddler's Song," for example, offers a pristine transcription of a type of folk expression that was soon to disappear:

> Good Lady,
> I have corn and beets,
> Onions, too, and leeks,
> And also sweet potat-y.
> (*Call and Response* 623)

As with his early versions of the spirituals, the cultural work that this poem performs (there are two more stanzas, not quoted here) may not be obvious. While the poem itself may be taken as nostalgic, it is also polemical. Such street cries, wrote musicologist Willis Laurence James, exhibited both "audacity and resourcefulness" as folklore creations. They may also have a deeper significance. "No matter how humble the crier is," said James, "even if he possesses only a basket of frowsy collard greens, he represents what all businessmen aspire to be—a man who fashions and operates his own business" (19). It may be worth remembering that Johnson's rich uncle Jesse Binga actually began his business career in Chicago as a peddler in the streets of the South Side (Reed, *The Chicago NAACP* 59).

If Johnson's exploration of folk forms accounts for his cordial reception at *Poetry,* both style and content won him a place in Alfred Kreymborg's *Others,* an avant-garde journal sponsored by poet and art patron Walter Arensberg (Crunden 412–413; Williams, *Harriet Monroe* 149–150, 195). Kreymborg, like others in Arensberg's circle, was the epitome of the avant-garde artist. In the decade before the First World War, Kreymborg enjoyed a typical bohemian existence in Greenwich Village, supporting himself by giving chess lessons (a profession similar to what billiards players call "hustling"). But Kreymborg considered himself a man on a mission, "the old Tolstoyan one of regenerating the world through art." An early literary effort, a work of "sentimental sociology" entitled *Edna: The Girl of the Street* (1916), created a bit of gratifying controversy when publisher Guido Bruno was arrested on a complaint from the New York Society for the Prevention of Vice. The society, which had been founded by Anthony Comstock in 1872, was a model of hyperactive intolerance. Working with a very broad definition of "indecent" literature, its agents stood ready to pounce on birth control pamphlets, medical studies of sexual behavior, and even Kreymborg's innocuous chapbook (*Edna* 4–9; Kreymborg, *Troubadour* 106–109,

Chauncey 138–139). Aside from the dreadful *Edna,* Kreymborg's early work—published in the collections *Mushrooms* (1916) and *Blood of Things* (1920)—are exercises in Modernism that eschew meter while often lapsing into old-fashioned poetic diction. "Improvisation" (1916) is a representative work:

Wind:
Play on.
    There is nor hope
nor mutiny
in you.
(10)

This is Imagist poetry without any images, its commonplace perception disguised by unconventional line breaks. Critic Louis Untermeyer was judicious, in 1919, when he observed that Kreymborg's poems until that time may have succeeded in surprising readers but displayed "an ostentation of simplicity, an ingenuousness that is both suspicious and affected" (*The New Era* 313). As an editor, however, Kreymborg was able to make *Others* into a journal that challenged Monroe's *Poetry* and Margaret Anderson's *Little Review* as the most interesting venue for the new poetic spirit.

Increasingly overlooked by today's textbook anthologists—though still doing better than Edgar Lee Masters, Amy Lowell, or Vachel Lindsay—Carl Sandburg was, perhaps, the most celebrated member of the New Poetry movement. More daring than Kreymborg, he had a voice that was brash and fresh; he was a poet with *attitude.* "Here is the difference between Milton, Dante, and me," he told audiences. "They wrote about hell and never saw the place. I wrote about Chicago after looking the town over for years and years" (Golden 116). Sandburg enjoyed tremendous popularity throughout his career, but popularity does not guarantee appearance in textbooks. In the early 1950s he could be seen occasionally on Arthur Godfrey's daytime television show. Tall, sallow, with long white hair, wearing one of Abraham Lincoln's suits, Sandburg was sort of a grandfatherly preappearance of Andy Warhol. He would theatrically pull guitar and manuscripts from a crocus sack, sing folk songs, or dramatically intone poems that had long since achieved the recognition of "greatest hits." By then, Sandburg had become so popular that people forgot why he was important.

The motto that Sandburg printed on the title page of his chapbook *Incidentals* (1905) pointed away from Romanticism and toward an as yet undefined Modernist aesthetic: "We feel and see a thing before we study it and explain it. Vision precedes analysis. That is why poets are as important as scientists" (Golden 112). Sandburg was also more concerned with politics than with any form of mystical seeking. Harry Golden pointed out that while Sandburg offered a strong socialist critique of capitalism, he also "welcomes the industrial society and forgives it. It brings to men a new source of pride and a new feeling of accomplishment" (119). As a result of these ideas, Sandburg's *Chicago Poems* (1916) reverberates with the optimism of the union organizer, avoiding the social analyst's usual note of despair.

The immediate impact of Sandburg's *Chicago Poems* on other writers was seismic—as can be seen on almost every page of the July 1917 "Chicago number" of *Others*, beginning with excerpts from Sherwood Anderson's *Mid-American Chants*. Contemporaneous critics such as Louis Untermeyer praised Sandburg's work as vibrant and vigorous poetry with "no trace of delicate languors, of passion extracted from songs or life that is gleaned in a library" (*The New Era* 109). Sandburg's influence was even felt in Miss Ethel Weimer's sophomore English classroom at Cleveland's Central High School, where fifteen-year-old Langston Hughes first encountered the new poetic style. His early poems reveal an excited response to the Sandburg idiom (Berry 16).

Not all of those who followed this path were successful. Though he was a regular contributor to *Poetry*, Max Michelson's hapless attempts to employ the Sandburg idiom produced poems that sounded like parodies. Eunice Tietjens, *Poetry*'s associate editor, did much better in her book *Profiles from China* (1917), which recorded impressions of an Asian journey in vigorously midwestern poems. Tietjens's work before 1917, collected in *Body and Raiments* (1919), demonstrates her ability with the sonnet and her mastery of metrical variations used to express melancholy moods. But her adoption of the Sandburg idiom results in powerfully ironic and effective portraits such as "The Dandy":

> Mr. Chu smiles the benevolent smile of one who
> satisfies both fashion and a tender heart.
> Does not a bird need an airing?
> (*Profiles* 41)

Another poem, "My Servant," comments on the ancient practice of foot binding but, carefully, offers no direct reproach.

Like Anderson and Tietjens, Fenton Johnson was able to assimilate Sandburg's model and added some interesting touches of his own. One of the elements that Johnson adds, surprisingly and quite effectively, is the sardonic worldview that is also found in the blues. "The Artist," published in the April–May 1919 issue of *Others,* at the start sounds an ironic note: "It is a wonderful world that greets me." Johnson follows this statement with images of the beauty of nature before introducing the troubling echo of "the songs my fathers chanted in the days of slavery." At this point, with an allusion to the extraordinary spiritual "I Know Moon-rise" (originally collected by Thomas Wentworth Higginson from black Civil War soldiers), Johnson turns the poem toward an Afrocentric or black nationalist statement that reflects the rhetoric of Marcus Garvey's UNIA:

> Sunlight, moonlight, dawn and dusk walk with me and
> talk with me, telling me strange tales of the jungle
> and the desert, of wild beasts and slave gangs, of
> kings and mighty warriors.
> In the dewdrop I see the eyes of a Pharaoh, angry at the
> desolation of his land by the hordes of Ethiopian
> warriors.
> In the mist I see the rise of a new Ethiopia, liberator of a
> world long stagnant.
> Who cares to hear my song of this wonderful world? Who
> cares?
> (20)

Johnson's poems in this mode continued to appear in *Others* and were later anthologized as a group under the title "African Nights." Several of them remain in anthologies and, it is fair to say, have had a significant influence on many younger African American writers. This influence is a matter of both style and content—Johnson's ability to transmit an Afrocentric message in a poetic vocabulary that is both stylistically current and indisputably connected to the vernacular of the African American community. It is important to understand that Johnson's title, "The Artist," was not intended to be ironic. The poem reflects and *enacts* the idea—shared by his Chicago contemporaries—best expressed by Sherwood Anderson when he wrote that the poet is obliged to "sit on the shaky rail of our ugly bridges and sing us into paradise," whether or not we want to hear the song (Anderson, "Song of the Soul of Chicago" 3).

Johnson's experiences as a magazine editor left him with a deep cynicism regarding the public's perception of the utility of art. In his short story "The Sorrows of a Stenographer," the female narrator confides: "I like rapid novels, don't you? And I like to have them printed on good paper, also. My hair is unable to endure a bad quality of paper when I curl it. The last novel I read had such a bad quality of paper it was necessary for me to purchase a copy of *The Favorite Magazine* to get my hair back in shape" (*Tales* 28). Precisely this note of self-mocking cynicism began to pervade the poems that Johnson wrote as the United States became more fully engaged in the First World War.

"Tired" (1919), Johnson's most frequently anthologized poem, is invested with an entirely unique kind of energy. In form, the poem resembles Sandburg's "The Poor" (1916), a radical appropriation of Whitman's faux biblical diction. Yet just as Sandburg discovers the millions of the world's poor to be as monumental as a mountain—"innumerable, patient as the darkness of night . . . and all broken, humble ruins of nations"—so does Johnson create a surprising reversal of his reader's expectations. In "Tired," the Bible, Volney's *The Ruins,* and Oswald Spengler's *Decline of the West* (1918) are reread from the perspective of the inner-city ghetto:

> I am tired of work; I am tired of building
> > up somebody else's civilization.
> Let us take a rest, M'Lissy Jane.
> I will go down to the Last Chance Saloon,
> > drink a gallon or two of gin, shoot a
> > game or two of dice and sleep the rest
> > of the night on one of Mike's barrels.
>
> (*Others* 8)

Later comes the startling line

> Throw the children into the river; civilization
> > has given us too many. It is better to die
> > than to grow up and find that you are
> > colored.

James Weldon Johnson—who probably knew better—was satisfied to read this as an expression of absolute despondency and suicidal despair (*Book of American Negro Poetry* 140–141). It is easy enough to see, however, that the word "tired" here is best understood as "fed up" rather than fatigued. In this sense, it is also clear why the poem would be more fully appreciated by the nascent proletarians of Alfred Kreymborg's *Others*—the young writers whom Untermeyer chided for "attempting to be both *bourgeois* and *bolshevik*" (329)—than by the militantly middle-class subscribers to the *Crisis,* the magazine of the National Association for the Advancement of Colored People (NAACP). Again, it is worth taking a moment to understand why.

Fenton Johnson's somber expression of distrust for the West's exploitative and imperialist version of civilization would be echoed in 1923 by Robert L. Poston, a journalist for the *Negro World*. For Poston, civilization was "not something to seek, but something to shun" (Gaines 241). For Countee Cullen, a Phi Beta Kappa scholar, the epitome of Du Bois's Talented Tenth, to be "civilized" was not a matter of choice but—as shown in his magnificent poem "Heritage" (1925)—a condition of repression. Johnson, however, does not use the word "civilization" to signify the genteel Victorianism that torments Cullen's persona. "Heritage" is concerned primarily with the Anglo-American racism that defined African people as "savage" merely because of their color; as well as with the problem that—as Sigmund Freud stated in 1930—"civilization is built up on a renunciation of instinct" (286). The dilemma faced by Cullen's persona is that, having struggled "to deprive an instinct of satisfaction," he finds that a racist society denies him any compensatory benefit whatever (see Freud 286–287). In this sense, Cullen's poem powerfully dramatizes the situation that Du Bois identified in *The Souls of Black Folk* (1903) as "double consciousness":

> All day long and all night through
> One thing only must I do:
> Quench my pride and cool my blood
> Lest I perish in the flood.
> Lest a hidden ember set
> Timber that I thought was wet
> Burning like the dryest flax
> (133)

"Heritage" is a deeply moving and complex poem, its crisis of Christian faith as central to its meaning as is the issue of color. Finally, Cullen's decision to clothe his message in a metrical scheme that evokes anxiety makes his poem as disturbing in its own way as Johnson's "Tired."

The most obvious difference between these two meditations on racial dislocation is that Johnson's speaker seems determined to escape becoming the victim of the inner turmoil that Cullen so graphically depicts. Yet while Johnson's poem seems to limit its discourse to the personal, that focus is as much a gesture of misdirection as Cullen's choice of formal meter to delineate psychological chaos.

There are at least two poetic precedents for Johnson's starkly Modernist poem. One is the hyperbolic dramatization typical of blues lyrics; the other, a durable Romantic convention. Though he claimed to have "cast aside" the language of the Victorian poets, Johnson was well versed in their lessons and ideas. Regardless of the poetic diction he adopted, Johnson was comfortable with the idea that poetry is most effective in the mode of melancholy philosophical reflection, a concept most vividly presented in Edgar Allan Poe's essay "The Philosophy of Composition" (1846) and popularized further by Arthur Symons in the 1890s. Indeed, Symons's "In the Wood of Finvarra" (1900) might be a precursor of Johnson's poem. "I have grown tired of sorrow and human tears," Symons wrote, seeking in the pastoral solitude of the Irish countryside "the peace that is not in the world" (886). The motif was not unfamiliar to generations of English-language poets.

The poem remains puzzling, however, if its historical context is ignored. "Tired" is a fascinating example of hyperbole on one level and meiosis on another. What is understated in the poem is Johnson's awareness of the grim carnage in Europe and the Afrocentric analysis of global political issues explicitly stated in Du Bois's "World War and the Color Line," published in the *Crisis* in November 1914. The poem's meaning, then, depends on the proper reading of the word "civilization." The civilization that Johnson's speaker so vehemently disdains is that which brags about Mozart but employs machine guns to slaughter its brightest young gentlemen, that prates about poetry while enlisting the world's darker and poor peoples as porters and cannon fodder. This self-proclaimed civilization is a rigged game run by perfumed thugs. Given this reality, the speaker of the poem exalts sanity, not suicide. What remains remarkable about "Tired" is its concise clarity, not its dark mood.

Alfred Kreymborg's "Red Chant," published in the *Crisis* for November 1918, may be read as a direct response to the anger expressed in Johnson's "Tired":

There are veins in my body, Fenton Johnson—
veins that sway and dance because of blood

that is red.
. . . .
Let us go arm in arm down State Street
Let them cry, the easily horrified:
"Gods of my fathers,

Look at the white man chumming with the black man!"
Let us nudge each other, you and I—
without humility, without defiance:
"We are red"—
(31)

The poem expresses a feeling of brotherhood across the "color line" and strives to convince Kreymborg's skeptical friend that such a brotherhood—such a revolutionary gesture—will prevail in the end. Indeed, the poem suggests that maintaining a friendship across the color line (such as his friendship with Johnson) was enough to earn him a reputation as a radical in those days, even in a city like Chicago. What "Red Chant" does not do, of course, is address the fact that Johnson's dismay is based upon his analysis of the *system* that oppresses black people, not the insults that remind them of their subordination.

In the preface to his *Songs of the Soil* (1916), Johnson had expressed both his cultural nationalist knowledge of his race as "builders of empires that have crumbled" and his dream of racial reconciliation. "The masses of white people," he wrote, "if left alone, would love the Negro, and the masses of black people, if they were not disturbed by the result of propaganda, would love the white man" (i–ii). There was a simple logic behind this statement: "There is no natural reason for bitterness when we must consider that a large proportion of our Negro population has Caucasian blood in their veins and that the Negro has contributed more than his share to American welfare" (iii). Perhaps it was too simple. Success in poetry might be the crafting of a single startling work such as "Tired," which, deceptive in its simplicity, contains a message that will continue to speak to individual readers for decades. Perhaps, the poet hopes, even for ages. Not much about this can be predicted, however. Curiously enough, it would not be Johnson's experiments with the Spirituals but his avant-garde prose poems—"The Banjo Player," "The Drunkard," and "The Minister"—that caught composer Robert Baksa's attention and became the texts of his song-cycle *Three Portraits* (1996).

Whatever the eventual fate of a poem, the value of journalism must be immediate influence—and it must impact on more than one solitary needful reader. Fenton Johnson's journalistic efforts did have an impact but not quite what he desired. Despite advertisements placed in the *Crisis* and the editor's claim of a readership of "250,000 every month [who] are the purchasing units of representative Negro homes," the

Champion Magazine probably achieved a circulation of about 1,000 and folded with the same issue in which this fanciful readership estimate appeared (April 1917; see Daniel 120). His next project, the *Favorite Magazine,* published between 1918 and 1921, represents an alarming decline into confusion and desperation. It is noteworthy chiefly because it published a number of excellent articles by the young J. A. Rogers. Under Johnson's sole proprietorship (see Statement of Ownership, October 1920), the magazine was certainly not as well capitalized as the *Champion Magazine* had been. Nor was it as well written. The editorials ranged from platitudinous rhetoric to an appeal for a political patronage job for Business Manager James H. Moody. In "The Way to Jericho" (June 1920), Johnson echoed both the gospel according to Jesse Binga and Garvey's dreams of economic development. "We desire the race to prepare for its materialistic needs," Johnson began. "Jericho cannot fall until we have built up our credit so that we have something to offer those who live beside us. The walls of Jericho are very hard to raze unless we have the money to raze them. *The Favorite Magazine* is very anxious . . . to see the race become a race of millionaires." Later that year Johnson's anxiety increased. In "For the Highest Good" (November–December 1920), he wrote: "We are anxious that the Reconciliation Movement in general should be adopted by the President and the United States Congress. We are anxious that the government should wipe out the race problem officially, and not only the race problem but the problem of labor and capital and the problems of the American home."

J. A. Rogers's article "Social Equality—What Is It?" in the same issue was a much clearer statement of the need for economic parity and equal opportunity. Rogers wasn't fretting about Congress. "A short, sharp way to clear out all the dead issues," he wrote, "to end forever all useless discussions, and get right down to business is for the Negro to decide to have EVERYTHING his white enemies do not want him to have" (519).

The rationale of the *Favorite Magazine,* however, was promoting Johnson's "Reconciliation movement." The instrumentality suggested for this cooperative movement is disarmingly simple and anticipates later "brotherhood" campaigns by groups such as the Congress of Racial Equality (a spinoff of the pacifist Fellowship for Reconciliation, founded in 1914) and the Commissions for Interracial Cooperation that were developed throughout the South in the 1920s and 1930s ("Interracial Activities" 235–237). Johnson merely proposed "Sunday afternoon clubs which are to be operated through a social settlement and a vigorous system of propaganda. At these meetings the ablest white and colored speakers are to lecture on the subject 'reconciliation' and in this way the uneducated within both races will be brought to a better understanding as to what constitutes true citizenship." The Reconciliation movement optimistically proposed that "social workers, scattered as they will be throughout the length and breadth of the United States, can show both the white man and the black man that the American nation cannot exist with one race fighting against the other, that America belongs to all the races and cooperation is the thing needed." While Johnson never specified the activities these settlement workers should promote, he greatly admired the work of Jane Addams at Chicago's Hull House and the Music School Settlement for Colored People, organized in Harlem in 1911 by David Mannes and Natalie Curtis Burlin with the support of orchestra leader James Reese Europe (Johnson, "David Mannes" 174; Badger 61–67). One would expect him, as a poet, to envision a primarily cultural program. In any case, Johnson's seemingly mild assertion of American pluralism must be viewed in the context of an era when many Americans endorsed the best-selling author Lothrop Stoddard, with his anxiety-ridden defense of "the white man's present position of political world-domination" (*Rising Tide of Color* 15). This element of the American public might have viewed Johnson's suggestions as a threat to the maintenance of the "color line," but Johnson's ideas also provoked resistance from black nationalists.

Perhaps the most important article published in the *Favorite Magazine* was Johnson's "The Negro Since the Armistice," which appeared in January 1921 and was immediately attacked in Cyril V. Briggs's *The Crusader*. During the war, writes Johnson,

> we thought that Africa could be set free, returned to the natives and a vast empire created, somewhat like Solomon's kingdom. I confess that I was a rabid "Africa for the Africans" spokesman and that Cyril Briggs, editor of *The Crusader*, was advocating it in a more scholarly manner than I was; and that I did not change, or at least become neutral, until Benjamin Brawley . . . discerned to me in his book that the natives needed occidental training to withstand occidental aggrandizement.

The article supposedly expressed disappointment that the Versailles peace conference had not fully addressed the desires of anticolonial and race leaders, but Johnson also used it to attack the *Messenger* of A. Philip Randolph and Chandler Owen as a "destructive" and inflammatory Marxist journal.

The book in question, Benjamin Brawley's *Africa and the War* (1918), was an essay suggesting that Germany's plan to seize the Belgian and French colonies in the Congo was the real issue of the First World War. With German defeat imminent, Brawley clearly renounces both Pan-Africanist and Garveyite demands for African self-determination, claiming that what the native African needs is "Christian education . . . so adapted as to make the African an intelligent citizen in his commonwealth" (40). Brawley sees a role for African Americans in the postwar development of Africa but ends with his own hand out by suggesting that the American colleges (such as Morehouse, where he was dean) that might be expected to provide the necessary expertise and trained personnel were themselves "five to seven years behind standard" and would need to be upgraded (41–44). Brawley did act on his own advice the next year, accepting a call to serve as visiting professor at Liberia College. Astonished by conditions there, he lasted barely a semester. The arrival in South Africa in 1922 of Max Yergan, a social worker representing the YMCA, was similarly inauspicious, but Yergan managed to work there for a decade (Spivey 21–31; Anthony 30–33).

The *Crusader* responded to the issue by ignoring the international question. Briggs merely denounced Johnson in sarcastic terms:

> Editor Fenton Johnson avers in the January "Favorite" that the radical preachments of the *Messenger* would have such an effect upon a weak mind that its possessor would arm himself and go hunting a Rockefellow or a Morgan. Er—was the editor's hunt successful?
>
> While speaking of Editor Johnson may we not be allowed to indulge ourselves in a definition of his "Reconciliation movement?" We won't take up much of his time. We can give our definition in just two words. It is: INTELLECTUAL SISSYISM! ("Fantasies" 11)

Briggs answered Johnson's "peaceable kingdom" vision of interracial reconciliation with a Marxist challenge: "The white bourgeois who happens to know the history of the Negro's contact with capitalistic civilization must tremble in his boots as he sees oppressed Negro and white proletarians approaching that unity without which the victory of the proletariat is impossible. . . . The Negro has much to avenge on the perpetrators of all his wrongs—the white bourgeoisie class" ("Fantasies" 11).

This falling out of former allies is not difficult to explain. In "The Negro Since the Armistice" we see Fenton Johnson desperately dancing to erase his militant footprints. A study of the black press published in the *Journal of Negro History* in 1944 noted that newspaper editorials "were unequivocally loyal in 1917–18" but that expressions of patriotism and support of the war effort often included a clear statement "that the Negro wanted the principles of Democracy applied to his role in society" (Jones 24–25). By 1919, however, white Americans found such statements provocative.

In November, Attorney General A. Mitchell Palmer released a report on "persons advising anarchy, sedition, and the forcible overthrow of the government." One section of the report, probably written by J. Edgar Hoover, documented what the author called "expressions of insubordination" and "insolence" in the black press. The report professed alarm at "the increasingly emphasized feeling of a race consciousness, in many of these publications always antagonistic to the white race and openly, defiantly assertive of its own equality and even superiority" (Foner 292, n. 407; *Investigation Activities* 162).

At about the same time, a committee of the New York legislature headed by state senator Clayton R. Lusk was preparing to publish its own four-volume report of a similar investigation into "revolutionary radicalism"—primarily among immigrants and blacks. "Unable to perceive the currents in the Black community," wrote J. H. Pawa, "the Lusk Committee treated all black leaders who were to the left of Booker T. Washington as potential Bolsheviki" (130). The *Favorite Magazine,* with its base in Chicago, did not concern the Lusk committee. But it *was* being read. It appeared on the Justice Department's list.

It should not be forgotten that the Justice Department and New York state's Committee on Sedition, headed by Lusk, were not avidly reading black poetry and magazines because they were literary critics. Their study of the black press was an investigation aimed at possible disruption of magazine mailing privileges or criminal indictment (Pawa 130, 132; Lewis, "Shortcuts" 92). Of all those monitored, the *Favorite Magazine* was a particularly vulnerable target.

James H. Moody, Johnson's partner in the *Favorite Magazine,* was a Republican Party community activist who had held various party patronage jobs such as federal marshal and bailiff in the Chicago municipal court. Johnson himself had no other employment. Nor did the magazine enjoy the kind of material support that Jesse Binga had afforded its predecessor. While the editors of the *Messenger* proudly used the attorney general's declaration that theirs was "by long odds the most able and the most dangerous of all the Negro publications" (*Investigation Ac-*

tivities 172) as an advertising blurb, Johnson quickly attempted to dissociate himself from the so-called radicals—most of whom he knew from his casual involvement with Harlem's 21st Assembly District Socialist Club (Turner and Turner 28–32). The machismo of the era's rhetoric notwithstanding, it's unfair to see Johnson's retreat as mere cowardice.

The intellectual climate of the period cannot be fully understood if we ignore the unrestrained power of intimidation exercised by President Woodrow Wilson's administration, an energetic campaign that makes the networks of innuendo seen during the McCarthy era seem like the work of dilettantes. The Post Office implemented the Espionage Act of 1917 and the Sedition Act of 1918 to deny mailing privileges to magazines and newspapers considered critical of Wilson's military gestures (Van Wienen 202–203). Max Eastman's journal the *Masses* was the voice of a bohemian avant-garde for whom socialism was only one element of a wide-ranging program of cultural radicalism. Nevertheless, the journal became a central focus for the federal government's active suppression of the political Left. The power that Postmaster General Albert Burleson wielded to put magazines out of business was clearly demonstrated by his treatment of the *Masses* in 1917. Having obtained a court injunction to prevent the bulk mailing of one issue, the Post Office was subsequently "able to revoke second-class mailing privileges altogether on the grounds that the *Masses* no longer qualified as a monthly periodical because it had skipped mailing an issue" (Zurier 59–61). Once this ploy had been successfully tested on the *Masses*, it became the Post Office's standard practice (Zurier 64).

Technicalities in postal regulations were not the government's only tools for censorship. Seven members of the *Masses* staff were indicted "for conspiring to obstruct recruitment and other vile deeds." As William O'Neill sarcastically comments, "The indictment of Josephine Bell, author of a poem mourning the arrest of Emma Goldman and Alexander Berkman, was dismissed after the court learned that she did not know any of her alleged co-conspirators. Though conspiracy was a vague and elastic charge, there was still some feeling that it required a person to have met the other plotters" (75). After this first trial under the Espionage Act ended in a hung jury, the prosecution mounted a second trial that achieved similar results. By the time all of the courtroom drama was over, the *Masses* had been permanently silenced.

The black press, of course, was much less able to defend itself than were affluent spokesmen for the proletariat such as Max Eastman. As participants in the Black Arts movement would grimly rediscover in the 1970s, some agencies of the U.S. government view race relations as an arena for serious Machiavellian politics. In 1918 the extent of government surveillance of the black press by the Justice Department, War Department, and Post Office was impressive, and these efforts were disclosed to the editors in order to intimidate them (Jordan 1576–1579). Additional persuasion was exerted by individuals such as Major Walter H. Loving, an African American officer in the U.S. Army's Military Intelligence Branch who compiled reports on activities in the black community and also conducted "interviews" with leaders such as Howard University professor Kelly Miller and Robert Abbott, the editor of the *Chicago Defender* (Lewis, *W. E. B. Du Bois* 559–560, 696 n. 58). Even the NAACP journal the *Crisis,* with a circulation of 80,000 and nationwide organizational support, found it expedient to "change the tone" of its editorials in June 1918. The "carrot" in a complicated negotiation was the possibility of a military commission for fifty-year-old editor Du Bois; the stick was obvious. In the end of this gambit, Du Bois escaped becoming a captain in the Military Intelligence Branch (MIB) by failing his physical exam (Lewis, *W. E. B. Du Bois* 552–555; Ellis, "Closing Ranks" 117). NAACP chairman Joel E. Spingarn, already serving as a major in army intelligence, was able to "warn" his board of directors that the militant editorial stance of the *Crisis* might lead to serious federal action. "To counteract the anti-NAACP reports in MIB files and to protect himself," concludes historian Mark Ellis, "Spingarn made a show of demanding assurances that the association recognized its patriotic duty" (105). Most historians agree that these negotiations, as they were inevitably discussed in the black press, damaged Du Bois's credibility among more militant African Americans. An editorial in the *Baltimore Afro-American,* referring to government pressure on Du Bois, bluntly informed readers, "*The Crisis* has a muzzle on it just as the *Afro-American* and all other colored newspapers." Major Spingarn's reward for his efforts was immediate reassignment to the battlefront in France (W. Jordan 1582; Ellis 118).

A relaxation of such efforts should have followed the end of the war, but other tensions soon emerged. The special unit headed by J. Edgar Hoover continued to monitor the labor and foreign-language press. The Chicago "race riot" in July 1919, when armed white mobs terrorized the city's black neighborhoods, refocused attention on the African American community (Robbins 34). "The Bureau of Investigation," wrote Max Lowenthal, "having started an inquiry at the end of World

War I avowedly to protect negroes from radicals," now saw an even greater need for undercover supervision. Hoover's Chicago superintendent was E. J. Brennan. In a telegram sent in July 1919, Hoover ordered an investigation to determine whether "race riots in your city [are] due to propaganda among negro element by radicals." Brennan's staff cited the militant weekly *Chicago Defender* and, reports Mark Ellis, "found *The Favorite Magazine* especially distasteful" primarily because of its protest of Chicago police behavior (Ellis, "J. Edgar Hoover" 45).

Surveillance by J. Edgar Hoover was a serious matter. The attorney general launched his campaign against dissent in Chicago with raids on New Year's Day 1920. Simultaneous strikes took place in other cities. Thousands of immigrants and suspected anarchists were arrested.

A dragnet is effective because it doesn't miss even little fish. The case of "Louis Wirth, radical alien"—as filed by Special Agent Branch Bocock—offers an interesting example. Wirth, then a twenty-two-year-old social worker for Chicago's Society of Jewish Charities (and later the chairman of the University of Chicago's Department of Sociology), became the protagonist of what Assistant Secretary of Labor Louis F. Post termed "a case on which any jury might well have disagreed" (*Investigation of Administration* 162). Wirth had been arrested in the raid and held for five days without a warrant. Interrogated by immigration inspector W. W. Poot after anxious days in jail, Wirth explained his "involvement" with the Communist Party in very simple terms. In the course of writing his master's thesis, he had collected several pamphlets and attended a political meeting. He added, "I had no idea it could be considered wrong to belong to the Communist Party of America. No one told me about that" (*Investigation* 165). Besides the question of whether or not Wirth's tenuous connection to the organization merited deportation, the fact is that federal courts had not declared the Communist Party illegal in 1920 (Whitehead 51–52). In his angrily eloquent and informative memoir, *The Deportations Delirium of 1920* (1923), Assistant Secretary Post would denounce the Attorney General's highly publicized "Red Crusade" as "hostile to American ideals of government and its methods defiant of American law" (327).

After he canceled more than 1,000 deportation warrants obtained through the raids, Post himself was called before the House Rules committee and threatened with formal impeachment proceedings (226–251). The high-handed behavior of Palmer's minions was soon denounced by a group of distinguished law professors led by Harvard Law School's Roscoe Pound and Felix Frankfurter, but little empathy is needed to understand why these efforts to stifle dissent of all types were chillingly effective (Post 297–298).

Besides political jeopardy, the *Favorite Magazine* placed its editor on the brink of bankruptcy and mental breakdown. In addition to his January 1921 mea culpa, Johnson had discussed his plight in a letter to the *New York Tribune* and an essay titled "The Story of Myself": "As I write this in the little furnished room that my wife and I call home, I wonder if the Reconciliation Movement is not a grand dream, *The Favorite Magazine* a foolhardy venture and I, myself a failure" (8). The *Favorite Magazine* was essentially a one-man operation, presenting a mostly emotional and ill-defined philosophy as a social movement with only two feet. As such, it could not hope to compete with journals such as the *Crisis* or the *Messenger,* which were, in actuality, well-funded political house organs.

Thus, at the age of thirty-three, Fenton Johnson—apart from the brilliant and troubling poems that Alfred Kreymborg, Harriet Monroe, James Weldon Johnson, and Arna Bontemps reprinted in their anthologies—vanished quietly from the literary scene. In 1927 a poem entitled "Sweet Love O' Dusk," its blank verse and lovely romanticism reminiscent of his early "The Vision of Lazarus" (1913), appeared in the *Crisis:*

> I who wandered through a maze of curse
> And know the scorn of those I strove to aid
> Have found a newer realm, a sacred grove
> Where I can woo the star-crowned maid of dusk
> Who brought to light a brood of sorrow folk
> (265)

Fenton Johnson's career is neither triumph nor tragedy. He did, however, end up a bitter man sadly embodying confusions that would continue to afflict many African Americans throughout the century. Proud of his education and middle-class manners, Johnson nevertheless felt that there was a cultural vitality among the black proletariat that he desperately needed to know and celebrate. Aware of this nation's seemingly intransigent and institutionalized racism, he alternated between justifiable outrage and a desire to seek the ameliorative path that he termed "racial reconciliation." He knew that the problems faced by black people in the United States required collective political action, and he nonetheless entered the battle as a concerned individual. In many ways, Fenton Johnson typifies both Du Bois's Talented Tenth and the generation of educated African Americans who came to maturity after the Civil Rights movement of the 1950s. His work constitutes an important key to understanding the development of the aesthetics of the Harlem Renaissance and the development of a militant race consciousness in the African American community. Yet after delving deeply into Johnson's work, the reader may recall Johnny Nash's plaintive song "There Are More Questions Than Answers."

Johnson, remarked James P. Hutchinson in 1976, "exhausted his wellspring of inspiration quite early." He adds that "the paucity of critical comment on the few poems worth considering [suggests] there must not have been too much of significance in that well-spring at all" (14). This judgment is, I think, undeservedly harsh. There are several ways of assessing Fenton Johnson's significance. Although Johnson was a minor poet, even in his friend William Stanley Braithwaite's estimation, he did become an enduring presence in anthologies, possibly the best thing any poet of any era can hope for. On the other hand, it would be simplistic to judge his personal failures and disappointments solely in the light of the relative success of a contemporary such as James Weldon Johnson—though the careers of both men reflect the complex cultural negotiations that would be required of all twentieth-century African American artists. It is most important to understand Fenton Johnson's literary career as it exemplifies Manning Marable's charge to scholars in *Black Leadership* (1998): "Political intellectuals as a social group have been central to the process of political, cultural, and social change within the African Diaspora. Further research should reveal even more extensive connections among black nationalist, labor, socialist and electoral political organizations and their programs, tactics, and strategies for empowerment" (107). Such connections are most clearly articulated—and communicated to the people—in the arena of the arts. Fenton Johnson's frustrations were personal and saddening, but they were also emblematic of the conditions that beset the entire African American community during the period. Furthermore, as we will see, Fenton Johnson's little light remained a beacon for many other African American writers who also saw themselves as "children of the sun."

2

William Stanley Braithwaite and Harriet Monroe

The Battle for New Poetry

> Tradition, however grand and old, ceases to be of use the moment its walls are strong enough to break a butterfly's wing, or keep a fairy immured.
> —Harriet Monroe

> The Negro race must come to a consciousness of itself before it can produce great literature. The civilization of a people is reflected in its literature.
> —William H. Ferris

Cultural inventories are usually excited manifestos or jeremiads. It is interesting and instructive to compare such pronouncements from various decades. By doing so, we can chart the movement of the glacier.

The United States has been enjoying a sort of poetry renaissance. Currently the "poetry slam," an event where drunken audiences hoot down sensitive poems about dying grandmothers or inevitable divorces and bestow twenty-dollar prizes on scatological doggerel, is sweeping the nation. It's an amusement that seems to be a goldmine for saloon keepers too sophisticated for "Hot Buns" contests. It has recently been possible to find at least three such events every week at different venues—even in a city like Houston. Perhaps, for a new generation, the poetry slam is the equivalent of the Beatnik coffeehouse scene. Not!

If the Beat Generation of the 1950s appeared to abandon all bourgeois values, it is clear—at least in hindsight—that its poets took their poetry seriously. Nor does the present situation much resemble even earlier times. At the turn of the century, while some popular journalists bemoaned American poetry's "inadequacy . . . to sustain a large and vigorous modern national life," the poets themselves were plotting an artistic revolution that would change both the voice of poetry and the terms of its popular reception. In Boston, the African American poet and critic William Stanley Braithwaite (1873–1962) emerged as the nation's most visible advocate of the new poetry. Through his column in the *Boston Evening Transcript,* he was able to launch the careers of Robert Frost and other major figures. For Braithwaite, the critic's job was making modern literature accessible to readers. Though many of his "mainstream" readers were unaware of his race, Braithwaite also exerted an enormous influence, through the NAACP's journal the *Crisis* and other publications, on African American literary developments that would culminate in the Harlem Renaissance. Some recent reevaluations of Braithwaite—excellent essays by Kenny J. Williams and Craig S. Abbott in particular—have attempted to avoid the political biases of earlier commentators, but Jean Wagner's severe and egregiously inaccurate dismissal of Braithwaite in *Negro Poets of the United States* (1973) continues to mislead scholars. Contrary to Wagner's often repeated claim, there is no evidence at all that Braithwaite indulged the slightest ambivalence concerning his racial identity. Nevertheless, W. S. Braithwaite has been undeservedly neglected by critics, and understanding his unique accomplishments plainly requires a clear-sighted investigation of the production of poetry in the half century 1880–1930.

Back in 1991 Dana Gioia was bemoaning the current state of poetic affairs in the pages of the *Atlantic.* "Outside the classroom—where society demands that the two groups interact—poets and the common reader," wrote Gioia, "are no longer on speaking terms" (100). Gioia longed for the popularity that poets apparently enjoyed in the nineteenth century when Longfellow and his peers produced volumes that were best-sellers. Apparently Gioia had no clue about such vital interactions as the "poetry slam." Yet even the depressing combination of the nightclub travesties and the closed-circuit boredom of writing in academic creative writing classes that worries Gioia can't approach the truly depressed state of the art at the beginning of this century. The period from 1890 to 1910, which historian Rayford W. Logan dubbed "the nadir of American race relations," coincided with what anthologist

Edmund Clarence Stedman in 1900 called "the twilight interval" of American poetry. It is almost tempting to think that the enervated condition of culture's best aspect somehow correlated with the mean-spiritedness evident in other social expressions of the times.

In its cultural ecology the United States at the end of the twentieth century is in some ways very different from the beginning. Not until the late 1950s, for example, did radio stations begin nonstop programming of both popular and classical recorded music—thereby creating a mega industry with economic dimensions undreamed of in any previous era. Poetry, like music, was mostly a part-time occupation at the beginning of the century. At that time—unlike today—the majority of published poets maintained careers as businessmen, lawyers, and journalists. Many were women who had the advantage of being married to supportive husbands who were also considerably more than "good providers." Some poets, apparently not as many as today, were teachers or college professors. Similarly, the audience for poetry ranged from those who simply enjoyed the patriotic, humorous, or sentimental verses that newspapers used as column fillers to readers who delighted in the serious study of literature both traditional and contemporary.

Nevertheless, the American "Poetry Renaissance" that began in 1912, followed by the Harlem Renaissance of the 1920s, definitely increased the size and diversity of the audience and readers' perception of the importance of the art. The socially engaged writing of the depression era and the oddly "mediagenic" Beat Generation of the 1950s continued to keep poetry at least newsworthy.

It is possible, however, that the basic cultural context for poetry in the United States has remained fairly consistent for more than a century. Poetry lovers expect poetry to offer both instruction and delight; those who don't read poetry think that this is precisely what it offers to those who do: people who are assumed to be smarter than themselves. Similarly, poets seem to maintain a bizonal concept of their craft, always aware of both its power and its privacy. In the 1840s John Greenleaf Whittier and Henry Wadsworth Longfellow used their verses to campaign for the abolition of slavery. They were as aware of literature's social and propagandistic function as were the African American writers of the Harlem Renaissance. From another angle, one can compare Longfellow's patriotic epics—composed in stanzaic forms borrowed from European tradition—to Walt Whitman's idiosyncratic experiments and those of a long list of later practitioners whose creative energies alternate between attention to matters of technical form and the need to document the elusive presence of the eternal in the quotidian. But this, after all, is precisely what the art of poetry is about.

The early years of this century, however, afford readers a period in the history of American literature that is notable for its exciting complexity and a sense of volatile change that mirrors other developments in society. Harriet Monroe, in Chicago, launched *Poetry: A Magazine of Verse* in 1912. Her journal became an influential force in the Modernist movement. William Stanley Braithwaite's work at the *Boston Evening Transcript* and as editor of an annual *Anthology of Magazine Verse* brought him recognition as the major proponent of poetry in the nation's press. The possibly inevitable clash of these literary titans in 1917 foregrounds important issues of artistic innovation, literary politics, editorial influence, and the mechanisms of cultural change.

In 1910, as Columbia University professor Joel E. Spingarn was calling for a "New Criticism" that would "recognize in every work of art a spiritual creation governed by its own law," contemporary poets were also seeking ways of avoiding the old classical conceptions that, according to Spingarn, had made literary genre into "a fixed norm governed by inviolable laws" ("New Criticism" 28). Ezra Pound and his Imagist co-conspirators found a way out by looking to Provençal folk song and Chinese court poetry and by exploring a radical reinterpretation of the Greek classics. Their activity was similar to that of the era's European painters, who turned to Oceanic and African tribal sculpture for inspiration. The poets felt that they were participating in something much greater than a revolution of literary style. Their optimistic attitude was expressed succinctly by Wallace Stevens. "You know," Stevens confided to Orrick Johns, "we *can* change it all" (Johns, *Time of Our Lives* 226).

Things began to change on the American poetry scene with the publication in 1912 of *The Lyric Year: One Hundred Poems,* edited by Ferdinand Phinny Earle. The book was first announced as a poetry contest with $1,000 in prizes. As fellow judges, Earle chose Edward J. Wheeler, president of the Poetry Society of America, and William Stanley Braithwaite (Earle iii–v; Rittenhouse 250–251). Earle's anthology included estimable works—chosen from 2,000 entries—by a hundred poets representing a wide range of occupations and located in all sections of the country, from New York and Chicago to Kentucky and Iowa, from big cities, small towns, and rural areas. The quality of the work is surprisingly high. Contributors readily recognized even today included William Rose Benét, Witter Bynner, Arthur Davison Ficke, Joyce Kilmer,

Vachel Lindsay, Edwin Markham, Josephine Preston Peabody, Sara Teasdale, Ridgely Torrence, Louis Untermeyer, and John Hall Wheelock.

Having read 2,000 poems to make a selection that he regarded as "representative . . . of the work done to-day in America," Earle announced that the "twilight interval" was over. "Our twentieth century poetry is democratic, scientific, humane," he wrote. "Its independence reveals the liberating touch of Walt Whitman, sweet with robust optimism" (viii). Though he himself thought Edna St. Vincent Millay's entry was the best poem submitted, Earle was somewhat taken aback by the reaction accorded the winning poem of *The Lyric Year* competition.

Orrick Johns, a St. Louis journalist, visited New York in 1911 and was delighted to be welcomed into the circles of people such as poet Sara Teasdale and social activist Emma Goldman (Johns, *Time of Our Lives* 202). Against the background noise of the nation's growing Nativist hostility toward immigrants, Johns's poem "Second Avenue" surveyed the tide of still-wretched humanity swirling through New York's Lower East Side ghetto and sounded a properly respectable note of intellectual sympathy:

Are you, O motley multitude,
Descendants of the squandered dead,
Who honored courage more than creeds
And fought for better things than bread?
(Johns, "Second Avenue" 132)

The dehumanization depicted in Edwin Markham's celebrated "The Man with the Hoe" (1896)—"Slave of the wheel of labor, what to him / Are Plato and the swing of Pleiades?"—has become, Johns notes (though somewhat less eloquently), an epidemic condition in this quarter of the nation's greatest city. All that a poet finds alluring, the natural beauties of earth and life, are denied these workers "who live from hour to hour" trapped in a city that is "a temple and a shrine / For gods of iron and of gilt" (135, 134). Worse yet, it was the people's own labor that had built their prison. The poem's conclusion offers tepid pseudo-Socialist hopefulness:

You, having brothers in all lands,
Shall teach to all lands brotherhood
(136)

It was enough to enable Johns to win *The Lyric Year* prize on points (Earle iii–v). As Jessie Belle Rittenhouse later recalled: "The social movement in poetry was then at its height; the catchword, the 'Time Spirit,' was in everybody's mouth. Poets were adjured to write of the thing immediately important in modern life. The twentieth century came in on a wave of social consciousness inspired by Whitman and crystallized by Markham in 'The Man with the Hoe.'" This mood explained Johns's prize. "It is not strange," Rittenhouse concluded, "that a social poem should have received attention wholly out of proportion to its poetic merit" (*My House* 250–251).

It should be noted that the much better 200-line poem "Renascence," by the nineteen-year-old Edna St. Vincent Millay, did not ignore social comment or politically correct empathy:

A man was starving in Capri;
He moved his eyes and looked at me;
I felt his gaze, I heard his moan
And knew his hunger as my own
(Millay, "Renascence" 182)

If the theme of the poem was actually meant to be social comment, one could fault Millay for conjuring an imaginary scene; Orrick Johns had, in fact, meditated upon the genuine plight of real people he observed in New York City. But Millay's bright rhyming couplets rapidly detour into an extraordinary scenario of imagined death and burial—a spiritual initiation—that leads to an astonishingly wise and beautiful epiphany:

The world stands out on either side
No wider than the heart is wide;
Above the world is stretched the sky,—
No higher than the soul is high
(188)

Even though Jessie Rittenhouse, one of the founders of the Poetry Society of America and a willing friend to young poets, had personally encouraged Johns to submit his prize-winning poem to *The Lyric Year* competition, she found it deplorable that his work should be preferred to Millay's (Rittenhouse, *My House* 251). Nor was she alone in her reaction. Orrick Johns himself later commented: "When the book arrived I realized that it was an unmerited award. The outstanding poem in that book was 'Renascence' by Edna St. Vincent Millay, immediately acknowledged by every authoritative critic as such. The award was as much an embarrassment to me as a triumph" (*Time of Our Lives* 203).

Rittenhouse and others, however, also realized that the great response of poets to Earle's announcement and the subsequent newspaper coverage of the debate over the winning entry had brought contemporary poetry to wider public attention and also indicated that an eager new generation of American writers was taking the form quite seriously. This sudden focus on the most ancient of literary forms was underscored by the simultaneous announcement of two ambitious new publications: *Poetry: A Magazine of Verse,* launched in Chicago by Harriet Monroe, and the *Poetry Journal* in Boston, edited by Braithwaite. In addition to affirming an increase in poetic activity, the coincidence of these projects provoked five years of controversy, rancor, and tantrums that made the debacle of *The Lyric Year* look tame.

The great American poetry heavyweight championship battle of 1917 emerged because the participants were ready for it. Miss Monroe saw herself—and herself alone—as the guiding star of what she christened the New Poetry movement. William Stanley Braithwaite, proud of his own contribution, was no stranger to literary infighting and could adroitly perform the understated news-column uppercut and the bread-and-butter-note jab. Conrad Aiken—a wannabe aristocrat from Savannah, Georgia—acted more as an instigator than a referee, writing essays in the *New Republic,* the *Dial,* and the *Poetry Journal.* He insisted upon attacking the New Poetry movement and, much to their mutual annoyance, always bracketed Braithwaite and Harriet Monroe as targets for his critical abuse.

As a poet, Aiken did not mind recognition, but as a critic he was unhappy with Braithwaite's annual anthology and with *Poetry* magazine's cash prizes for the best poems published during the year. Aiken castigated "Mr. Braithwaite's annual parade and Miss Monroe's annual graduation exercises" and felt that, between the two of them, poetry was "too much rather than too little recognized in this country" ("Prizes" 99; Williams, *Harriet Monroe* 178). In his view, no contemporary poetry was worthy of prizes or honors. "In all this," he wrote, "it is perhaps possible to detect a central fallacy—the belief that poetry can be made essentially popular, in this time and place. Mediocre poetry—yes. . . . But the finer poetry, now as always, needs time for valuation" ("Prizes" 99). Like James Fenimore Cooper and Ezra Pound, Aiken was unhappy that America was not the Europe of an earlier, grander century.

The New Poetry movement of the first decade of the century usually brings to mind the energetic American vernacular of Carl Sandburg and Vachel Lindsay, renovations of the classics attempted by H.D. and Ezra

Pound, or an infatuation with Asian poetic forms as (mis)understood by Ernest Fenollosa and Amy Lowell. The interest in Asian poetry paralleled visual artists' curiosity about African and Polynesian sculpture and, later—led by Mary Austin, Alice Corbin Henderson, and Witter Bynner—a similar infatuation with Native American cultural artifacts. Encouragement from Monroe's *Poetry* resulted in an anthology of translations and "interpretations" of American Indian poetry published by Boni and Liveright in 1918 (Cronyn viii).

Such cosmopolitanism was not necessarily reflected in the era's criticism. Some readers did, however, enjoy a short but intense fling with the "cutting edge" European critical theory of the time. Italian philosopher Benedetto Croce's *Aesthetic* was an immediate success among American avant-garde literary circles when it appeared in Douglas Ainslie's translation in 1907. The popularizer of Croce's theory was Joel E. Spingarn, a controversial Columbia University professor and one of the founders of the National Association for the Advancement of Colored People. Croce's attack on the conventional definition of literary genre and the "intellectual error" of assigning external values to works of art could only delight those interested in Asian poetic forms and Imagism (Croce 34–38; Spingarn, *Creative Criticism* 176). As Amy Lowell wrote in *Tendencies in Modern American Poetry* (1917): "I quite agree with that brilliant disciple of Signor Benedetto Croce, Mr. J. E. Spingarn, that the criticism of art should be first, foremost, and all the time, aesthetic. As I have already said, its aesthetic value is, in the final summing up, the only value of a work of art" (viii). The error of critics working from definitions of genre was clear to Croce: "instead of asking before a work of art if it be expressive and what it expresses, whether it speak or stammer or is altogether silent, they ask if it obey the *laws* of epic or of tragedy, of historical painting or of landscape" (36–37). Artists themselves, said Croce, have never been limited by such definitions: "While making a verbal pretence of agreeing or yielding a feigned obedience, artists have really always disregarded these *laws of the kinds*. Every true work of art has violated some established kind and upset the ideas of the critics, who have thus been obliged to broaden the kinds, until finally even the broadened kind has proved too narrow, owing to the appearance of new works of art, naturally followed by new scandals, new upsettings and—new broadenings" (37).

Spingarn, edging into territory later explored by Ezra Pound, further interpreted Croce to mean that "the critic should concern himself with the poet's own intentions and not with rules laid down by others." The poet's intention, he said, is found "not in one or another of the various ambitions that flit through his mind, but in the actual work of art which he creates. His poem is his 'intention'" (166–167). In his essay "Prose and Verse" (1917), Spingarn employed Crocean ideas in a vigorous defense of vers libre. Spingarn regarded poetic rhythm and meter as "aesthetically identical with style, as style is identical with artistic form, and form in its turn is the work of art in its spiritual and indivisible self" (47).

Fifty years later, of course, such ideas would appear in the correspondence of Charles Olson and Robert Creeley as a rejection of traditional English-language poetic forms under Creeley's maxim "Form is only an extension of content." At the time, however, the Crocean suggestion of the natural revolutionary potential of art greatly appealed to poets experimenting with free verse. It had little impact on the aestheticism championed by a critic such as Braithwaite. He would not, however, have disagreed much with Spingarn's statement, in "The New Criticism" (1910), that "the poet's only moral duty as a poet is to be true to his art" (35). By the 1930s, of course, Spingarn's New Criticism would be eclipsed by another critical approach that used the same name but had rather different goals.

Aiken's critical reservations did not, of course, prevent him from publishing his poems in both Monroe's *Poetry* and Braithwaite's *Poetry Journal*. In addition to his complaints regarding the editors' policies, Aiken issued an even more direct attack on Braithwaite's concept of criticism. He accused Braithwaite of "the express belief that poetry is a sort of supernaturalism" (*Skepticisms* 127–128).

Aiken's comment is disingenuous. Braithwaite's criticisms—including the introductions to his annual anthology—compare more than favorably with the writings of Edmund Clarence Stedman and Brander Matthews, who dominated the literary scene at the time. It was a period when Matthews, a reviewer for the *New York Times* and a professor at Columbia University, promoted an approach to literary criticism consistent with Matthew Arnold's ideas (some of which anticipate Du Bois's concept of the Talented Tenth). In 1909 Matthews served as president of the Modern Language Association but chastised his academic colleagues for writing "books which are not only unreadable by the average reader, but which are frankly not intended to be read by anybody except by a very limited circle of fellow-specialists" (*Gateways* 67). True enough, Matthews's sunnily complacent efforts "in behalf of the general reader" eventually prompted Randolph Bourne to dub him "the most naively worldly soul who ever got himself recognized as a man of letters" ("A Vanishing World" 234). In the first decade of the century, however, Matthews was an important figure, and Braithwaite was not particularly out of step in feeling comfortable with the earlier, time-honored notion of the critic's role as a careful and selective reader who perused books for wisdom and delight, directing other readers to works of value. Indeed, such was the very purpose of his book page in the *Boston Transcript*.

While he seemed uninterested in fashionable critical theories, Braithwaite was a meticulous literary historian and—perhaps as a result of his journalist's training—a writer capable of synthesizing and expressing ideas with elegant and concise effectiveness. It is true, though, that popularizers always run the risk of becoming mere promoters. Monroe was, in the cause of Modernism, an effective and tireless promoter. Her *fiat lux!* did not, however, instantly illuminate what Stedman had called "the twilight era" of American poetry. By the 1980s verse in open form and vernacular speech rhythms so completely dominated American poetry that some writers felt compelled to publish polemical essays calling for "a New Formalism." Given the recent state of the art, then, it is easy to forget how long it actually took for the old formalism to be displaced. In fact, it took a generation for poets, editors, and readers to accept fully the revolutionary ideas of the century's first decade.

For her part, Miss Monroe was a formidable contender. The slight, middle-aged former schoolteacher's appearance was deceptive. Harriet Monroe, born in 1860, was the daughter of a prominent Chicago attorney and became a powerful woman in her own right. If anyone could be called a "poetry activist" it was she. When Chicago's 1893 World's Columbian Exposition neglected to include poetry in its showcase of the nation's arts, Monroe persuaded the officials to allow her to organize a Poetry Day. When the *New York World* reprinted her ode celebrating the World's Fair without permission—a practice that was standard among newspapers of the period—she initiated a copyright infringement lawsuit and won a $5,000 judgment two years later. In her view, the result established that the copyrights of poets were as important as those of other artists. After 1899 she was daring enough to make her living as a freelance journalist and art critic for several newspapers and magazines. Indeed, Monroe did everything with a flair. Upon deciding to publish *Poetry: A Magazine of Verse,* she turned to civic leader H. C. Chatfield-Taylor for advice and built the magazine with an endowment from a group of subscribers that mirrored the Chicago Symphony's founding patrons (Williams, *Harriet Monroe* 8–17).

Monroe was also good at holding grudges and loved a fight. Not everyone, however, appreciated the amusement she apparently found in literary disputations. John G. Neihardt was among her early enthusiasms, but when in 1913 he reviewed Pound's contributions to *Poetry* harshly in his column in the *Minneapolis Journal,* he found himself the target of Monroe's wrath. Neihardt, who is best known today for his excellent oral history *Black Elk Speaks* (1932) rather than for his epic poems on the American West, backed away from the fight and forfeited Monroe's friendship (Aly 64–65). The fuss did not, however, prevent Monroe from including Neihardt's poems in her anthology *The New Poetry* (1917).

At the risk of a charge of guilt by association, it also seems clear that Miss Monroe took pleasure not only in Ezra Pound's poetry but also in his pugnacity. She must have been entertained by the ranting correspondence that he conducted as her magazine's "European editor." She herself was never inclined to shrink from a battle. Visiting New York City in 1917, Monroe reported: "As for the poets, they seem as numerous as sparrows . . . and almost as quarrelsome. This is not to deride but to declare! I have always admired the vigor and enthusiasm with which battles of the intellect are fought in Paris" (*A Poet's Life* 404–405). In William Stanley Braithwaite, Monroe found a worthy opponent.

Monroe and Braithwaite had first faced off in 1912 when each independently announced the establishment of a journal devoted to contemporary poetry. Monroe assumed that Braithwaite's *The Poetry Journal,* funded in part through the efforts of their mutual friend Amy Lowell, was an "impudent" attempt to compete with her own plan for *Poetry: A Magazine of Verse* (Williams, *Harriet Monroe* 26). As Braithwaite, decidedly unmellowed, remembered forty years later, the dispute was not simply a matter of jealousy or of motives misunderstood. "This was the revolt of the West against the East under the leadership of Harriet Monroe," he wrote in his Introduction to *Anthology of Magazine Verse for 1958:* "They felt that the supremacy of the 'effete' East in poetic matters had to be challenged and overthrown because, to them, it no longer had the vitality nor the insight to express and celebrate American life and character" (xliii). The feud built in intensity over the

THE ANTHOLOGY OF MAGAZINE VERSE

FOR 1914

Including "The Magazines and the Poets: A Review"

DEAR MR. *Leland* :—

This second annual issue of the "Anthology of Magazine Verse for 1914," will be published in November. The reception given the issue for 1913 was evidence of the importance and value of this publication as a record of the quality and achievement of contemporary American poetry. The contents of the volume this year are, in many respects of more varied interest and appeal. The discovery of some hitherto unknown names in American poetry — which has always been a feature of the annual summaries in the "Transcript," and emphasized more permanently in this volume — will result in the presentation of some very fine work, while the best work of familiar poets will maintain a high standard of achievement.

The most distinctive, and in every case poetically excellent selections by American poets inspired by the European war, with a note especially emphasizing the idealism and aspiration for peace, have been included in this volume.

The volume will contain the text of about sixty selections. In each case the poem has been selected purely in regard to its excellence as a poem, but the themes are of varied interest and significance; they are expressed in a variety of poetic forms.

Beside the text, the volume supplies the only source of reference to what has been accomplished in American poetry for the period. There is a separate list of all the "distinctive" poems and their authors estimated in the magazines, and a list of the titles of every poem and their authors appearing in all the leading American magazines. Also there is a critical summary of every important book of poems published during the year. All of this constitutes what is practically, and never before attempted, a Year Book of American Poetry.

All interested in the progress of American poetry can do it a special service by making the "Anthology of Magazine Verse for 1914," a Christmas gift-book for which it is admirably suited. For this purpose I am glad to offer the following special rates: three copies for $4.00 — five copies for $6.00 — ten copies for $11.00 — single copies $1.50. The book will be uniform in all respects with the 1913 issue but containing more material.

May I request that you will oblige me with an order at your earliest convenience, so that it may be determined how large an edition would be necessary to print. Fill out subjoined subscription blank and return with check or money order payable to the undersigned.

Yours very truly,

William Stanley Braithwaite
7.

- -

To WILLIAM STANLEY BRAITHWAITE
27 Ellsworth Avenue, Cambridge, Mass.

Date..191

Please send me on publication............cop........of the Anthology of Magazine Verse for 1914, including "The Magazines and the Poets: a Review," in boards at $1.50 each, carriage extra. Parcel post rate. 3. zone. 6. 0.

NAME ....

CITY OR TOWN .... STREET ....

STATE ....

Special rates three copies for $4.00, five copies for $6.00, ten copies for $11.00.

3. William Stanley Braithwaite's direct mail announcement of his anthology reached a growing community of poetry lovers. Courtesy of the Schomburg Center for Research in Black Culture.

next two years even though neither magazine was successful in market terms. Braithwaite's *The Poetry Journal* struggled on for a few years under the editorship of Edmund R. Brown (Williams, *Harriet Monroe* 85).

In 1913 Braithwaite began editing his annual anthology of the best poetry appearing in magazines. Evident from the beginning was his intention to refute E. C. Stedman's low valuation of contemporary poetry. In his introduction to the anthology (which he published at his own expense), Braithwaite wrote: "Our poetry needs, more than any-thing else, encouragement and support to reveal its qualities. The poets are doing satisfying and vitally excellent work and it only remains for the American public to do its duty by showing a substantial apprecia-tion" (xiii). Some readers argued, however, that the editor bestowed lau-rels too easily. In a review of Braithwaite's *Anthology of Magazine Verse for 1917* in the *Bookman,* his old friend Jessie Rittenhouse cautioned, "American poetry stands in much more danger of inflated praise than of balanced, judicious, even negative, criticism." Nevertheless, she noted, "Mr. Braithwaite has given to poetry a devoted, single-minded, unselfish service which all must appreciate, however they differ from his opinions" (Rittenhouse, "Contemporary Poetry" 679–680).

Conrad Aiken, of course, truculently dissented. In *Scepticisms: Notes on Contemporary Poetry* (1919), Aiken announced that he was not at all impressed with either Braithwaite's critical judgments or his generosity. "If in the presence of a piece of poetry the critic is content merely with the exclamatory," Aiken wrote, "he is not doing his work." Aiken was also displeased with the presence in Braithwaite's critical vocabulary of "such expressions as 'reverence for life,' 'quest for beauty,' and 'mystic illumination.'" To Aiken this was evidence of the editor's "belief that poetry is a sort of supernaturalism" (Aiken, *Scepticisms* 127–128). It would be a serious error, however, to think that Aiken's attack on Braith-waite involved issues related to Modernist aesthetics or an endorsement of the rigorous (if self-serving) critical stances espoused by T. S. Eliot or Ezra Pound. Indeed, when Aiken himself took on the role of popular-izer—as he did in editing *Modern American Poets,* published in London in 1922 and curiously including the very traditional and mediocre Anna Hempstead Branch among Modernists such as Eliot, John Gould Fletcher, and Alfred Kreymborg—his own critical vocabulary embraces flimsy boilerplate such as "American poetry, like any, must obey the principles of poetry; and they, whatever they may be, are presumably constant" (*Modern American Poets* vii).

Despite Braithwaite's own rather conventional poetic style, as an edi-tor he seemed quite receptive to newer, experimental poems. As the Imagists and other young poets associated with what Monroe was call-ing the New Poetry movement began to fill more of the pages of Braith-waite's anthology, the Braithwaite-Monroe feud boiled over into vicious acrimony. In the spring of 1917 Monroe's beef with Braithwaite was not merely that he had ignored her favorite protégés in 1913 but that, when

he enthusiastically included some of them in later years, he meticulously avoided acknowledging that Miss Monroe's *Poetry* had been the
proving ground of their genius.

Braithwaite may have had reasons to resent Monroe's sniping. Many
others were also annoyed by her proprietary stance. Jessie Belle Rittenhouse, author of *The Younger American Poets* (1905), poetry critic for the
New York Times and the most energetic founder of the Poetry Society of
America in 1910, was sometimes peeved with Monroe's possessive attitude and particularly resented Monroe's claim to have "discovered"
Vachel Lindsay in 1913. "He might have been a discovery to Miss Monroe," wrote Rittenhouse, "but he was no discovery to many others,
since . . . he had been writing verse for seventeen years" (*My House of
Life* 300).

With Conrad Aiken's sallies as overture, Monroe attacked Braithwaite as "the Boston dictator" in an intemperate editorial in *Poetry* that
(alluding to Shakespeare's *Merchant of Venice*) she entitled "Sir Oracle."
"Last year," she wrote, "Mr. Braithwaite was almost a convert to 'radicalism.' This year his mind is at sea, wondering whether it should venture further out into the unknown, but on the whole steering shore-
wards, reverting to type" (212). Monroe made sure that her criticism of
his editorial judgment was understood to be personal. "Mr. Braithwaite's tardy and reluctant recognition of our 'influence,' " she wrote,
"is perfectly comprehensible. *Poetry* has from the first taken exception
to his autocratic tone and criticized his somewhat provincial opinions"
(212).

Clearly, the issues that Braithwaite and Monroe clashed over were
extremely personal—and basically inconsequential, since both individuals were instrumental in advancing the careers of the same group
of poets. Their dispute primarily reflected considerations of ego and
power, not aesthetics, but it also made poets choose sides, bringing out
their true colors and their worst behavior. There has never been any
ambiguity about what poets think of editors and critics. As Spingarn
perceptively noted, "what each mainly seeks in his own case is not
criticism, but uncritical praise" ("The New Criticism" 9). Nevertheless,
the role assumed by the poets in the 1917 dustup was somewhat extraordinary.

Alice Corbin Henderson, co-editor of *Poetry,* had poems of her own
included in Braithwaite's *Anthology of Magazine Verse for 1916* but chose
to stick with Monroe and began to organize poets to "boycott" future
editions. Willard Wattles, editor of *Sunflowers: A Book of Kansas Poems*

(1918), responded to her campaign with a satirical poem accusing those who appeared in Braithwaite's book of shaming themselves (52):

> All the poets have been stripping,
> Quaintly into moonbeams slipping,
> Running out like wild Bacchantes
> Minus *lingerie* and panties,

Carl Sandburg, whose recent work had been negatively reviewed by Braithwaite in the *Boston Evening Transcript,* offered to help spread the boycott, writing to Henderson that "a pathetic personage has been permitted to grow into a fungus mistaken for what it grows on. The popery and kaiserism of it, the snobbery, flunkyism and intrigue, I'm on to it" (124). The opportunistic Robert Frost, whose popularity had been boosted by Braithwaite's articles in the *Boston Evening Transcript,* did not have Sandburg's excuse. Nevertheless, like Ezra Pound, Frost was not reluctant to call Braithwaite a "nigger," and though never missing an opportunity to advance his own career, Frost hyperbolically complained to a correspondent that he resented "the climbing of every black reviewer's back stairs for preferment" (Thompson 542–543 n. 32). Much earlier, Frost had expressed his resentment of Braithwaite in even uglier terms in a letter to Louis Untermeyer (Frost 21–22).

Alice Corbin Henderson's own "race card" was viciously played in an April 1916 satire on contemporary poets that she mailed to Ezra Pound for critical comment. Regarding Braithwaite, she wrote:

> It is very like Boston
> To accept as poetic arbiter
> . . . .
>   in a country where all men
> Are created *free and equal,*
> One so obviously handicapped
> By nature.
> (Nadel 178)

The slur recalls a letter from Pound to Henderson on 16 January 1913 that described Braithwaite's race as an "affliction." Though Pound asked Henderson to destroy the slanderous page, it is now in the Harry Ransom Humanities Research Center at the University of Texas and is reprinted in Ira B. Nadel's meticulously edited volume *The Letters of Ezra Pound to Alice Corbin Henderson* (1993). This letter and others suggest that while Pound was fluent with racist remarks, he may also have seen an opportunity to reinforce his alliance with the *Poetry* ladies by appearing to share their hatred of a man he had never met (Nadel 14–16; Nielsen, *Reading Race* 66–67).

A proper assessment of Braithwaite as an anthologist must take into account the available material from which he made his selection. Clearly Monroe's quarrel with Braithwaite reflected her desire to promote her own editorial choices (and her position). Braithwaite, if honestly attempting to produce anthologies containing the "best poems" published in a wide range of widely circulated magazines, could not devote his book to a single coterie. With this point in mind, it is illuminating to compare Braithwaite's selections with the usual contents of the period's magazines. From a total of 506 poems published during the year in *Harper's, Scribner's, Century, Forum, Lippincott's,* the *Smart Set,* and a few other journals, Braithwaite selected 86 as worthy of anthologizing in his initial 1913 volume ("Introduction," *Anthology of Magazine Verse for 1913* viii–ix). Critic Clara Parker, interested in charting the advance of Modernism, published a study of poetry in major magazines in a 1920 article in *Texas Review.* In her survey of *Harper's* for the decade 1910–1919, Parker noted: "The most obvious indication of modernity in poetry is, of course, free verse form. When we find that only two of the five hundred poems published in *Harper's* during these ten years are written in free verse, we cannot avoid the conclusion that its editors have manifested little desire to see unfettered cadences substituted for regular rhythm. These two poems are 'The Superman' (1916) by Albert B. Paine and 'Quincunx' (1919) by Amy Lowell" (Parker 56–57). *Scribner's* during the same period was somewhat less conservative and published most of the better writers included in Monroe and Henderson's *The New Poetry* (1917), yet Parker found that "striking examples of the new poetry are rare. The only poems [written in free verse out of works contributed by more than 250 writers] are four by Amy Lowell, all of which are modern in content as well as form, and one, a war poem entitled 'Candles' by Allen Tucker. Irregular metrical compositions combined with blank verse are found occasionally, but in general the form of the verse is conservative, including common lyric forms, 'Tennysonian' blank verse, and many sonnets" (63). Not surprisingly, Harriet Monroe's two poems that appeared in *Scribner's* were not exercises in vers libre.

Atlantic Monthly, despite the frustration of poetry editor Bliss Perry regarding the space available, was hospitable to the newer voices (Williams, *Harriet Monroe* 4). Parker found only this magazine "abreast of the times," though it was not spilling over with Imagist poems. "None of the poems it has published could be said to furnish a contribution to great world literature," Parker carefully concluded, "but some of them are representative of the best poetry of the present day as measured by its own standards" (Parker, "The New Poetry" 56).

Indeed, the range of forms found in a magazine such as *Scribner's* could also be seen in the pages of Monroe's own journal. Parker, while sympathetic to the experimentation that Monroe championed, was not overwhelmed by everything that the most daring members of the movement produced. "It would appear" she remarks, "that one may put on any sort of poetical garment he chooses provided only he doffs the thread-bare Victorian garb. The result is that the new-clad crowd appears in motley" ("The New Poetry" 46).

Braithwaite's choices show that as an anthologist he was clearly more receptive to the experimental poets than were the editors of the major magazines. Monroe's animosity toward Braithwaite was not shared by all poets. Indeed, as Margaret Widdemer recalled, many desired Braithwaite's notice and inclusion in his anthologies. "If you were in it," wrote Widdemer, "you were on your way or more likely arrived. The poems chosen for the *Transcript* page, and the reviews there, were an accolade" (*Golden Friends* 39). Braithwaite did not only support other poets in print. Along with Brander Matthews, he mentored James Weldon Johnson's transition from popular songwriter to poet (E. Levy 161; Fleming 20). He could also be exceedingly generous to aspiring poets who knocked on the door of his Boston home. In 1916 a young New Yorker named Glenn Clairmonte dropped by and later recalled that Braithwaite "allowed me to visit in his studio for several days while he sonorously read poetry to me" (102).

The charges and countercharges from Boston and Chicago went on, actually, for about three years (1915–1918) and eventually had a beneficial result for poets. As Braithwaite noted in 1958, perhaps with purposely exaggerated gentility: "The publicity given to poetry in the press, the appearance of other poetry magazines in different parts of the country, and the space given in general periodicals like *The New Republic* and *The Freeman,* made the public so conscious of the art that the renaissance took full stride" ("Introduction" xl). The African American poet Fenton Johnson, editing the *Champion Magazine* in Chicago, had come to Braithwaite's defense on his editorial page, but otherwise the numbers seem to have been on Miss Monroe's side. Braithwaite, however, emerged from the fracas as powerful and arrogantly genteel as ever, continuing to turn out new annual anthologies for the next decade.

William Stanley Braithwaite was no victim of racism. The confrontation with Harriet Monroe in 1917 was really of the nature of a family squabble among supporters of the Modernist movement in American poetry. If some of the printed comments and private correspondence took unsavory tones, it is merely more evidence of what Aldon Lynn Nielsen has identified in his fine work *Reading Race* (1988) as the ingrained anti-Negro attitudes of the period, attitudes that were reflected even in those we have been taught to consider our most sensitive and advanced intellects. In the case of Sandburg, otherwise known to have been sympathetic to the African American cause, the opportunity to retaliate for a bad review may be understandable even if his vituperative response seems excessive. We may lean toward caution; it is possible to make too much of this.

From Braithwaite's perspective, however, the racial implications of the affair might not have been so easily dismissed. It would, therefore, be useful to know what elements of character or pragmatic outlook shaped his responses.

"Braithwaite's view of poetry was pre-modern," contends Craig S. Abbott. "He was more poetry-lover than critic" (151). This is not quite the whole story. Despite his tendency toward a rhapsodic assumption of unquestioned and eternal verities, a reading of Braithwaite's critical commentaries suggests that he was interested in poetry not as a purely metaphorical discourse but as an effective and elegant means of preserving and transmitting the multivalent complexities of human existence and of what Matthew Arnold had called "the best that has been thought." In 1922, for example, Braithwaite became an enthusiastic supporter of Hughes Mearns's pioneering high school creative writing classes at New York's Lincoln School. In a properly Arnoldian mood, Braithwaite wrote that "even if [the students] do not become expressed poets later on, they will become possessed of that culture whose spirit is poetry" (Mearns 3; Myers 102–103). In Braithwaite's writings it becomes clear that he does not believe that the culture transmitted in English-language poetry is *essential* or that one can avoid "the technical elements of the science of versification." In an article titled "Some Contemporary Poets of the Negro Race," published in the *Crisis* in 1919, Braithwaite identified the source of much bad poetry: "It is the hard and laborious task of mastering the subtle and fluctuating rhythms of verse that the average individual tries to escape which produces such a mass of mediocre work, often choking and wasting the substance of a passionate and imaginative poetic spirit" (55). This statement is not a specific criticism of African American writers; it is advice from an accomplished poet to beginners of any racial background. In this context, Braithwaite's praise of "the glorious and perfect instrument of English poetic art" (51) refers to the *language* and to the techniques developed over centuries that can be learned by anyone dedicated enough to do the work required.

Rather than being measured as an early integrationist, however, Braithwaite might best be understood as a person who actually lived— or, at least, worked—in a racially "integrated" milieu. This did not mean that he was ignorant of the harsher aspects of the racial status quo. Though his father died when he was only seven years old, Braithwaite felt that he was firmly anchored by his family heritage. He was as proud of the grandfather, who had "the reputation of being the best Latin scholar" in Barbados, as he was of his maternal grandmother, who "found her way to Boston from North Carolina with three young daughters" amid the chaos of 1865 (*Reader* 159, 162). Completing four years of school, Braithwaite went to work at age twelve performing duties "reserved for a colored boy" in various firms (*Reader* 168). But young Braithwaite was smart, hard working, ambitious, and—in no small degree—lucky.

Like Mark Twain and William Dean Howells, Braithwaite began his literary apprenticeship and advanced education in the print shop. He began writing poetry while learning to set type at the Boston publishing firm Ginn and Company. In the time-honored tradition of young poets, Braithwaite was not shy about writing to literary notables such as Howells and Edmund Clarence Stedman, asking for attention to his poems (*Reader* 238–242). In April 1899 he also drafted a straightforward letter to publisher L. C. Page: "I am an American Negro, a Bostonian by birth, and received my M. A. from Nature's University of 'Seek, Observe and Utilize' and am now in my 20th year." Having revealed a sense of humor, the poet next tried a touch of modesty: "without advantage of even a high school education and teeming with the faults inherent to youthful poetical genius, I beseech you to be indulgent of the minor imperfections that pervade my work" (*Reader* 237). A rejection slip was not long in arriving.

Armed with impeccable manners and dignified carriage, Braithwaite seems to have had better luck presenting himself in person. Beginning around 1901, he busied himself as a contributor to William Monroe Trotter's newspaper, the *Boston Guardian,* the *Colored American Magazine,* edited by novelist Pauline E. Hopkins, and J. Max Barber's militant *Voice of the Negro* (*Reader* 11, 114; Johnson and Johnson 23). By 1903 he had met several of Boston's "mainstream" literati and had compiled a collection of poems. With the help of poets Frederic Lawrence Knowles and Jessie Rittenhouse he was introduced to literary doyenne Louise Chandler Moulton, whose astonishingly long-running salon had been attended by Longfellow and John Greenleaf Whittier, and to Thomas Wentworth Higginson, the famed abolitionist who encouraged Emily Dickinson's poetic efforts. Encouragement and subscriptions for his volume *Lyrics of Life and Love* (1904) came from Boston luminaries such as Julia Ward Howe, Thomas Bailey Aldrich, Bliss Perry, and Edward Everett Hale. Braithwaite's reputation grew rapidly. The year 1906 found him involved in editing several book projects and beginning an association with the *Boston Evening Transcript* that would result in one of the most influential book columns in the United States (*Reader* 182–186).

Braithwaite belonged to that group of literary men who wrote for a living. Like Langston Hughes later, or early Boston associates Isaac Goldberg and Henry Thomas Schnittkind, Braithwaite was always pursuing the next publishing contract—for editing a volume, for writing prefaces or newspaper columns, or for any other literary commission such as biographies. Only in 1935 at the age of fifty-seven did he succumb to the lure of a comfortable academic position and its regular paycheck by accepting an appointment at Atlanta University. Despite Braithwaite's lack of formal academic credentials, university president John Hope enthusiastically recommended his appointment as professor of English. "I suppose," Hope wrote, "that there is no Negro living who is so steeped in English and American Literature and who has had such unusual opportunities for acquaintance with contemporary writers of prose and poetry. He has encouraged many young American authors of both races and by his friendly criticism has helped to make them writers of note" (Bacote 290). The transition to academia was not necessarily easy for the veteran freelancer. In 1940, for example, Braithwaite received a stern letter from university president Rufus Clement emphasizing the importance of attending faculty meetings.

In earlier days, Braithwaite not only wrote his literary surveys and book reviews for the *Boston Evening Transcript* but also briefly held editorships at Boston magazines such as the *Stratford Magazine,* founded the *Poetry Journal,* and was on the editorial boards of African American journals such as the short-lived *Citizen* (1915–1916) and the NAACP's *Crisis.* He also edited anthologies of British poetry aimed at a popular audience.

These projects are worth close examination because of the quietly oppositional quality of some of Braithwaite's productions. If, as T. M. Pearce noted, the poetry of the 1890s was devoted to "pleasant selections" that never managed "the surge of Walt Whitman or the cryptic condensation of Emily Dickinson" (3), Braithwaite and his peers—regardless of stylistic differences—wanted twentieth-century poetry to play a more significant role in public intellectual discourse. Mark W. Van Wienen, in *Partisans and Poets: The Political Work of American Poetry in the Great War* (1997) points out an interesting facet of Braithwaite's influence. Attempting "to represent the best of American magazine verse by featuring war verse and especially verse favoring the cause of England, France, and Belgium, his anthology of 1915 is representative of the partisan and interventionist sentiments coming to dominate attitudes among America's political and intellectual elite" (116–117). There is, however, another strain that counterpoints Braithwaite's support of the Allied war effort. By the end of the war, Braithwaite made an even more forthright statement.

Victory (1919), an anthology of World War I poems, opens patriotically enough with an introduction by Theodore Roosevelt and sonnets in praise of Allied heroes such as Marshall Ferdinand Foch. But soon one encounters Mary Carolyn Davies's "Fifth Avenue and Grand Street," which depicts two Red Cross volunteers—a socialite and a shop girl—packing medical supplies for army field hospitals. Their moment of sisterhood lasts only a moment:

> But now that peace is here again
> And our boys safe, I can't help wondering—Well,
> Will she forget, and crawl back in her shell
> And if I call, say "Show this person out"?
> Or still be friendly as she was? I doubt
> If Grand will sit beside Fifth Avenue
> Again, and be politely spoken to.
>
> We're sisters while the danger lasts, it's true;
> But rich and poor's equality must cease
> (For women especially), of course, in peace.
> (Davies 27)

Fenton Johnson's contribution, "The New Day," was later cited by Robert T. Kerlin as an example of "the newer methods of verse, and yet with a splendid suggestion of the old Spirituals" (Kerlin 102). For this elegiac meditation on the war experience of black soldiers, Johnson chose not to use the prose poem form, skillfully employing a variety of line lengths and rhetorical patterns. The editor's real agenda becomes apparent in the poems by Davies, Johnson, Louis Untermeyer, and others, focusing on class issues in the United States that remained unresolved while the nation pursued Woodrow Wilson's "war to make the world safe for democracy."

It is significant also that some of Braithwaite's associates on various editorial projects were men like Schnittkind (later a prolific author of popular nonfiction under the name Henry Thomas) and Goldberg, both of whom were involved with Jewish working-class education movements and Socialist literacy efforts such as Emanuel Haldeman-Julius's *Little Blue Books*. It is not unreasonable to suppose that Braithwaite shared similar enthusiasms. For his own part, he was never inactive in the African American press and maintained close contacts with race leaders such as Benjamin Brawley, W. E. B. Du Bois, George W. Ellis, and Kelly Miller.

While he was editing the *Poetry Journal* and feuding with Harriet Monroe, Braithwaite also worked as editor of the *Stratford Journal*. In the fall of 1916, the first issue of this handsome bimonthly included an editorial signed by Henry T. Schnittkind, Braithwaite's associate editor and a shareholder in the publication ("Statement" 86). Schnittkind clearly announced the editorial board's view of the important functional role of literature in society: "Who has not thrilled with the poetry, the tenseness, the homeliness, the living, throbbing *humanness* of the one-act plays of the Irish players? Who of us, on seeing these plays, has not exclaimed, 'Give us more and more of this, for this is the sort of stuff that life is made of.' Well, this is the sort of 'stuff' that we are going to publish in each issue of *The Stratford Journal*." The editors were not interested in merely exciting their readers with powerfully poetic exoticism: "After reading that sort of drama, our visions are broadened, are they not? We no longer sneer at the benighted Russians, the hot-headed 'dagos,' the slimy 'Chinks' but we feel a reverence for them, for in their eyes we recognize a gleam that reflects the soul of God" (Schnittkind 5–6). The editors did not, of course, intend any notion of religious brotherhood; rather, they saw that literature could be useful in promoting the sort of cultural pluralism that sociologist Horace M. Kallen discussed in 1915 in a series of important articles in the *Nation*. The contents of the *Stratford Journal* certainly delivered on the editors' cosmopolitan promise, offering poems by the young Louise Bogan, translations of the Mexican poet Luis G. Urbina, stories by Knut Hamsun, and critical essays on American poetry and fiction. The editors also directed readers' attention to the works of Bengali poet Rabindranath Tagore, to Bertrand Russell, and to Gilbert Cannan's novel *Mendel,* described as "a sympathetic study of a Jewish immigrant" ("Books" 86).

If Braithwaite's role in an enterprise such as the *Stratford Journal* has been previously unmentioned, neither has his role in the development of African American literature been adequately assessed. In a sense he was a forerunner of the Harlem Renaissance, yet he was also seen by some of the younger participants in the movement as one of their more antagonistic critics. Braithwaite shared Du Bois's distaste for some of the more sensationalized depictions of black life that were encouraged during the period. Some commentators, however, suspected that—unlike Du Bois—Braithwaite was not concerned primarily about strategies for presenting the race in a flattering light. Robert L. Poston, writing in Marcus Garvey's UNIA newspaper the *Negro World* in 1922, noted: "Braithwaite, because of his anthologies and his connection with a great white daily and because he does not in his poems indicate his racial extraction, is taken by many, who do not know him personally, to be a white man." Poston felt that such a mistake was understandable, since "Braithwaite has become so Caucasianized in his writings, that he has lost his racial identity entirely, if he ever had any, and the white people claim him as their own" (70). Poston admitted, however, that Braithwaite was a good poet whose work had universal appeal.

William H. Ferris, literary editor of the *Negro World,* did not agree with Poston. Ferris had first met Braithwaite in 1896 and recognized in the ambitious teenager a "voracious reader, an ardent lover of poetry." By 1913, when Paul Laurence Dunbar was dead and James Weldon Johnson was struggling (with Braithwaite's help) to make the transition from popular songwriter to poet, Ferris had pronounced William Stanley Braithwaite "the poet laureate of the colored race" (*The African Abroad* 870). In 1922, in the pages of the *Negro World,* Ferris cited Braithwaite as living proof that "the world of literature, art and music knows no color line" ("Negro Composers" 302). Such a statement did not compromise Ferris's Garveyite Pan-African nationalism. Like Du Bois and Alain Locke, Ferris wished to demonstrate that the higher intellectual realm of culture might accomplish what seemed to be impossible in the meaner political arena. The example of Braithwaite's career—anomalous though it might have been—armed Ferris with evidence that he could use in his newspaper's ongoing assault on the irrationality of racism, evidence that refuted white supremacist doctrines.

Scholarly assessments of African American attitudes are frequently more self-serving than accurate. It is not that the African American, as Norman Mailer and others have quite arrogantly suggested, remains a projection of suppressed white desire. Rather, as Claude McKay eloquently stated in his poem "In Bondage" (1921), black people in the United States have been merely "simple slaves of ruthless slaves." From the Moynihan Report to the recent spate of affirmative action survival narratives on the best-seller list, intellectual discussion usually describes the "mood of Black America" in terms that suit the political establishment's own desired self-image. For this reason it is both important and difficult to understand the implications of Braithwaite's racial identity—or its ambiguity. Robert L. Poston's idea that Braithwaite simply identified with the Caucasian status quo is insufficiently convincing and, in fact, incorrect. Others have suggested that, even though Braithwaite did not come from a privileged background, the Boston milieu stifled the development in him of a militant race consciousness.

In nineteenth-century Boston, writes sociologist Oscar Handlin, "Negro awareness of race derived not from differences they desired to cherish, but rather from a single difference—color—which they desired to discard" (175–176). Whatever Handlin's motives may have been in formulating such a statement, his words are misleading. The African American community in Boston campaigned for the elimination of color as a *handicap* to advancement. Militant leadership was personified by William Monroe Trotter and his newspaper, the *Boston Guardian*. Trotter's adventures included a 1914 confrontation with President Woodrow Wilson in the White House over the issue of legalized segregation in government employment. In 1915, Trotter and the Boston community led the nation in protests against D. W. Griffith's vicious portrayal of Negroes in *The Birth of a Nation* (Weiss 133–137; Rogers "William Monroe Trotter" 399–405; Fox 188–197).

Where Handlin discerns a lack of ethnic pride, a better understanding of the African American mood during this period might be gleaned from J. Max Barber's May 1907 editorial in Atlanta's *Voice of the Negro* announcing that his journal "is devoted to the unraveling of the snarl of the Color Problem and is published to the end that justice may prevail in the land, that lawlessness and bigotry may be wiped out and that the fetish of color prejudice may pass away forever" (Johnson and

Johnson 17). African American race consciousness based on the recognition that "the color line" should *not* be the boundary of opportunity certainly did not arrive with the turn of the century; indeed, this type of race consciousness can be said to have formed the character of those born in the 1870s and 1880s. Judith E. B. Harmon suggests, for example, that the talented, highly educated James Weldon Johnson with his "self-perception as a cosmopolite" effectively made a bold personal statement that "defied political restrictions" intended to limit his creative expression (1). A similar view may be accurate in the case of William Stanley Braithwaite and others of that generation.

It is important to understand that the intellectual color line was more complex than simple exclusion. Braithwaite's friend Benjamin Brawley, dean at Atlanta's Morehouse College and author of "The Negro Genius" (1915), *The Negro in Literature and Art* (1918), and other important works of the period, complained in a 1919 letter to Braithwaite that he was having trouble marketing a history of English drama that he felt would be suitable for adoption as a high school text. Brawley felt that the manuscript was "the best thing I have ever done." Nevertheless, the response from publishers was "very good, but we are not in the textbook business. Send us more of the Negro stuff" (Brawley, Letter 4). Paul Laurence Dunbar complained to James Weldon Johnson that publishers had forced him into the almost schizophrenic position of dividing his poetic energies between Negro dialect verse and attempts at a more "universal" expression in traditional forms. Writers of the sensibility shared by Johnson, Brawley, and Braithwaite struggled to avoid Dunbar's dilemma.

Braithwaite's own poems are skillful and elegant, usually cast in the philosophical mood popular in late nineteenth-century verse. His volume *The House of Falling Leaves* (1908) included meditations on death and life, titles such as "A Little While Before Farewell" (which can be compared without judgment to the effective—and predictable—musical "hooks" of today's pop songs), and well-turned lines intended to go directly into the reader's personal treasury of favorite quotations:

Failure is a crown of sorrows,
Success a crown of fears
(*House of Falling Leaves* 79)

The reader will not find racial identification in Braithwaite's poetry. The nearest thing to it in *The House of Falling Leaves* is a poem titled "La

Belle de Demerara," an answer to Oliver Wendell Holmes's wonderful "Dorothy Q" (1871):

> O Poet who sang of Dorothy Q.;
> I have a Great-Grandmother too,
> Born in a British colonial place,
> Sent to learn Parisian grace;
> Who won all hearts in her demesne
> By the Caribbean's warm blue sheen:
> And large is the debt I owe to her,
> La belle de Demerara.
> (*House of Falling Leaves* 88)

Some might mistake this for "Caucasianized" values, but it seems more clearly to be Braithwaite's assertion of his own heritage, full of contradictions though it may be, and his willingness to present that heritage as the full functional equal of any Boston brahmin's. An invented African heritage may be purer and more politically useful, but Braithwaite is satisfied to celebrate his genuine roots. It would be an error, however, to conclude that Braithwaite was unconcerned about broader racial issues; in fact, he felt that the proper subject matter of poetry was not to be found in a category as limiting as race—especially as it was conceived during that era. "I am not one who believes," he wrote in 1919, "that a Negro writer of verse—or of fiction, for that matter—must think, feel, or write racially to be a great artist; nor can he be distinctively labeled by the material he uses" ("Some Poets" 276). For Braithwaite as an artist, the quest for the universal should be the goal of artistic expression. This was the same principle that directed his editorial hand in his annual poetry anthologies and the *Stratford Journal,* and he followed this principle in composing his own poems.

Recent critical opinion of Braithwaite—what little there is—is nowhere near as harsh as was J. Saunders Redding's 1939 assessment. "The world beyond the walled world of Negro life was not ready," said Redding, for African American writers of "kinless verse" that—while excellent in technique—did not depict the expected Negro themes. Furthermore, though he certainly abhorred racist stereotypes, Redding did not himself hold "color blind" attempts at universality in high esteem. Braithwaite, Redding concluded, "is the most outstanding example of perverted energy that the period from 1903 to 1917 produced" (*To Make a Poet Black* 89).

Current views are more along the lines of a recent comment from

Michael Bérubé. According to Bérubé, unlike Jean Toomer and Melvin B. Tolson, who "sought a negotiation of African American cultural forms and Anglo-American modernist experimentation," Braithwaite was merely old-fashioned enough to assume confidently that the word "universal" embraced all particularities (*Marginal Forces* 186, 171). Negative judgments aside, the critics are at least accurate about Braithwaite's staunch position as a universalist. In his work as an editor and anthologist, Braithwaite was able to promote the avant-garde while also supporting African American writers because he operated from a clearly stated premise: "to respect the vitality and variety of present-day poetry" while carefully understanding its place in an ancient tradition (*Reader* 91). And, of course, he encouraged all efforts that were consistent with his vision of social justice and racial equality.

The type of race consciousness that shaped both Braithwaite and the emerging "New Negro" at the turn of the century gave rise to two distinct but related strategies. One, of course, was the type of political activism and social comment literature that was associated with William Monroe Trotter, W. E. B. Du Bois, Ida B. Wells-Barnett, J. Max Barber, and others. This approach—and these very individuals—established first the Niagara movement and then the NAACP. The second approach was more personal and was expressed as an engaged and committed desire to live one's own life free of the bonds of a racist system. Both of these approaches, of course, would be the driving forces of the Harlem Renaissance of the 1920s. Indeed, Benjamin Brawley's 1915 essay "The Negro Genius," first published in Hampton Institute's *Southern Workman,* is an early statement of an aesthetic argument that would often be repeated by Du Bois, James Weldon Johnson, and Alain Locke. Brawley declared that "America should realize that the Negro has peculiar gifts which need all possible cultivation, and which will one day add to the glory of the country. Already his music is recognized as the most distinctive that the United States has yet produced. The possibilities of the race in literature and oratory, in sculpture and painting, are illimitable" ("The Negro Genius" 330–331). A writer such as Braithwaite hoped that this realization would be possible without rancorous conflict, that it might be spurred by the example of artists, like himself, who genuinely believed—though socially and politically hampered by racial discrimination—that their artistic possibilities could not be segregated. It was, in fact, on the strength of such a personal creed that W. S. Braithwaite was able to achieve his unprecedented position of literary eminence at the *Boston Evening Transcript.*

The teenaged Willie Braithwaite, reading his way through the great Boston Public Library, would have shared Du Bois's epiphany about the power of art. "I sit with Shakespeare," Du Bois wrote in *The Souls of Black Folk* (1903), "and he winces not. Across the color line I move arm in arm with Balzac and Dumas. . . . they come all graciously with no scorn nor condescension" (76). Braithwaite, having experienced overt racial discrimination while seeking a job in the book business in New York in 1900, became determined, as William H. Ferris noted, "to make his living solely with his pen" (*The African Abroad* 869). "The resolution I formed," Braithwaite recalled in 1941, "was to express myself on the common ground of American authorship, to demonstrate, in however humble a degree, that a man of color was the equal of any other man in possession of the attributes that produced a literature of human thought and experience, and to *force* a recognition of this common capacity and merit from the appreciation of the reading public and the authority of critical opinion" (*Reader* 179, emphasis added).

This resolve, and the fact that William Stanley Braithwaite was able, over five decades, to bring his dream close to reality, mark him clearly as a philosophical mentor of the Harlem Renaissance. Just as clearly, his efforts on behalf of the new poetry—whether or not he was, as Conrad Aiken charged, more of a drum major than a critic—gave substance to the hope of James Oppenheim, the editor of *Seven Arts,* that America could be "regenerated by art" (Kazin 172), and they helped justify Wallace Stevens's belief that poets, indeed, *can* change it all.

Though Braithwaite is not usually considered a participant in the Harlem Renaissance, by his eminence he contributed to its luster—as did his critical essays in the *Crisis* and in Alain Locke's anthology *The New Negro* (1925). Indeed, Braithwaite's criticism reflected a central tenet of the movement—the redemptive or recuperative power of art for the African American image—even when he appeared to be resisting the idea of "a Negro idiom." "All great artists," he wrote in the *Crisis* in 1919, "are interracial and international in rendering in the medium of any particular art the fundamental passions and the primary institutions of humanity" (*Reader* 54).

James Weldon Johnson lucidly articulated the instrumental potential of this idea. In a column for the *New York Age,* published 7 September 1918, Johnson encouraged his readers to buy books of poetry and argued that "the production of literature by colored writers" might have a significant effect on the improvement of race relations. "The world does not know that a race is great," he wrote, "until that race produces great literature" ("Some New Books" 271–272). The axiomatic source of Johnson's idea had been expressed, with broader intent, by Braithwaite in the introduction to his *Anthology of Magazine Verse for 1913*. There is, Braithwaite declared, "no achievement more vital in registering the soul of a people than its poetry" (v). While the statement can be taken as "universal," Braithwaite's 1919 *Crisis* article "Some Contemporary Poets of the Negro Race" shows that he was not averse to applying the principle specifically to African American literature. Johnson liked his own formulation of the idea so well that he repeated it in his remarks at the Urban League's May 1925 *Opportunity* Literary Awards banquet— where the young prizewinners included Countee Cullen, Zora Neale Hurston, Langston Hughes, and Dorothy West ("Opportunity Dinner" 176). Johnson's statement would effectively, concisely, and officially enunciate the raison d'être and strategic politics of the Harlem Renaissance.

As an individual who had achieved unequivocal success in his chosen field despite society's racial prohibitions, Braithwaite—whatever the views of Harlem's younger firebrands—personified one goal of the developing New Negro movement. The younger writers (as Claudia Tate has pointed out) promoted an exaggerated depiction of Braithwaite, Georgia Douglas Johnson, Jessie Fauset, and even Du Bois, as representatives of "a rigidly defined bourgeois conservatism" in order to "highlight their own originality, liberalism, and self-assertiveness" (Tate xxiii). At the same time, they depended on Du Bois and Fauset to publish their poems and hoped that Braithwaite might anthologize them.

When the 1920s dawned, poetry was in glorious bloom. "On every hand, from every locality," wrote Louis Untermeyer, "a fresh scattering of voices is heard. It is in this rich diversity that a new era in American poetry is being made manifest" (354). Braithwaite's assessment of two exciting literary decades stands as testimony to Harriet Monroe's efforts as well as his own. "The twenty years between 1904 and 1924," he wrote, "will always present the most paradoxical records in American literary history. The currents of song came from every source from which the national character was forming; all, more or less striving to present a unified consciousness of native art" (quoted in K. Williams 540).

PART TWO

Too Close to Turn Around

3

Margaret Walker and the Contest to Define America

In 1920s America the nation's myriad voices raised in song seemed to echo the recipe for cultural pluralism advanced by the sociologist Horace M. Kallen. In the following decade, however, it became apparent that these voices were not always singing in unison and that the various artistic forces were strenuously competing for an impact on the national character. An understanding of the high stakes involved can be gained by a study of the career of Margaret Walker (1917–1998), a poet who was first celebrated for her precocity and who was later revered for her wisdom and generosity to younger artists.

Margaret Walker's *For My Children* (1942), an extraordinary first book of poems, has become one of the classic works of twentieth-century American literature. The word "classic" requires explanation. There is, as we all know, the general understanding that a classic is a work that withstands the test of time—which often means a book that doesn't fall to pieces while languishing on a shelf in silent testimony to the truth of Mark Twain's definition of a classic as "a book which people praise and don't read." In contrast, Walker's volume went through six printings by the Yale University Press between 1942 and 1968, was reprinted by Arno Press, and is included in *This Is My Century: New and Collected Poems,* published in 1990 by the University of Georgia Press.

Donald B. Gibson's very specific meditation on the term is most appropriate. "A classic," he writes, "exists in relation to the needs of a particular culture and will remain a classic only as long as it fulfills those needs" (8–9). Gibson further instructs us that the critic's job in

4. Margaret Walker at the Washington, D.C., opening of Brian Lasker's exhibit entitled "I Dream a World," 1983. Photo by Roy Lewis.

determining what is indeed classic "is to describe and evaluate the value system informing literary works . . . by means of analysis of its social dimension" (ix). In other words, as the French writer Maurice Olender puts it, we seek a practical method to "arrest a thought in its flight by identifying the questions that gave rise to a particular text" (17). *For My People* was the first book by an African American poet to be published in the prestigious Yale Series of Younger Poets. As we shall see, however, Walker's achievement was more heroic than this honor indicates.

Walker was born in Birmingham, grew up in New Orleans, and moved to Jackson, Mississippi, in 1949. Eventually she became a distinguished professor at Jackson State College. The daughter of a minister and a music teacher, both on the faculty of Dillard University, Walker while still a child met luminaries such as W. E. B. Du Bois and Roland Hayes.

"I grew up at a time when we talked about race pride," she has said, "and in my family, in my house, we were always reading *Crisis* magazine and *Opportunity*. My father's friends were Garveyites. My mother believed in Booker T. Washington, but my father believed in W. E. B. Du Bois" (Ward, "A Writer" 526).

At seventeen, Walker wrote a fine essay in support of Booker T. Washington's educational theories. "True" she wrote, "we have a hard road before us with many heavy odds against us but we are encouraged when we think of the splendid progress made so far and know that in proportion to the difficulties our fathers faced and the hindrances we face today, we are indeed fortunate" (*On Being Female* 176). Published in the August 1932 issue of *Our Youth* magazine, Walker's "What Is to Become of Us?" was, of course, precisely what was expected of a bright, "well-trained high school graduate" (171). In less than a decade, however, she would be a nationally acclaimed poet.

Undergraduate study at Northwestern University and a subsequent job with the Chicago office of the Federal Writers Project (part of the Works Progress Administration, or WPA) broadened Walker's cultural outlook even further. Music had always been important to her, but as she told Jerry Ward, "It was not until I went to Chicago that I had a chance to see many art exhibitions. I remember being so awe-struck and excited at the Art Institute of Chicago. I saw great paintings and great masterworks of art for the first time. I heard a symphony for the first time when I was seventeen in Chicago, and I heard José Iturbi playing with the Chicago Symphony" (Ward, "A Writer" 519). Margaret Walker's first poem was published in the *Crisis* in 1934 while she was still a student at Northwestern University. Echoing an 1895 poem by Frances E. W. Harper, the nineteen-year-old poet accepted her vocation. "I want to write the songs of my people," she declared (113):

I want to catch the last floating strains from
  their sob-torn throats
I want to frame their dreams into words; their
  souls into notes.

Her goal would be eloquently realized over the ensuing decade. *For My People* would be a signal achievement.

The poet enjoyed significant early attention. Some of the poems in the manuscript of her book had appeared in the widely read Urban League magazine *Opportunity.* Others were welcomed by editor George Dillon at *Poetry,* the "formidable influence" on Chicago's Erie Street (Walker, *Richard Wright* 79).

Stephen Vincent Benét, editor for the Yale Series of Younger Poets, wrote to a young aspirant in 1940: "Every year I read for the Yale Series about 50 book-length manuscripts by poets under thirty, who haven't published before. I'll say about 30 of them usually were by women. A great many of them are fluent, technically proficient and essentially pretty-pretty" (*Letters* 341). Benét must have been pleasantly surprised by Margaret Walker's submission. Technically proficient indeed, but the book was also innovative—and not a bit "pretty-pretty." In his foreword, Benét hailed Walker as "a contemporary writer, living in a contemporary world," whose poems yet contained "the voices of Methodist forebears and preachers who preached the Word, the anonymous voices of many who lived and were forgotten and yet out of bondage and hope they made a lasting music" (7–8).

To understand Walker's work it is important for us to appreciate the milieu in which it was written. *For My People,* on one level, depicts a young poet in her relationship to other writers. In this case, Margaret Walker actually wrote the poems while in contact first with the South Side Writers' Group in Chicago between 1936 and 1939 and later at the renowned Iowa Writers' Workshop. Her association with both groups had an impact on what she wrote, but the ideas expressed in the first section of *For My People* most clearly reflect the influence of the South Side Writers' Group. In a sense, too, this group's manifesto, published as "Blue Print for Negro Writing" by Richard Wright in *New Challenge* in 1937, informs the folk ballads that were actually written while Walker pursued her master's degree at Iowa.

The South Side Writers' Group—which included playwright Ted Ward, poets Frank Marshall Davis, Walker, Marian Minus, and several others—was pulled together by Richard Wright following the National Negro Congress held in Chicago in 1936. Though the South Side Writers' Group was a black organization, the members (a number of whom, like Walker, also worked on the WPA's Federal Writers' Project) were not isolated from other literary circles. Walker's title poem "For My People" shows the technique of Kenneth Fearing's wonderful breathless Whitmanesque catalogues (such as "Twentieth Century Blues") but is more carefully controlled and—in the end—much more optimistic about the human condition. In "A Dollar's Worth of Blood, Please" (1938), Fearing examines a cross section of American society, people

> sure of tomorrow's pleasant surprise,
> and the stranger, who knows there is nothing on
>   earth more costly than hope, and nothing
>   in all the world held one-half so cheap as
>   life

(176)

Walker, however, is gifted with a lyrical and metrical virtuosity, a sureness, that Fearing seldom achieves, as is demonstrated in the ringing hexameters that turn vigorously within the long line that constitutes the final stanza of "For My People" (7).

In subject matter, "For My People" parallels the montage presented in Richard Wright's "I Have Seen Black Hands" (1934) but eschews that poem's concluding Marxist blazon in favor of a call for African American solidarity (Walker and Giovanni 89). Margaret Walker exhibits a determined optimism that transcends political movements in its deepest implications. Unsurprisingly, she differs in tone from contemporaries who used similar poetic approaches.

In Fenton Johnson's blues-tinged later poems, in the work of Kenneth Fearing and Frank Marshall Davis, the long line of Whitman is tuned to the darker mood of the psalmist, producing a tone of cynical lamentation. Walker's lines, however, gleam with an inner light. Consider the elusive healing song that weaves through her poem "Delta":

> Nights in the valley are full of haunting murmurings
> of our musical prayers
> of our rhythmical loving
> of our fumbling thinking aloud
> (*For My People* 17)

From these mingled sounds Walker would compose an anthem: "If only from this valley we might rise with song! / With singing that is ours" (16).

The first section of *For My People* ends with "Today," a jeremiad that contrasts the complacency of white middle America with the spreading war in Europe. The point of the poem is that, for African Americans and the poor, a war is already under way at home. The attitude of the poem is similar to that of Tolson's "Grandma Lonigan," whose response to the economic cataclysm of the Thirties is a decided lack of alarm because "us black folks was borned in a depression" (*Gallery* 42). Walker ends her poem with an allusion to Exodus:

> pray for buttressing iron against insidious termite
> and beetle and locust and flies and moth and
> rust and mold

(25)

Darkness need not be summoned, for Walker's Americans already dwell in self-imposed benightedness.

Margaret Walker's journey to Iowa did not represent a retreat from reality or from the issues confronting social realist art. John T. Fredrick, a unit editor for the Chicago WPA, had nothing but good intentions when he urged Walker to attend the Writers' Workshop. Still, upon her arrival she must have experienced a classic case of culture shock as she encountered issues far more significant than the loneliness and insecurity of a black student on the isolated campus of a white college. The University of Iowa was not exactly an ivory tower; it was, rather, another rampart in the American cultural controversy of the 1930s (Corn 44).

At the center of the Iowa graduate program in creative writing was Professor Norman Foerster's idea of regionalism, which held that "writers who draw from their own experience and the life they know best are more likely to attain universal values than those who do not" (Wilbers 49). The books published by the program's graduates between 1937 and 1941 attest to the workshop's encouragement of regionalism. They range from novels of Texas cattle country and small town New England to a narrative about "Tennessee mountain life" and an epic poem about the Mormon trek (Wilbers 58 n. 24). The poet and folksong collector Edwin Ford Piper was also an influential figure in the department (Stegner 17).

Regionalism, in the words of Iowa professor Frank Luther Mott, sounds at first like cultural pluralism or a precursor of today's multicultural ideal. "The believer in American regionalism," Mott wrote in 1944, "may even argue that one of the few distinctive characteristics that unite to make American literature American is the variety which comes from differences ethnological, climatological, topographic—in short, from the scope of our land and people" (403).

The limitations soon become apparent. Consider Mott's appreciation of one black poet: "Sterling Brown's blues songs are real, for they represent the actual life and aspirations and tragedies of folk along the lower Mississippi" (404). What Mott seems most to appreciate is the tenacity of these folk in their struggle with merciless sun and periodic flood, not the pointed political messages of Brown's "Old Lem" or the Slim Greer series.

Robert L. Dorman identifies regionalism in his excellent study *Revolt of the Provinces* (1993) as among "a loosely defined range of modernist movements" that flourished in the 1920s and 1930s. "Together with several of those other movements—the makers of the Harlem Renaissance, the *Partisan Review* cosmopolitans, the *New Masses* communists—regionalists would share a common faith in cultural radicalism," Dorman contends, "the belief that artistic and intellectual production (especially social art) can in itself help to bring about dramatic social change" (22). This broad overview does not, however, show that regionalism served as a *counterforce* to the other movements cited.

For most of the public, regionalism was identified with the robust or taciturn rustics depicted by Grant Wood, Thomas Hart Benton, and a group of colleagues later known as the "American Scene" painters. At the university, Wood's regionalism also exerted some influence on friends in the English department's Writers' Workshop such as Frank Luther Mott and Paul Engle (Corn 44). These artists and writers may have been cultural radicals in Dorman's sense, but they worked in a decidedly conservative atmosphere that Margaret Walker must have found disturbing.

In 1928 Charles Atherton Cumming, founder of the art department at the University of Iowa, published a pamphlet entitled *Democracy and the White Man's Art*. Cumming attributed development of "the art of realistic representation" in painting to "the Nordic branch of the Aryan race" and thought that abstraction was, conversely, "characteristic of all colored and primitive races." Assessing trends in twentieth-century American art, Cumming pessimistically doubted "if democracy will ever be able to continue the white man's art because it was born and maintained only during periods of the Nordic white man's highest culture" (quoted in Firestone 150). Such ideas, it should be understood, were hardly Cumming's unique property.

While C. A. Cumming might have considered even Grant Wood (who succeeded him at the university) something of a Modernist, the persistence of his reactionary ideas in the department might account for an incident in 1939 when, according to Evan R. Firestone, lecturer H. W. Janson, "although soon reinstated, was fired in mid-semester by the dean of the College of Liberal Arts for taking his students to Chicago to see a Picasso exhibition" (Firestone 158). Later, Janson enjoyed a terrible revenge when he published "Benton and Wood, Champions of Regionalism" (1946), an article arguing that their work showed similarities to the newly discovered Nazi propaganda paintings of wartime Germany. Though Wood was already dead when Janson's article appeared, the critic was determined to bury Wood's reputation as well (Doss 391, 420 n. 46; Corn 59). But even if Janson's comparison may have been spiteful, the ideological concepts of race and culture expressed by Cumming—and some of the nativistic sentiments in Wood's 1935 pamphlet *Revolt Against the City* (Dennis 229–235)—reflect some of the era's most disturbing tendencies.

Indeed, regionalist painting was never regarded as merely decorative or pictorial, and the political issues it raised were highly publicized and controversial. Far from being confined to academic circles, the debate became part of the general public's discourse. Painter Thomas Hart Benton, for example, became in December 1934 the first artist to appear on the cover of *Time*. Since the cover art is a self-portrait, the enterprising Benton must have collected a paycheck in addition to the honor. A few years later Benton's murals in the Missouri state capitol kept his name in the newspapers for most of 1937. Some viewers were unimpressed by Benton's draftsmanship, but most were irritated by his subject matter. The former head of the Kansas City Chamber of Commerce remarked: "Missouri is not proud of hangings and Negro honky-tonks. She is not proud of the whipping of slaves, the slave block and Jesse James hold-ups. There are still many subjects in Missouri which would supply mural material without resorting to such subjects as those" (quoted in Priddy 84). Invited to appear at a Chamber of Commerce luncheon in February, Benton listened as a member declared that Illinois would hardly immortalize a figure such as Al Capone in its capitol. "If Illinois had any regard for the truth," Benton replied, "it would have to include Al Capone in the mural" (Priddy 101).

While working on the project, Benton headed off possible opposition from the African American community by employing flattery in a form worthy of a fifteenth-century Italian master. When a powerful black St. Louis politician complained about one of the slavery scenes, Benton spread his oils on the troubled waters by including the deal maker's portrait in a section celebrating the rise of electoral democracy after statehood (Priddy 254–257). Though many people remained unpleased with Benton's depictions of African Americans—often in what seemed stereotypical settings—his work was included in an NAACP-sponsored exhibit of works protesting lynching that was mounted at New York's Newton Galleries in 1935 (Powell 73).

There are subtle undertones of ugly prejudice in the regionalism of Wood and Benton. Despite his association with many Iowa artists of Scandinavian descent, for example, Wood—revealing basic sympathies that recall the ideas of C. A. Cumming—made a point of arguing for the Anglo-Saxon heritage of "the farmers that I know" (Dorman 233). And it is easy to understand why Benton attracted hecklers whenever he spoke in public, for there was always an undercurrent of bigotry in his arguments. A number of anti-immigrant and anti-Semitic remarks appear in Benton's *An Artist in America* (1951), where they preface an odious attack on the "aesthetic-minded homosexuals" who Benton claims controlled the New York art galleries (*An Artist* 264–266).

While sophisticated art critics such as Robert Hughes insist upon the satirical nature of Grant Wood's best-known work, others see it quite differently. "The stern father and equally serious daughter of *American Gothic*," writes E. Bradford Burns, "radiated traditional values. They reminded viewers of a simpler past with a well-defined ethic. The visual simplicity embedded in complexity of meaning fascinated the public. Americans immediately acclaimed the painting that eventually became the most famous and reproduced canvas in American art history" (153).

Midwestern Regionalism, exemplified by Grant Wood's confections—idealized landscapes with cotton-puff clouds and lollipop-shaped trees—became a short-circuited form of social commentary. Genuine social realism, of course, did not please the public. Although they could see the model outside their own windows, for example, Texas businessmen were outraged by Alexandre Hogue's beautifully sere "dustbowl" landscapes. After his *Drouth Stricken Area* (1937) had been exhibited in Dallas, some museumgoers proposed a public collection so that they could buy the painting and burn it (Bywaters 305). Midwestern radicals such as H. H. Lewis also claimed to be regionalists. Known as "the plowboy poet," Lewis was widely published between 1930 and 1936 (Nelson 48). His Missouri farmer persona, sometimes expressed in dialect verse, was outspoken:

I don't give a damn for Uncle Sham,
I'm a left-wing radical Red

Reviewing four of Lewis's books in *Poetry,* William Carlos Williams was hesitant to praise his poetic skills but unequivocal about his honestly delivered message. "If Lewis' subject matter should distress some readers," Williams wrote, "it's about time they learned what makes their fruits and vegetables come to ripeness for them—and what kind of thoughts their cultivation breeds in a man of revolutionary inheritance" (229).

Another aspect of the regionalist movement was much more menacing, however, and it is worthwhile to consider it more closely. *I'll Take My Stand: The South and the Agrarian Tradition* (1930)—an anthology of polemical essays by professors at Nashville's Vanderbilt University, most of whom had been associated with the little magazine *The Fugitive* (1922–1925)—was the primary expression of a type of regionalism that made a tremendous impact on academia and the general public. The Southern Agrarians, as they called themselves, took an anticommunist, anti-industrial position that they hoped would "support a Southern way of life." "The South," they declared defiantly, "scarcely hopes to determine the other sections [of the United States], but it does propose to determine itself, within the utmost limits of legal action" (*I'll Take My Stand* xix–xx). The supporters of this intellectual secessionist movement included John Crowe Ransom, Donald Davidson, Allen Tate, Andrew Nelson Lytle, and Robert Penn Warren. Former expatriate John Gould Fletcher, one of the original Imagist poets, was also associated with the group.

The *American Review,* edited by Seward Collins, became something of a "house organ" for the Nashville Agrarians as well as a platform for the Distributist movement, anti-Marxist intellectuals who endorsed poet Hilaire Belloc's theory that "freedom involves property" (Penty 457). For someone like Donald Davidson, such philosophical theories complemented nostalgia for the slave system of the antebellum South. In an *American Review* article in 1936, Davidson defends the white lynch mob's "reciprocal savagery" while deploring the efforts of sociologists affiliated with the Commission on Interracial Cooperation "to set the Negro up as an equal, or at least more than a subordinate member of Southern society" ("A Sociologist in Eden" 181, 200).

Donald Davidson, the least gifted poet of the group, became their most aggressive apologist for racism and the reactionary social program. Davidson romanticized the exiled and defeated, dreaming—as in "Sanctuary" (1938)—of eventually reversing history. The quintessential exponent of "the Lost Cause," a desk-bound guerrilla, he never stops fighting the Civil War:

> This is the secret refuge of our race
> Told only from a father to his son,
> A trust laid on your lips, as though a vow
> To generations past and yet to come
> There, from the bluffs above, you may at last
> Look back at all you left, and trace
> His dust and flame, and plan your harrying
>
> If you would gnaw his ravaging flank, or smite
> Him in his glut among the smouldering ricks
> (Pratt 84)

During the 1930s, in his essays, he was even capable of blaming the evils of the sharecropping system on northern banks (Agar and Tate 118–122). Davidson's allegiance to a mythic concept of the aristocratic southern gentleman led him into genuine absurdity. At one point in *I'll Take My Stand*, for example, he declares that "public libraries, which tend ever to become more immense and numerous, pervert public taste as much as they encourage it. For the patrons are by implication discouraged from getting their own books and keeping them at home" in the plantation big house (40).

The most charitable recent assessment of *I'll Take My Stand* views the Nashville Agrarians' position on race as a sort of genteel avoidance of the issue. D. A. Hamlin nonetheless equates this reticence with slavery's "benevolence myth, through which the entire community attempted to limit the psychological burden of complicity with such an obvious evil" (71). But a careful reading of Robert Penn Warren's "The Briar Patch" in *I'll Take My Stand*, and other writings by members of the group, suggests that they were at the time active proponents of racism. In *I'll Take My Stand*, the Nashville Agrarians were simply working ground already prepared by popular works such as *Re-Forging America* (1927) by the Harvard-educated racist Lothrop Stoddard. In that work, Stoddard attempted to describe "how the bright promise of our early days was darkened by the disaster of the Civil War and by the blight of alien factors"—by which he meant Reconstruction and the massive European immigration of the 1880s (vii). Stoddard was obsessed with race; he did not pretend to be either an economist or a cultural critic.

Lacking only his explicit Aryanism, this version of American history has been continuously recycled since his day, and *Re-Forging America* eerily prefigures right-wing "conservative" rhetoric of the 1990s.

There was little direct black response to the Nashville manifesto. African American critics opted to promote attention for sympathetic white southern writers such as Julia Peterkin and Dubose Hayward. Sterling A. Brown, writing in *Opportunity,* dismissed *I'll Take My Stand* as pretentious journalism hardly worth binding in cloth. The review did permit Brown to exhibit his own erudition and fine-tuned sarcasm. Recalling Donald Davidson's poetry collection *The Tall Men* (1927), Brown reminded his readers that the Twelve Southerners had hashed over this material before. Davidson's poem, "Geography of the Brain," for example, is crowded with caricatures. Notes Brown, "While it takes no perspicuity to see the present evils of industrialization, it does take a great imagination to see this peasant's paradise" ("A Romantic Defense" 118). It is a strange pastoral paradise indeed that includes, as Davidson's poem does, the thrill of watching "Ku Klux riders all in white parading" while taunting "frightened negroes" (*Poems* 138).

Margaret Walker claims to have understood little about the Left during the 1930s, but she would have had little trouble decoding the Southern Agrarians' message. Her course work at Iowa involved reading a great deal of southern history. "I was trained as a child in the South," says Walker, "to read books at school from the southern viewpoint and books at home from the Negro viewpoint." Her Iowa research complicated this schema; she discovered that "southern historians claimed slavery was a beneficial system with benign masters; northerners did not oppose slavery as long as it was 'contained' in the South and did not spread into the territories; while Negro historians regarded slavery as a cruel, inhuman system. White southerners claimed they fought a war between the States for independence; white northerners claimed it was a rebellion of the southerners against the Union, and Negroes said it was a war of liberation." Such conflicting interpretations of history and society made it difficult for a reader "to maintain an 'objective' point of view. Obviously she must choose one or the other—or create her own" (*How I Wrote Jubilee* 52–53).

Walker was neither confused nor intimidated by the South's regionalists, nor, of course, would she relinquish her own southern birthright. Her poem "Southern Song" (1937) begins—as do most such works, dating back to Jefferson's *Notes on the State of Virginia*—with a passionate evocation of the region's beauty:

> I want my body bathed again by southern suns, my soul
>> reclaimed again from southern land. I want to rest
>> again in southern fields, in grass and hay and clover
>> bloom; to lay my hand again upon the clay baked by
>> a southern sun, to touch the rain-soaked earth and
>> smell the smell of soil.

This bucolic note soon, however, reveals a sterner undertone of pointed social comment:

> I want no mobs to wrench me from my southern rest; no
>> forms to take me in the night and burn my shack and
>> make for me a nightmare full of oil and flame.

> I want my careless song to strike no minor key; no fiend to
>> stand between my body's southern song—the fusion of
>> the South, my body's song and me.

"Sorrow Home," published in *Opportunity* in 1938, directly challenges and dismantles the rhetoric of the Agrarians to reveal the brutal reality silenced by their idealized depiction of the rural South. "My roots are deep in southern life," the speaker declares, "deeper than John Brown or Nat Turner or Robert Lee." In Whitmanesque verses she again describes the natural beauty of "a tropic world" yet, poignantly, admits that it is tainted:

> O Southland! Sorrow home, melody beating in my
> bone and blood! How long will the Klan of
> Hate, the hounds and the chain gangs keep
> me from my own?
> (139)

Another poem, "Delta," expresses an angry response to environmental disaster, industrial exploitation, and political frustration. Even the victims of terrorism reinforce Walker's determination to reclaim her land:

> We with our blood have watered these fields
> and they belong to us.

and to the future:

> Neither earth nor star nor water's host
> can sever us from our life to be
> (*For My People* 17)

While Grant Wood and his circle enjoyed folk music and the spirituals as elements of the country's homegrown culture (Corn, *Grant Wood* 40), Walker viewed African American folk culture as a communal and actively political expression of resistance. Her poem "The Spirituals," published in *Opportunity* in August 1938, conflates the historical slave songs and work songs that continue to be created because "mills of oppression grind songs of the poor" (237). All such songs, the poet seems to say, are a response to actual inequities of capitalism rather than an outpouring of naive Christian fervor. In this sense, Walker's "The Spirituals" proposes a direct contradiction of James Weldon Johnson's "O Black and Unknown Bards" (1917), prefiguring the interpretation of the spirituals offered in Miles Mark Fisher's controversial *Negro Slave Songs in the United States* (1953).

In a 1986 address to the Tennessee Council of Teachers of English, Walker recalled that the Nashville Agrarians had purposely "revived old and raw wounds" in 1930 by "continuing an ostracism of black writers and all our creativity, [and by pursuing] the successful suppression of our southern literature and our substantial contribution to American culture in language, religion, music, art, dance and literature" (*On Being Female* 112). Though she did not say so explicitly, it was clear that undoing this damage had occupied her own creative efforts in the subsequent decades.

Indeed, the legacy of all of the regionalist movements of the era deserves careful reassessment. By 1942, the midwestern school of regionalist art was in the service of corporate profit, with Thomas Hart Benton and other prominent painters commissioned to provide original works for a Lucky Strike advertising campaign. The way in which race became an issue showed—as did Howard W. Odum's *Race and Rumors of Race* (1942) and Walker's *For My People*—how far the nation had moved away from the Old South fantasies promoted in *I'll Take My Stand* and also indicated how much battle remained to be waged. Benton's sketches of black Georgia sharecroppers sorting tobacco leaves were rejected by the advertising agency. Their rejection, Benton wrote later, was based on an intriguing argument. The executives told him: "We don't want realism that will foul up our sales. The Negro institutions would boycott our products and cost us hundreds of thousands of dollars if we showed pictures of this sort. They want Negroes presented as well-dressed and respectable members of society. If we did [that], of course, the whole of the white South would boycott us. So the only thing to do is avoid the representation of Negroes entirely" (Doss 234). As Walker noted in a 1950 article in *Phylon,* the emerging poets of the period—Frank Marshall Davis, Robert Hayden, Owen Dodson, and Gwendolyn Brooks—were all "poets of social protest who began to catch a glimmer of a global perspective [and] did not beg the question of their humanity" (*How I Wrote Jubilee* 107). The anecdotal evidence collected by Odum affirms that such work accurately reflected the consciousness of the black community. In some ways, then, this militancy and intensified assertions of African American agency had made a difference—even if the ironic result was another type of invisibility.

If the intellectual debates at Iowa in some ways recalled (perhaps antagonistically) ideas current in the discussions of the South Side Writers' Group, Walker's personal situation was far from comfortable. "I suffered a lot of trauma that year," she wrote later, "through no one's fault other than my own, but I was miserable and I kept thinking how awful it was not to have *any* money and being ill all the time, despondent and depressed to the point of tears" (Wilbers 57 n. 23). Nevertheless, she accepted Paul Engle's encouragement to work on the ballads that form the middle section of *For My People* (Rowell 7).

The second section of the book consists of ten folk ballads. Cary Nelson sees these as portraits of "self-affirmation through violence," like Walker's 1944 poem "Harriet Tubman." In my opinion the figures portrayed more closely parallel the episode in Wright's *Black Boy,* to which my father was fond of alluding, where Wright concludes that an uncle in Mississippi is not an example but a warning (176). Of the figures depicted only the notorious ladies' man Poppa Chicken appears to have a lick of sense (30):

Poppa met a pretty gal
Heard her name was Rose
Took one look at her and soon
Bought her pretty clothes

One night she was in his arms
In walked her man Joe
All he done was look and say,
    "Poppa's got to go."

A book of poems may be assembled by accident or convenience and may even be ordered by numerological design. In any case, once it has been completed, it can be read in sequence—since a sequence exists. *For My People* is a lesson book. By framing the folk poems, the mythologies of both southern and urban Negro Saturday nights exemplified by

> lost disinherited dispossessed and happy people
> > filling the cabarets and taverns and other
> > people's pockets

with the contemporary social realist voice of section one and the seemingly (subversively) conventional sonnet sequence that closes the book, Walker fulfills what in the 1960s we would have termed the "revolutionary" requirements of the South Side Writers' Group's "Blue Print for Negro Writing": "Reduced to its simplest and most general terms, theme for Negro writers will rise from understanding the meaning of their being transplanted from a 'savage' to a [so-called] 'civilized' culture in all of its social, political, economic and emotional implications" (47). For Wright this transplanting had yielded a sere harvest of "people who have lost their individuality, whose reactions are fiercely elemental, whose shattered lives are burdened by impulses they cannot master or control" ("The Literature of the Negro" 86). This view, of course, has been reiterated by the social scientists of the last three decades. What Margaret Walker calls our staggering "struggle for . . . bread, for pride, for simple dignity" (51) continues unabated, and we may give thanks that our children don't get weary. "Shall Negro writing be for the Negro masses," asked the South Side Writers' Group, "moulding the lives and consciousness of these masses toward new goals, or shall it continue begging the question of the Negro's humanity?" ("Blue Print" 40). Walker's poems and the very title *For My People* deliver her resounding and unequivocal answer. "The gospel of social justice, freedom, peace, and human dignity," she noted in a 1976 essay in *Freedomways,* "has been preached in all the art of Afro-America from its beginnings to the present. The slogan 'Art for the People' is not a new nor radically different tag from what it has always been among Black people. African art from its ancient beginnings has always been functional in its highest spiritual sense" (*How I Wrote* 115).

In her sonnet "Our Need," the poet says: "We need a wholeness born of inner strength" (*This Is My Century* 50). In the current period—when we have developed an African American popular culture that is often misleading, irresponsible, confused and confusing, and aimed directly at young people—Margaret Walker's struggle a half century ago to make a healthful synthesis of similarly conflicting materials can only be instructive. And because she succeeded in her endeavor, her work stands as a model for us in our own search for what she delightfully termed "a beauty full of healing" (7).

To look again at Donald Gibson's definition, *For My People* remains a classic because it continues to fill a social, cultural, and political purpose. It would be simplistic and inaccurate to suppose that we are today, as we were half a century ago, merely confronting the same racial or economic struggle. Walker's book records and presents her successful negotiation of conflicting political forces, a negotiation that measures the difference between survival and destruction. *For My People* is both a diagnosis and a remedy.

For My People, then, was a book that gave American letters a poet of both astonishing precocity and avid diligence. It remains a book that represents its era, capturing the mood of the period and transmitting to today's readers a clear sense of the intellectual and emotional conflicts of that time. The book is a classic and remains vital because Walker's message speaks to each new generation of Americans.

"Life is real and life is earnest," says Longfellow ("A Psalm of Life" 371). And Margaret Walker adds that it must, in fact, be lived, that though "the struggle staggers us," we will, with vision such as that she offers, find strength to communicate with each other and to fulfill our promise as individuals and as a nation.

For My People, finally, is an early testament of Margaret Walker's lifelong personal philosophy. As she told Jerry W. Ward, Jr., in an interview for the *Mississippi Quarterly*, "I have no desire to separate myself from what I am . . . , from my race, from my gender, from my nationality, [or] from my consciousness. I'm black, woman, writer" (Ward 527). In a 1992 interview with Alferdteen Harrison, Walker noted that the poems collected in *For My People* were, in fact, social commentaries on the 1930s: "We were literally outcast from the general society. But then there were poor white people, too, and poor working people. It was a time when the unions were struggling to have collective bargaining, to have a forty-hour week, and all these entered into the picture of economic depression. A number of my poems indicate that" (Harrison 9).

With the notable exception of the deeply personal "October Journey" (1973), all of the poems that Walker published after *For My People* can also be called social commentary. Political poems are often considered ephemeral and forgettable. That Margaret Walker's are not attests to the brilliance of her language and the humane integrity of her vision.

4

Literary Criticism and the Color Line

Melvin B. Tolson's Eloquent Accommodations

Few people asked to think of a way of measuring alienation between the races in the United States would think first of literary criticism. Nevertheless, literary criticism as clearly as any other area of inquiry bears out W. E. B. Du Bois's prediction nearly one hundred years ago in *The Souls of Black Folk* (1903) that "the problem of the Twentieth Century is the problem of the color-line" (12).

In a sonnet that is quoted as often and as widely as any ever written by Shakespeare, the Harlem Renaissance poet Countee Cullen considered the harshness of segregated black life and the Romantic calling of lyric poetry. "I doubt not God is good, well-meaning, kind," wrote Cullen:

Yet do I marvel at this curious thing:
To make a poet black, and bid him sing!
("Yet Do I Marvel" 915)

So it is that, for almost half a century, our critics have chosen to confront the modernist poetry of Melvin Beaunorous Tolson as a conundrum. The reason is not that Tolson's work is difficult and dazzling in its erudition—John Ciardi believed that it could induce "dizziness" (Flasch 90)—but that the author of such work was a black man from the South.

In his preface to Tolson's 1953 publication of *Libretto for the Republic of Liberia*, Allen Tate, dean of the New Critics, perhaps unconsciously alluded to Cullen's lines. Comparing Tolson's long ode to Hart Crane's

The Bridge, Tate enthusiastically declared, "Here is something marvellous indeed."

This praise of Tolson has troubled many critics inasmuch as Tate was hardly reticent about his racist belief in the natural inferiority of black people. But what are we to make of the fact that, twenty-five years after the civil rights legislation that was intended to make the Thirteenth and Fourteenth Amendments reality at long last, most white Americans continue to view African Americans as outsiders? In a 1990 paper documenting the remarkable scarcity of black poets in the pages of *Poetry,* Michael Bérubé managed somehow to fault Tolson for *his* presence there! Bérubé seemed to blame Tolson for assimilating what he termed "the dominant literary discourse." This, of course, is a loaded term for what might better be described as contemporary poetic fashion. And one might wonder why it should seem strange that any young writer— black or white, male or female—should try to learn the craft by imitating the models found on library shelves or the local rack of literary magazines. Only the legacy of American apartheid could give birth to such an opinion.

If we are to appreciate Tolson as something other than "an historical anomaly," we must find a proper context for reading him (Bérubé, "Avant-Gardes" 192). As a brief comparison shows, the careers of Tolson and Amiri Baraka—both black Americans, both skillful Modernist poets, and both above all Afrocentric poets—illuminate each other.

Tolson and Baraka are the legitimate heirs of Fenton Johnson (1888– 1958), the first African American poet to explore the Modernist style in the years before the First World War and also, naturally enough, the first—and (as Michael Bérubé's research shows) for many years the only—black poet to appear in the pages of Harriet Monroe's *Poetry.*

It is also significant, for our comparison of Tolson and Baraka as Afrocentric modernists, that Fenton Johnson was also engaged in an attempt to make the African American spirituals, what Du Bois called "the sorrow songs," the basis of a new poetic form and diction. Fenton Johnson's poetic explorations were, in his break with nineteenth-century poetic conventions and interest in adapting a pristine vernacular to literary ends, entirely consistent with the developing Modernist aesthetic.

Modernism in art is, of course, precisely the opposite of the more general and still current belief in the efficacy of science and the technological precision of an industrialized, electrified society (Adas 414).

Modernism actually represents an attempt to survey the new twenti-eth-century landscape and, by a radical reinterpretation of myth and tradition, to rescue the classical values of so-called Western civiliza-tion. This is clearly what Ezra Pound and his cohorts were all about in the 1910s and 1920s.

The concept of Progress as inevitably linear and ascending, coupled with capitalism in its imperialist stage, led to a crisis in Western cul-ture. This crisis, not coincidentally named in the title of the journal of the newly established National Association for the Advancement of Colored People and edited by Du Bois, was the machine's need for "raw materials." Modernist artists might glorify Western sophistication, yet they also realized that the system needed constant infusions of "new blood" and energy. Consequently, there was a strain of exoticism in the Modernist movement that, at various times, invoked African sculpture or Native American ritual. One might see in this the West as spiritual vampire or, more humanely, consider the arts of the period as a parallel enterprise to capitalism's appropriation of the political and economic energies of the non-European world. Eliot's *The Waste Land,* which Tol-son read in the 1930s, appealed to his interest in technical experimen-tation. He was intrigued by Eliot's use of what he called the "inverted participial phrase, because I was grounded in grammar, and I knew Eliot was 'doing something'" (Flasch 33). But it was only Eliot's tech-nique that attracted Tolson. "My work," he wrote in 1961, "is certainly difficult in metaphors, symbols, and juxtaposes ideas. There the simi-larity between Eliot and me separates. . . . when you look at my ideas and Eliot's, we're as far apart as hell and heaven" (Flasch 134–135).

Similarly, the young Amiri Baraka recognized two distinct traditions of Modernism during the late 1950s. In his introduction to *The Mod-erns: An Anthology of New Writing in America* (1963), Baraka noted that for the avid readers among the Beat Generation, "William Carlos Wil-liams, Ezra Pound, The Imagists, and the French symbolist poets were restored to importance as beginners of a still vital tradition of Western poetry. It was an attempt to restore American poetry to the mainstream of modern poetry after it had been cut off from that tradition by the Anglo-Eliotic domination of the academies" (*The Moderns* x–xi). The writers that he assembled for this anthology used the tradition of ex-perimentation as a structure of rebellion against social conventions of the 1950s: "Selby's hoodlums, Rechy's homosexuals, Burroughs' ad-dicts, Kerouac's mobile young voyeurs, my own Negroes, are literally not included in the mainstream of American life. These characters are people whom Spengler called *Fellaheen,* people living in the ruins of a civilization . . . , but they are nevertheless Americans, formed out of the conspicuously tragic evolution of modern American life" (xiv).

Baraka—unlike Fenton Johnson, who disappeared from the national literary scene in the early 1920s, or Tolson, who despite the honors bestowed on him late in life remained a somewhat isolated voice at Oklahoma's Langston University—had a tremendous impact, both as editor of *Yugen* and as a close advisor to Donald Allen's seminal anthology *The New American Poetry, 1945–1960.* "Being in a position to pass judgement, however marginally, on the work of the most adventurous younger white writers in the nation," notes Arnold Rampersad, "he held a place of authority virtually unprecedented among black Americans. Only William Stanley Braithwaite early in the century, with his Boston newspaper reviews and his influential annual anthologies of magazine verse, had enjoyed a similar prestige" (310).

Even more important was Baraka's influence on an entire generation of African American poets through the Black Arts movement of the late 1960s and the 1970s. William J. Harris notes that Baraka's "avant-garde ideas of form," drawn from his studies of the William Carlos Williams branch of Modernism and Charles Olson's *Projective Verse,* "cohered perfectly with the new black artist's need to express his or her own oral traditions; the free verse and the eccentric typography of the white avant-garde were ideal vehicles for black oral expression and experience" ("Introduction" xxvii). In this technical development, however, the poets of the Black Arts movement were actually returning to a development that had occurred forty years earlier, when Modernist poetics met up with African American cultural consciousness during the Harlem Renaissance. As noted above, there are some very good reasons why black American writers became interested in Modernist aesthetics. Pound's investigation of Provençal balladry, for example, parallels the interest most African American poets took in their own folk heritage. The Modernist dimension of the Harlem Renaissance directly inspired Tolson's poetics, though he seems always to have taken his time studying—and eventually mastering—new techniques.

The Harlem Renaissance of the 1920s was a high point in American cultural history. While it intersected with the developing Modernist movement at several points, it was primarily an expression of African American cultural nationalism. Like the literary Modernist movement, too, the Harlem Renaissance abounded with contradictions. As David Levering Lewis has pointed out, while the leaders of the Harlem Renaissance "frequently wrote as cultural nationalists and Pan-Africanists, the ultimate goal of their Renaissance was assimilation" ("Shortcuts" 96). Racial pride and the black experience were the subject matter of most Renaissance poems and novels, but thanks to publishers such as Alfred Knopf, Horace Liveright, Albert and Charles Boni, and Bennett Cerf, the books reached an avid interracial audience. The literature itself ranged from the striking Modernism of Jean Toomer's *Cane* (1923)—a work that continues to resist assignment to any traditional genre—to Claude McKay's exquisitely crafted sonnets protesting racist atrocities. The universal appeal of McKay's "If We Must Die," written in response to the lynchings of 1919, may be judged by the fact that Winston Churchill quoted it to build morale during the Luftwaffe's blitz of London (Tolson, "Claude McKay's Art" 287, 290).

Despite their differing choices of poetic idiom, the poets of the Harlem Renaissance shared a desire to express themselves with dignity. For Cullen and McKay, this intention meant demonstrating their mastery of forms such as the Shakespearean sonnet; others used the Modernist idiom to invent new ways of recording African American speech, African American inflections, and, as with Langston Hughes, the music that was the most highly developed expression of African American creativity.

In his autobiography, *Along This Way* (1933), James Weldon Johnson, both a poet and an NAACP official, recalled a paper he had prepared for a meeting of the Intercollegiate Socialist Society in 1917. He had chosen to speak about the African American contribution to American culture in order to counter what he termed "the common-denominator opinion in the United States about American Negroes": "These people are here . . . to be shaped and molded and made into something different and, of course, better; they are here to be helped; here to be given something; in a word, they are beggars under the nation's table waiting to be thrown the crumbs of civilization" (326). This, of course, was the benign view. As Nielsen has vividly shown in *Reading Race* (1988), it was just as common during the period to find virulently racist opinions fueled by a set of derogatory and vicious racial stereotypes dating back to the 1820s.

An attempt to destroy such stereotypes led James Weldon Johnson to Modernist technique in his own work. His brilliant *God's Trombones* (1925) solves the problems with which Fenton Johnson had wrestled in early attempts to use the spirituals as a formal poetic structure. *God's Trombones* is an entirely satisfying series of dramatic monologues (sermons, actually) that capture the voice of the black old-style "country preacher" in free verse that allowed the poet to replace conventional nineteenth-century dialect—and its dangers of caricature—with carefully controlled syntactical line breaks. In his choice of poetic technique, the author of *God's Trombones* clearly articulated the social problem that black artists and intellectuals of the 1920s accepted as their personal challenge.

Facing the resurgence of a frequently antiblack populism after World War I, black leaders found their options "limited to the obvious strategy of redoubled advocacy before the courts and in Congress, and to the novel game plan of harnessing art and literature for civil rights" (Lewis, "Shortcuts" 93). The movers and shakers behind the Harlem Renaissance, says David Levering Lewis, conceived of the movement "as serious racial politics, as art for politics' sake, or civil rights by copyright" (95).

The strategy was simple enough. Though neatly and eloquently stated by Howard University philosophy professor Alain Locke, the program of the Harlem Renaissance was also a renovation of the eighteenth- and nineteenth-century abolitionist attempt to demonstrate the immorality of slavery by forcing recognition of the African's humanity. Art, of course, was convincing evidence, and the slave poet Phillis Wheatley was often cited. Thomas Clarkson in his prize dissertation at Cambridge, *Essay on the Slavery and Commerce of the Human Species, Particularly the African* (1786), noted that "if slavery should be determined by [intellectual] ability, in comparison with Phillis Wheatley most of the inhabitants of Great Britain must lose their claim to freedom" (Fladeland 19). Alain Locke and the artists of the Harlem Renaissance believed that relief from legal segregation and racism would allow the African American to exchange the degrading—and, in fact, erroneous—"status of a beneficiary and ward for that of a collaborator and participant in American civilization." "The great social gain in this," Locke wrote, "is releasing of our talented group from the arid fields of controversy and debate to the productive fields of creative expression. The especially cultural recognition they win should in turn prove the key to that revaluation of the Negro which must precede or accompany any considerable further betterment of race relations" ("The New Negro" 15).

If the goal clearly is to achieve the civil rights promised by the Thirteenth and Fourteenth Amendments, also evident in Locke's statements is what we might today call the Afrocentric theme of the Harlem Renaissance. Locke identified what he called two "constructive channels . . . into which the balked social feelings of the American Negro can flow freely": "One is the consciousness of acting as the advance-guard of the African peoples in their contact with Twentieth Century civilization; the other, the sense of a mission of rehabilitating the race in world esteem for that loss of prestige for which the fate and conditions of slavery have so largely been responsible" ("The New Negro" 13–14).

To apply the term "Afrocentric" to Alain Locke's sense of "a mission of rehabilitating the race in world esteem" might confuse those who understand the word "Afrocentric" only to mean groups of men in kente-cloth hats and yarmulkas arguing about who really built the pyramids. But the mission of which Locke spoke is the best definition of the Afrocentric tradition in the United States, a tradition that extends from David Walker in the 1820s to Frederick Douglass and William Wells Brown to the Harlem Renaissance and encompasses poets such as Melvin Tolson and Amiri Baraka. Locke's definition also explains how these poets felt free to choose or develop their poetic styles with an equanimity that some recent critics have found difficult to grasp. As Playthell Benjamin pointed out, "turn-of-the-century black intellectuals like W. E. B. Du Bois, James Weldon Johnson and Kelly Miller . . . believed high culture was the heritage of all who were educated enough to appropriate it" (56).

The custodianship of the African American vernacular culture is also a prominent Afrocentric principle. As George W. Ellis put it in 1914, "the Negro should explain his own culture and interpret his own thought and soul life, if the complete truth is to be given to the other races of the earth" (19).

The third element of Afrocentricity, which was carefully coded in Alain Locke's essays but could easily be discerned in much Harlem Renaissance poetry, is a sort of millenarianism that perfectly matches the gloomier visions of Modernism. All three of these principles of Afrocentricity are clearly evident in Tolson's work but may confuse us if we are expecting one-dimensional sloganeering. It may be useful to think of Afrocentricity as *positional* rather than merely polemical. Certainly, though, the Afrocentric position is an Archimedean attempt to correct a biased concept of *universality* developed by nineteenth-century Europeans who, says Wilson Jeremiah Moses rather charitably, "were so involved in the myth of progress, and so delighted with the progress of their own society as to be unaware of their ethnocentrism" (*Golden Age* 21). The most excessive expression of this European ethnocentrism is, of course, the theory of Aryan supremacy, and its operational aspect is known as *racism*. To identify a work as primarily Afrocentric is, therefore, to identify its relationship to a Eurocentric discourse that has suc-

5. Melvin B. Tolson. Courtesy of the Schomburg Center for Research in Black Culture.

ceeded because it is too often taken for granted—an unexamined aberration purporting to be universal. In many ways Tolson's work offers the most significant example of the Modernist aesthetic in the service of an Afrocentric philosophical position.

Melvin Beaunorous Tolson (1898–1966) was for most of his life a highly respected and effective college teacher. A gifted elocutionist, he produced national championship debating teams at a small black Texas school called Wiley College and continued his career at Oklahoma's Langston University (where he also served four terms as mayor of the town in which the school was located). In the early 1930s he attended Columbia University and wrote a master's thesis on the poetry of the Harlem Renaissance.

Tolson delighted in maintaining the most rigorous and treasured tradition of historically black colleges. As a teacher, he was boisterously intellectual and demanding. James Farmer, later director of the Congress of Racial Equality (CORE), got the full treatment in Tolson's freshman English class at Wiley College in 1934. The professor called him aside for a conference, saying, "You're doing good work. In fact, you're doing A work, but if you don't do better, I'm going to flunk you." Those who made the extra effort were often rewarded by invitations to gatherings at Tolson's home, evenings when he entertained them with talk and with animated recitations of his new poems (Farmer 118–119). Those who studied with him at Langston University in the 1950s and early 1960s reported much the same exuberant and unwavering quest for excellence.

Tolson's own published poetry appears in three distinct styles. His early *Gallery of Harlem Portraits* is a collection that drew for its style on the colloquial free verse of Sandburg and was organized somewhat like Edgar Lee Masters's *Spoon River Anthology*. These poems are notable for strong social protest with a Marxist slant. The collection did not appear in book form during the poet's lifetime. His first book, *Rendezvous with America,* appeared in 1944, partly as a result of attention he received when his long poem "Dark Symphony" was awarded first prize at the 1941 American Negro Exposition in Chicago. This poem recounts the history of the African American people in a series of finely wrought stanza forms that display Tolson's virtuosity. The collection also contained a sonnet sequence, ballads, and a variety of unrhymed metrical poems in addition to free verse. The book-length poems *Libretto for the Republic of Liberia* (1953) and *Harlem Gallery* (1965) are extended suites in the manner of "Dark Symphony."

By definition, anything that deserves the name poetry must *last,* yet it is useful to take the metaphor of Tolson's title as a directive and to confront *Rendezvous with America* in its temporal context. In the title poem, the speaker travels back in time to Plymouth Rock, to the Boston massacre, to Valley Forge, and to other significant moments in American history. *Rendezvous* deserves a critical reevaluation. For our purposes, we need to understand—as if we were there—what the late 1930s and early 1940s meant to black Americans. As demonstrated in the 1930s, when high art dares to go among the people, the result can be the cosmic grandeur of Diego Rivera—or the reactionary kitsch of Grant Wood. Tolson's panoramic *Rendezvous* aspires to the stature of Rivera, sounding the themes that African Americans found most significant during the World War II era. In creating a perceptively accurate record of the period's passions and struggles, Tolson also produced excellent poems.

The literary work that best captures the emotional atmosphere and the ambiguous obligations of loyalty during the years of the Second World War is unmistakably John Oliver Killens's superb novel *And Then We Heard the Thunder* (1963), but Tolson's poems also illuminate the collective guilts and angers that shadowed the nation's political and intellectual discourse. Tolson's critics are not particularly enamored of *Rendezvous with America* (1944). Joy Flasch comments that many of the poems "seem to have been exercises in poetic technique which Tolson regarded as a challenge" (48), and while no one would ever find Tolson's verse clumsy, some reviewers thought the sonnets included in *Rendezvous* were "mechanical" and overly literary in allusions and subject matter (Flasch 67). More recently, Michael Bérubé has called the book "an uneven volume" and has asserted that "Tolson's current and future recognition cannot rest, even slightly, on the achievement of *Rendezvous*" (*Marginal* 157). Nevertheless, *Rendezvous with America* is an interesting example of engaged political poetry—even if the politics it offers may seem dated to contemporary readers.

In poems written in the 1930s—later published as *A Gallery of Harlem Portraits* (1979)—Tolson offers straightforward Marxist studies such as "Jack Patterson," where the speaker of the monologue asserts, based on his experiences as a merchant seaman, that everywhere on earth "Big fish eat up little fish / An' the color of the fish don't count" (*Gallery* 127). But in *Rendezvous* we encounter a poet who sings of America

> *Here,*
> *Now,*
> At Pearl Harbor, I remember
> I have a rendezvous at Plymouth Rock and Valley Forge
> This Seventh of December.
> (11)

The nation that Tolson sings is

> An international river with a legion of tributaries!
>
> A magnificent cosmorama with myriad patterns and colors!
>
> A giant forest with loin-roots in a hundred lands!

A cosmopolitan orchestra with a thousand instruments playing
America!
(5)

A comparison of these sentiments suggests a number of questions. Is
Tolson insincere or merely someone who embraces the practical politics
of his moment? He was, in fact, enough of a politician to be elected
mayor of Langston, Oklahoma, for several terms. Is Tolson a writer who
sees poetry not as the most personal form of verbal expression but as
merely another—albeit powerful—form of public discourse? Did Tolson's experience as an award-winning collegiate debating coach reflect
a person for whom the joy of spirited argument was primary, with ideology and sincerity of belief taking second place? Did Tolson simply
replace the Marxist theme of his unpublished 1930s poems with a suitable wartime patriotism?

While the concept of nationhood or even community is subject
to continuous negotiation, civic mythologies are constantly being re-
vised—primarily so that we may lie to ourselves. The memories recalled
in Studs Terkel's magnificent oral history *"The Good War"* (1984), for
example, are remarkably different from the conventional ignorance
documented in Howard W. Odum's 1943 study *Race and Rumors of Race.*

Tolson's *Rendezvous with America* (1944) is socially engaged, though
hardly Marxist. But while the title poem, which is deeply involved in
World War II patriotism, and several others (such as "Ballad of the
Rattlesnake," "The Man Inside," and "Esperanto") present ideas that
might be called a plea for "international brotherhood," there are also
several stinging rebukes of racism both at home and abroad.

While it was de rigueur in the war years, even in the African American press, to denounce Nazism, Tolson's "The Furlough" (*Rendezvous*
23–24) tells of a soldier who returns to find that his beloved has been
unfaithful—or, at least, so he imagines. The poem is a cynical turn on
Odysseus's Penelope, but it can also be read as an allegory of the treatment that black American servicemen were often forced to endure in
the segregated South:

I stitched the gash of fate to serve my country,
His treason stabbed the trinity in the back.
A soldier fights for Honor, Love, and Duty:
A man's castle is a palace or a shack.

His treason stabbed the trinity in the back,
His life was rubbish bargained in a fraud.
A man's castle is a palace or a shack:
A victory lost at home is lost abroad.
(*Rendezvous* 23)

Few African American readers would have seen these lines as simply a poet's ostentatiously clever naming of Jody, the proverbial sneak who preys on lonely girls back home. Black GIs in the South, even in uniform, suffered racist humiliation that was pointedly dramatized in stories such as Frank Yerby's "Health Card" (1943). Numerous complaints from soldiers and outraged civilians eventually resulted in a much publicized fact-finding tour of military bases by General Benjamin O. Davis, Sr., the army's highest-ranking black officer. As early as 23 September 1939, for example, an editorial in the *Pittsburgh Courier* warned: "Before any of our people get unduly excited about SAVING DEMOCRACY in Europe, it should be called to their attention that we have NOT YET ACHIEVED DEMOCRACY HERE" (James and others, *Fighting* 44).

If Tolson, in Texas, had been called upon to celebrate American democracy, to what might he have turned his eyes? Reading pre–World War I issues of the *Crisis,* one finds Texas to be primarily an uncivilized locus of particularly heinous lynchings. By 1928, however, Henry Nash Smith was noting in the *Southwest Review* that, the frontier having been settled and the bounties of leisure time showered upon the inhabitants, Dallas could boast of record-breaking sales of season subscriptions to its (segregated) symphony orchestra and Houston could brag about its ambitious four-year-old (segregated) Museum of Fine Arts. Smith, naturally, suspected that these developments were less likely genuine outbreaks of sweetness and light than examples of displaced "boosterism" that ordinarily concerned oil field bonanzas and record-breaking auction prices for champion bulls (Smith 249). The directors of the Houston museum were able to accommodate demands from the city's colored YWCA and set aside a special time on Thursday evenings for black people to attend, but the mood of the region was generally more hostile. As late as 1937 a writer in *West Texas Today,* the magazine of a chamber of commerce, found it impossible to praise the accomplishments of Baptist-supported Hardin-Simmons University in Abilene without also characterizing the west Texas region as "the last frontier of pure, unadulterated white Americans" (Shabazz 20–21; H. West 15).

There is no better poetic documentation of these attitudes than Tolson's poem "The Town Fathers" in *Rendezvous:*

> At the Courthouse Square
> On the Fourth of July,
> Beneath Old Glory's
> Pyrotechnic sky,
> The town fathers met,
> Minus Bible and rye.

> Against the statue
> Of Confederate dead
> The Mayor spat
> His snuff and said,
> "We need a slogan!"
> And he palmed his head.

After some deliberation, a solution is found:

> On a neon billboard,
> As high as a steeple,
> The travelers puzzle
> The amazing sequel:
> *The Blackest Land*
> *And The Whitest People.*
> (*Rendezvous* 22)

This is straightforward reportage. "Woodcuts for Americana," the title of the section in which it appears, is Tolson's sarcastically nostalgic euphemism for a series of poems that include graphic snapshots of racism, stupidity, and the frustration of those who know better.

With such racist attitudes extant and accepted by presumably educated white people, it is not surprising that on 19 December 1942, Langston Hughes reported in his *Chicago Defender* column: "I asked a Negro soldier on furlough in Chicago how he liked Texas. He said, 'Like a Jew likes Germany'" (DeSantis 142). A year later, race riots in Beaumont, Texas—fueled by local race prejudice as well as by competition among black and white workers flooding into the east Texas shipyards and defense plants—seized national media attention. There were also several military training bases in the South, including Louisiana's notorious Ft. Polk (the actual location of Yerby's short story and Charles Fuller's award-winning play *A Soldier's Story*). The mistreatment of black soldiers at these bases also created national headlines. Again, Langston Hughes reported: "I haven't seen a Negro yet about to be inducted into the army who did not say, 'I hope they don't send me down South.' Being sent to North Africa or New Guinea doesn't seem to phase them" (DeSantis 142).

The tension between patriotism and protest in Tolson's *Rendezvous* was not idiosyncratic; indeed, the general mood of the African American public in the 1940s reflected deeply ambiguous feelings regarding the war. "It is cold comfort," Roi Ottley wrote in 1943, "to tell the Negro his lot will be worse if the cause of democracy falls. Negroes want tangible assurances that the loud talk of democracy is in fact meant to include them" (343). Few such assurances were forthcoming. Press reports simultaneously fueled and explained a widespread dissatisfaction that could hardly be diagnosed as anxious "double consciousness." The *Crisis* cover girl for the September 1944 issue was defense plant worker Aurelia Carter, proud and patriotically chic in welder's gear. Inside the magazine, however, former army chaplain Grant Reynolds bluntly declared that black GIs were "damned tired of the treatment they are getting" ("What the Negro Solidier Thinks" 289). More disturbing than enduring racial slurs from southerners was the fact that black troops, regardless of aptitude, were being "trained" to dig ditches but denied entry into the military's technical occupations. "The Negro soldier," Reynolds declared, "will not give his life for the perpetuation of this outright lynching of his ability, nor for the right of domestic nazis to make of him a military scapegoat" (290–291).

Such bitter outspokenness did not go unnoticed by the white South. Defense mobilization also affected civilians and, as with other sections of the labor market, black domestic workers looked for economic improvement. The urban folklore of white southerners created a fascinating explanation for this turn of events, attributing "uppity" and independent attitudes among formerly meek and exploited black women to their membership in a recently established nationwide network of clandestine Eleanor Clubs. In North Carolina, one of sociologist Howard Odum's informants reported, "This Eleanor Club is spreading like wildfire all over the South and their motto is 'a white woman in every kitchen.'" Elsewhere it was a known fact that Eleanor Club members were probably the mothers of organized and impudent youths who wore zoot suits as uniforms (Odum, *Race and Rumors* 74–77). Supporting these stories was the belief among Odum's informants that the First Lady "is the most dangerous individual in the United States today" because of her vocal and widely publicized antagonism toward racial discrimination (84–85).

In Florida, legend had it that "when a Negro applied for a job she first asked if the head of the house liked Eleanor Roosevelt. If not, she replied that she belonged to the Eleanor Club and couldn't work for her" (*Race and Rumors* 74). This humor, or widespread rumor (among more slow-witted gossips), masked the white South's own recognition of the unfair racial system that it intended to maintain—regardless of how far that system diverged from the national creed of *democracy*.

African Americans did not simply sit still for mistreatment or racist jokes. In 1940, A. Philip Randolph's alliance of labor unionists threatened a massive "March on Washington" to demand a fair share of jobs in defense industries. Later, the left-wing press vilified Mrs. Roosevelt as "an enemy disguising herself as a friend" for her role in defusing the planned march. It seemed that Eleanor Roosevelt just couldn't win! The president, of course, bought off the militants by issuing Executive Order 8802, establishing the Fair Employment Practices Commission (James, *Fighting* 112; Brown, "Count Us In" 70). Political scientists agree that Randolph's threat of massive direct action forced Roosevelt's hand in the issuing of Executive Order 8802. But as Acklyn Lynch has suggested, the black public felt that "they had put President Roosevelt back in the White House for the third time" and, proud of their demonstrated voting strength, "pushed their leadership to react militantly" (57).

The militant mood of black Americans was not at all difficult to discern. The Atlanta-based Commission on Interracial Cooperation—which many African Americans viewed as decidedly conservative in both aims and methods and which certainly was so in comparison to A. Philip Randolph's supporters—convened a conference of black southern leaders at Durham, North Carolina, in October 1942. The conferees' report included the unequivocal statement: "Our loyalty does not, in our view, preclude consideration of the problems and situations that handicap the working out of internal improvements in race relations essential to our full contribution to the war effort" (Odum, *Race and Rumors* 186). Blunt as it was, such a statement was weak tea compared with similar position papers issued by black trade unionists or newspaper columnists such as Langston Hughes and Tolson (whose commentaries appeared in the *Washington Tribune,* with columns published between 1937 and 1944 collected in the volume *Caviar and Cabbage,* edited by Robert M. Farnsworth).

The South's racist stupidity approached genuinely tragic dimensions in 1942 when the Red Cross, in the wake of Pearl Harbor, refused to accept blood from African American donors: "Against the medical authorities who stated that there was no such thing as Negro blood, that blood from the veins of whites and Negroes could not be told apart, the Red Cross sided officially with [Mississippi congressman John Rankin,] who saw, in the proposal that Negroes too might contribute much needed blood, a communist plot to 'mongrelize America'" (Brown, "Count Us In" 70–71). "Democracy for many," wrote Sterling A. Brown in disgust in 1944,

> seems to be symbolized by this message, printed under a large red "V" on a bus in Charleston, South Carolina:
> VICTORY DEMANDS YOUR COOPERATION
> If the peoples of this country's races do not pull together, Victory is lost. We, therefore, respectfully direct your attention to the laws and customs of the state in regard to segregation. Your cooperation in carrying them out will make the war shorter and Victory sooner. Avoid friction. Be patriotic. White passengers will be seated from front to rear; colored passenger from rear to front. (Brown, "Count Us In" 76–77)

In response to such ludicrous notions of what Americans should be fighting for, the *Pittsburgh Courier* and other black newspapers launched an outspoken "Double V" campaign—demanding "victory for democracy at home and abroad" (James, *Fighting* 157–158).

On this historical point, of course, literary critics and cultural must answer some serious questions. If what I have described was indeed the real mood of the country, how could someone like Tolson, who wrote newspaper columns denouncing racism, also publish a poem such as "Rendezvous with America"—a poem that the *Raleigh Observer* praised with the words "Only a Negro whose spirit rises above so-called racial problems of today could write a poem so unprejudiced and so full of thankfulness to be an American, regardless of color, creed or kind" (Flasch 53)? A good critic, of course, would also wonder whether the editor of the *Raleigh Observer* had actually read Tolson's book or had merely scanned the blurb on the book's dust jacket. Tolson's eloquent "accommodation" and his outspoken militant criticism appear side by side not only in *Rendezvous with America* but in a *Washington Tribune* column of 31 July 1943 that, perhaps immodestly, advertises the poem to Tolson's weekly readers: "A Negro who thinks this country—the United States—is not his country is a damned fool. My native land!

Where is it? It is where my mother gave me birth. My hometown is where I was born. Jesus was a Nazarene, because He was born in Nazareth. I am just as much an American as President Roosevelt. And for the same reason. We were both born in the United States" (*Caviar and Cabbage* 99). Among the many metaphors that Tolson tests in his attempt to come to grips with America's racism, the most powerful of all occurs in the poem "Babylon." Tolson retranslates the writing on King Nebuchadnezzar's wall—or the bus placard discovered by Sterling Brown—in terms that are, finally, not ambiguous at all:

A people divided
Against itself
By the Idols of Race
And Caste and Pelf
Writes its own epitaph
With the fingers of doom:
"Here lies a nation
In a suicide's tomb."
(*Rendezvous* 94)

Rendezvous is Afrocentric in terms of its presentation of the collective desire of black Americans to achieve full recognition as capable and willing participants in their society. *Libretto for the Republic of Liberia* (1954), however, mounts a defense of Africans and African Americans against the derogations of white supremacist propaganda. It is, in this sense, an important text in a tradition that begins in the late eighteenth century with scholars such as Johann Friedrich Blumenbach and works such as Abbé Henri Grégoire's *On the Cultural Achievements of Negroes* (1808). But these Tolson books have more in common than their exploration of aspects of the Afrocentric project. From our privileged position as the "vertical audience" that Tolson hoped would eventually learn to appreciate his works, we can see how the historical scheme of poems such as "Rendezvous with America" and "Dark Symphony" prepared him for his grand assignment.

Commissioned by Liberian president William V. S. Tubman in 1947 and intended as an epic poem in the tradition of Vergil's *Aeneid*, Tolson's *Libretto* employs a simple framework to recount the significant events of Liberia's history and add mythological resonance to the deeds of "founding fathers" such as Reverend Jehudi Ashmun, the American Colonization Society's Reverend Robert Finley, and Joseph Jenkins Roberts, the country's first president. Each section of the poem is given the title of one of the notes of the do-re-mi musical scale, suggesting that a mere reading of the work will result in the production of music.

The *Libretto* begins by questioning the Eurocentric view of Africa as a mysterious continent, while later sections (based on documentation from the works of J. A. Rogers and W. E. B. Du Bois's *The World and Africa*) depict precolonial achievements. There is also a dramatic telling of the struggle and hardship involved in the effort to establish the Liberian Settlement in the early 1800s. Section 5, "Sol," suggests that the former slaves were not only required to survive on a hostile coast but also bore the burden of refuting Europe's racist condemnation of black people as inferior. Later, in the 232-line tour de force of literary allusions and intricate rhyme that constitutes section 7, "Ti," Tolson directly confronts and denounces European imperialism and the intentional misreading of world history that allowed Western nations to rationalize the plunder of other peoples' past, present, and future.

The epic genre necessarily encompasses vast spans of historical (or mythological) time. Think of Milton's *Paradise Lost* or Pound's *Cantos*. The classical Greek epics, recited today, perform a ritual re-membering of heroes whose deeds were accomplished in an epoch that was ancient even to Homer. Taking advantage of this feature of epic form, Tolson's *Libretto* represents an effective "correction" of white supremacist ideas. Perhaps the most interesting gesture used to facilitate this goal is Tolson's deliberate attempt to demonstrate parity between the wisdom and eloquence of the great texts of European literature and the proverbial wisdom of the African griots—the oral historians and traditional bards that he describes as "living encyclopedias." Naturally this tactic also undermines the "universal" authority claimed for such European texts by so-called scholars who, in the 1920s and 1930s, were actually propagandists for the concept of Aryan supremacy. As Martin Bernal explained in *Black Athena* (1987), even the teaching of ancient history was tainted. Thus Tolson pointedly warned his readers to beware of any account—historical or literary—that chose to ignore the "dusky peers of Roman, Greek and Jew" (*Libretto* 1343, l. 294). In a sense, Tolson anticipates Molefi Kete Asante's call for an academic discourse open to transcultural analysis in order to oppose Eurocentric definitions of history that constitute an "aggressive seizure of intellectual space" (Asante 9). Unlike some recent Afrocentric scholars, however, Tolson is not interested in claiming superiority for a non-Western viewpoint; instead, he cautions against the distorted perspectives provided by "the ferris wheel / of race, of caste, of class" (*Libretto* 1348, ll. 474–475).

Interestingly, Tolson's gesture has been effective even if a number of readers seem to have misunderstood his purpose. Karl Shapiro's statement that Tolson's works "are the Negro satire upon the poetic tradition of the Eliots and Tates" may be the source of Richard Kostalanetz's bizarre characterization of Tolson as "a poet who raised nonsensical parody to high literary levels. He was the great American Dada poet who could ridicule the allusive techniques of the great moderns in the same breath as certain African-American myths about Africa" (Bérubé, *Marginal Forces* 166; Kostalanetz 217). This attempt to enlist Tolson in the ranks of a 1990s concept of "transgressive" literature does him a disservice; indeed, it is dismissive. Tracing the history of Modernist intertextual reference, Elizabeth Gregory has written that, during the Middle Ages, when "reverent quotation flourished in both Christian and scholastic texts, parodic quotation also flourished, in opposition to the authoritative mode. Parodic quotation builds on the impulse to irreverence and undermines the same authority that reverent quotation means to evoke and continue; it equalizes where the other works hierarchize" (Gregory 7). While there is obvious ironic purpose in many of Tolson's quotations and allusions, it would still be a mistake to see his method—as Langston Hughes did momentarily—as entirely parodic.

Tolson's *Libretto* is surprising in a number of ways, not least the author's choice of Allen Tate to write the book's preface. Aldon Neilsen reminds us that in 1924 Tate had expressed the opinion that the American literary tradition was "utterly alien" to black writers. Tate, says Nielsen, "offers no explanation of why the tradition should be alien to an entire race of people whose presence in this nation extends as far back in time as that of white people. Nor does Tate recognize that he has confused a culture's rendering of itself alien to the outsider with the outsider's ability to comprehend that culture" (*Reading Race* 109). Reading Tolson in 1953, however, Tate thought that he had found an exception, "a Negro poet [who] has assimilated completely the full poetic language of his time and, by implication, the language of the Anglo-American poetic tradition."

Tolson, being educated enough to appropriate the tradition for himself, apparently felt flattered by Tate's statement, ridiculous though it was. If Tate thought that Tolson was the first African American poet to achieve such stature, the reason could only be that he was ignorant of Phillis Wheatley, who, for all her international fame, had been criticized for her adherence to the neoclassical style popular in the 1770s.

Indeed, the only American poet before Wheatley who had a wider readership was Anne Bradstreet.

In his preface to *Libretto,* Tate also complained that the majority of black poets were imprisoned by their reliance upon the black experience for subject matter, which he characterized as "the plight of the Negro segregated in a White culture." This charge certainly would not fit Tolson's poem, though Tate might not have understood why. In fact, *Libretto* is partly the history of the American Colonization Society's efforts to establish Liberia as a place to return free Africans and emancipated slaves, but Tolson uses the topic as a staging area for the presentation of the millenarian agenda of the Afrocentric tradition. If Liberia is, as stated in the poem's first section, "A moment in the conscience of mankind" (line 56), it is also as Nnamdi Azikiwe wrote in 1934, "the hope of an African civilization which should emphasize spiritual values, and should apply the African ideal of hospitality, of friendliness, of honesty, of truth, of justice, and of the brotherhood of man" (*Liberia* 396).

What Allen Tate did not know is that for Azikiwe, as for Melvin Tolson and other Afrocentric thinkers, this African civilization is intended to *replace* the one that Tate held so dear. "Day by day," Azikiwe had written, "it is becoming obvious that the civilization of the West could not withstand the reverberation of the civilization that is to be—and that is a *Risorgimento* of the majesty that was Ethiopia in antiquity, and the glory that was Songhay" (*Liberia* 396).

Most surprising about *Libretto* is the style that Tolson chose to celebrate the centennial of Liberia as the symbol of the "civilization that is to be." Tolson, says Rampersad, as "poet laureate of an African country had written probably the most hyper-European, unpopulist poem ever penned by a black writer." Langston Hughes thought that the style of the poem was a clever stratagem to ensnare just such as Allen Tate. In a letter to Arna Bontemps, Hughes chuckled, "More power to tongue-in-cheek Tolson! He told me he was going to write so many foreign words and footnotes that they would *have* to pay him some mind" (Rampersad 235).

Critical responses concerning Tolson's "difficulty" may seem peculiar, though, when one considers the context in which his work first appeared. Indeed, difficult poems were highly prized in the early 1950s. In a year when William Carlos Williams's *Paterson: Book III* received the National Book Award, *Poetry* magazine published not only an excerpt from Tolson's *Libretto* but also works ranging from the hermetic eroticism of Judson Crews to the stanzaic elegance of Richard Wilbur. A poem by Babette Deutsch in the June 1950 issue demands of readers a recognition of Dante, Delacroix, and St. Augustine. The latter is first introduced merely as "The saint from Africa" and then, as if to reward the allusively literate reader, is named in the following stanza. A later stanza offers an excellent description of what *Poetry*'s readers and contributors expected of the genre:

> The rhymes are slant, of course, the rhythms free
> Or sprung, the figures moving through the mind
> Close as a caravan across country
> Often unkind.
> It is magnificent in its privacy.
> (Deutsch 136)

In a way, this might be a description of Tolson's *Libretto* or of the very poem in which these lines appear. Certainly, without questioning the originality of either poet, it is clear that the work of both Tolson and Deutsch in 1950 reflected the accepted stylistic fashion of the day—the very thing that poets such as Frank O'Hara and Kenneth Koch (as in his hilarious poem "Fresh Air") were attempting to undo, Koch by burlesque and O'Hara by simply ignoring fashion's demands. In 1955, for example, *Poetry* carried a spirited debate between O'Hara and Harry Roskolenko on the question, as phrased by Roskolenko, "Is Mr. Koch's poetry valid or is it childish?" (177). The work of Tolson and Deutsch was sophisticated but, according to the standards of the period, not excessively difficult.

The most important thing about the language Tolson chose for *Libretto*, however, is that it is very consciously a development of the style first explored in "Dark Symphony" (1941) and an attempt to incorporate the discursive method of the African oral tradition of the griots whom the French linguist Maurice Delafosse called "living encyclopedias": "There are all categories of griots: some are musicians, singers, poets, story-tellers, mimes, dancers, mountebanks; others have the task of learning by memory the genealogies of noble families, the important facts relating to great personages, the annals of States or of tribes, political, juridical or social customs, religious beliefs, and their transmission to the next generation" (268–269). Tolson had drawn a sensitive portrait of the griot in a poem from the 1930s included in *Rendezvous with America*. "The Bard of Addis Ababa" (83–87) confronts the 1936 invasion of Ethiopia by Mussolini's air force and motorized legions. This event galvanized most black Americans. Journalist J. A. Rogers, a frontline correspondent for the black weekly *Pittsburgh Courier,* wrote in his widely distributed pamphlet *The Real Facts About Ethiopia* (1936): "Whatever be the outcome of the threatened Italian aggression against Ethiopia the world consciousness of the darker races against white exploitation has been intensified and will not subside. . . . The avalanche is on its way and it will not stop until the last vestiges of the brutal and debasing color-line imposed on the world by the white race shall have been shattered into irretrievable fragments" (3). For Africans and African Americans, the Italian invasion of Ethiopia was as shocking a challenge as Guernica was to the rest of the world.

Tolson's poem, however, is not a dirge. The traditional bard that he describes is

A blooded Amharic scholar
With the lore of six thousand years—
Yet he wears a sackcloth shamma

But the bard is no outcast:

The battle-cry of his ballads,
The meters' blood-spurring pace,
The star-reach of his spearing forefinger,
The eloquence of his face,
The seven-league boots of his images—
Stir the palace and the marketplace
(*Rendezvous* 84)

The second section of the poem reproduces the bard's song with its exhortation, "Rise up, ye warriors, do or die," as sung to "the backboned men" of Ethiopia:

The Fascist jackals shall die on the dunes,
    From Gambela to Danakil,
And the rain and the sun shall rot their thighs
    From Gojjam to Bodobo Hill.
(85)

The poem's final section leaps forward to a victory parade where "Along the Imperial Highway / The heroes of Takkaze ride" resplendent with medieval shields and swords, while

The Black Shirts slump on the camels,
Haggard and granite-eyed;
No longer the gypsying Caesars
Who burnt-faced breeds deride:
In the river Takkaze their vanity
Lies with the Caesars who died.
(86)

Significantly, the victory of the Ethiopians over the invaders is also a victory over the myth of racial superiority and European imperialism. The poem, of course, identifies the Ethiopians' "secret weapon" as the Bard of Addis Ababa, who is both the bearer of tradition and the people's inspiration. It was a role that Tolson coveted for himself.

It may be possible, as Joyce Ann Joyce suggests, that "the theoretical foundations of African-American poetry are of African origin" (6), but any actual connection would be a matter of carefully studied technique and poetic practice rather than atavistic inheritance. To the extent that poets of the Black Arts movement aspired to create works in what they understood to be an African tradition, one of the ways of reaching it was through Tolson. There are two sections of *Libretto* that show exactly how Tolson interpreted his commission as an opportunity to assume the role of a modernist griot. The section titled "Sol" in fact consists of a number of proverbs spoken in the *deepi-talki,* or "deep talk," used by the Zo's (or men of wisdom) of the Liberian Poro ritual societies. In his note to lines 163 and 168, Tolson sarcastically comments: "Delafosse feared that the mass production technics introduced by missionaries and traders would contaminate art for art's sake in Africa." But this section of the poem makes clear that the proverbial wisdom is timeless, accurate, and imperishable. Furthermore, the poem and footnotes make very clear that carnage is Europe's true *art pour l'art* (see notes to lines 42, 148, and 422) in much the same way that Pound makes this point in "Hugh Selwyn Mauberley" (1920).

The way that Liberian "deep talk" operates has recently been explained by Beryl L. Bellman's anthropological monographs, though Tolson was probably familiar with George W. Ellis's 1914 study *Negro Culture in West Africa.* Understanding the narratives of the wise men, Bellman writes, "involves the same interpretive procedures as does the discovery of intended meanings in parables, proverbs, chants, ritual metaphors, and dilemma tales. These procedures are the primary methods of communicating concealed knowledge without being accused of exposing secrets" (54). "When listening to 'deep talk,'" says Bellman, "hearers must attend to it as an analogical description that refers to meanings other than those contained in the narrative itself" (60). This requires locating an "interpretive key" either in the *text* itself or its immediate *context* (what is told before or after the tale).

Charles Bernstein has usefully suggested that we review Ludwig Wittgenstein's concept of poetry as "a language game" being played. When we apply this notion to Tolson's *Libretto,* we see that the poem is an extraordinary display not only of the author's mastery of "the Anglo-American tradition" that Allen Tate applauds but also of Tolson's knowledge of German, Latin, Greek, and numerous other traditions. The poem, indeed, suggests clearly that Liberia is heir to the combined wisdom of the world, or at least to planetary erudition. By providing the reader with footnotes, Tolson suggests an idea quite the opposite of the one entertained by his critics. *Libretto* is not a poem that needs deciphering but one equipped with its own bibliography. As with the references and citations in Pound's *Cantos,* the text and footnotes of *Libretto* constitute Tolson's own indispensable curriculum, complete and self-contained. Indeed, what is offered here can be seen as an Afro-centric alternative to Pound's syllabus—not because the poets chose different sources, but because Tolson offers a quite different perspective for reading them. Though it is written in imitation of the Liberian Zo's "deep talk," *Libretto* is delightfully an encyclopedic history of the intellectual sources of Liberia's century of existence. A recitation of the poem is a recitation of the nation's (and the author's) pedigree; in the process, Tolson consciously performs the African griot's age-old function.

5

Roots of the Black Arts Movement

New York in the 1960s

> New York City is a death festival.
> —David Henderson

For the sporting man, it's the city so nice they had to name it twice. New York New York. To many others it's not quite so nice. The Last Poets said it is "a city that don't mind fucking over a brother." Cold-blooded. Still, in spite of or because of its congestion of horrors, New York has a dynamic magic. Dynamic and decadent. Shyless and maddening. Her fancy airs polluted with sighs of desperation.

One writer spoke of looking under Miss Liberty's gown only to discover that she don't wear no drawers. Well, if you ever lived in New York, you always knew. Just like Barney. As the white man's mastery of men dwindles, New York has become more of a mess than a mecca, but it is still the premier city of planet Earth under the present regime. Strangest place on the planet. Ornette Coleman said, "New York is now!" A metapresent, total living, with the lights on twenty-four hours a day.

Personal life, though, has a much lower voltage. *Crawdaddy's* Peter Knobler suggested that "having to put up with *anything* is a New York pre-requisite." The atmosphere that results is perhaps what Ishmael Reed was talking about when he said of New York that "it always looks like the final days there." It looks like that because New York City began a grim decline just after World War II, a decline that paralleled the disintegration of the economic and political hegemony the city represents.

In everyday life, the glamor of New York is all shadow, and the danger does not cast a shadow. That's one of the tricks of the trade.

New York's decline was reflected in the side streets long before it reached the financial headlines. By 1960, the once bright neighborhood of Harlem had become a ghetto filled with trash-lined streets, callous muggers, and stumbling junkies. Formerly fashionable outlying suburbs like Forest Hills had grown narrow and insensitive. People were robbed and killed on the streets and in the subways while "good" white and black citizens drew their window shades or turned their heads, afraid to become "involved." On the other hand, younger people agitated for peace and civil rights. The city still had an atmosphere of urgency and creative energy. These impulses blended to create a unique and compelling environment.

The sharp ambiance of New York in the early 1960s was the thump on the rump that forced the new black poetry into breath. This is not to say that Chicago, Cleveland, Los Angeles, and other cities lacked significant movements. The New York experience, however, possessed an energy and direction that remain remarkable today. A great source of this energy was the Harlem Writers Guild, directed by John Oliver Killens; another was *Umbra* magazine and the Umbra Workshop, founded in 1961 by a younger group of writers. When we look back at the period, it is clear that, despite the normal diversity of personal tone and style, these writers all exhibited a common orientation. The young black writers in those years approached their world with a sense of outrage and with a missionary zeal borrowed from the southern civil rights struggle and heightened by an urgency bred by their surroundings.

The various writers' groups each had their own, often overlapping, concerns and orientation. Members of the Harlem Writers Guild stood solidly within the black literary tradition; another group of writers, clustered around Daniel Watts's powerful *Liberator* magazine (including Woodie King, Lebert Bethune, Larry Neal, Clayton Riley, and others), interpreted the African American literary heritage in more immediate and militant terms. Amiri Baraka (then known as LeRoi Jones) and A. B. Spellman, who tended toward the avant-garde, managed to be powerful figures in both black literary circles and white ones—without compromising their blackness. The Umbra Workshop, for its part, included many writers with a strong commitment to "nonliterary" black culture: David Henderson, Ishmael Reed, Tom Dent, Calvin C. Hernton, Joe Johnson, Charles Patterson, Al Haynes, Raymond Patterson, and Steve Cannon, among several others. Another member of the Umbra group,

N. H. Pritchard, investigated the African underpinnings of "Black English" before most of us even understood the significance of the term. Pritchard's early experiments, which were to lead to a "transrealism" that resembles concrete poetry, resulted in poems written in tampered English in which the combination of sounds approximated vocal styles and tones of African languages. Pritchard's poem "Aswelay" is a fine example of the experiment.

An excerpt from the poem shows one aspect of its innovations:

> in this boundlessvastly hours wait
> in gateless isn't fleshly smelling
> muchly as a golden on the crustishunderbrush of where
> no one walked were unwindishrustlings mustingthoughts
> of illtimed harvests
>
> and as we lay and as
> welay and as welay
> andaswelay
> aswelay   aswelay
> andaswelay
>
> above a bird watching we knew not
> what cause his course of course we
> lay we lay in the rippling
> soundlessboundlessvastly

(64)

Pritchard's rhythmic recitation of "Aswelay" on *Destinations* (1964)—a record album produced by Wilmer Lucas with readings by Pritchard, Hernton, Jerome Badanes, and Paul Blackburn—reveals to full effect the poem's beauty and deep, nostalgic sadness.

All of the young black writers in New York shared a sense of cultural crisis that was to become the basis of the Black Arts movement. They were basically concerned to effect the re-turning of a purely African sensibility and a style that would develop organically from this feeling and stance. They did not know exactly what to do. All were alienated, lacking a direct connection with African culture simply because they had grown up as black Americans with fundamentally American tastes and sensibilities. Most of them felt that an understanding of the most traditional black lifestyles and folkways available to them here would lead to a greater comprehension of the African way of life. This way of life interested them, but they did not idealize it as some militant blacks did in later years. They did share an intuitive knowledge that the ordinary private and communal life of black people was the key to a certain African integrity that most of their intellectual contemporaries lacked. If the force of this feeling can be understood, it seems quite logical that, in later years, most of these writers would reject the delusion of "literary New York" and turn toward home—Baraka to Newark, Tom Dent to New Orleans, and Spellman to lovely Atlanta—taking with them a brand new sense of urgency, black culture, and nationalism. But such cultural and political activism was the fruit of their New York experience. In the early 1960s, New York City and its unique scale of the typical informed the work of most of these pioneers of the Black Arts.

One might significantly begin to study the new Black Arts movement by reading A. B. Spellman's profoundly interior landscapes of the far edge of Manhattan, so distant from safety and sanity in every sense but Spellman's hoard of feeling. Almost nothing else can be kept in a Manhattan apartment anyway. Spellman, best known for his book *Black Music: Four Lives in the Be-bop Business* (1966), managed in his poetry to record the tone of black life in a soft and poignant voice. In one of his best poems, "For My Unborn and Wretched Children" in his book *The Beautiful Days* (1965), Spellman writes:

> if i bring back
> life to a home of want
> let it be me.
>
> let me be,
> if i come back, new, hands in first,
> the mouth in.
>
> if hands & mouth are in,
> the belly, filled, clothes
> the body. *then* want.
>
> if want & hurt are clothed, bring
> back life to home. if want decides,
> let it be me.
> (n.p.)

This is already Black Art in full maturity and strength—an African song in American English, drawing upon the syntax of traditional proverbs and the tersely sentimental tone of Rhythm and Blues. The self-sacrificing willingness to accept the weight of suffering is derived from an

African American legacy that goes back to slavery days. In more recent times, the old folks would tell us, "Things gon' get better. . . . I may not see it, but you children will." This sentiment may be the result of an attitude, prevalent in parts of Africa and the West Indies, that gives children latitude in behavior (and misbehavior) because "they don't know any better, they just children" and because they, as the incarnation of the community future, must be nourished and *allowed* to grow. In the United States, children are valued in this way by the stable black middle-class family and by the victims of the rough street life as well. Elliot Liebow recorded a moving and characteristic incident in *Tally's Corner* (1974): "On a Saturday morning, after a visit from his wife, Stoopy stands on the corner with three other men, watching his wife disappear down the street with their two school-age children on either side of her. 'There goes my heart,' says Stoopy, 'those two kids, they're my heart.' The other men nod understandingly. They would have felt and said the same thing had they been in his place" (81–82). This idea entails something more than the standard American desire to give one's children advantages in life that their parents were deprived of. A deeper tone is sounded here, one that recalls the real sufferings of slavery, genuinely abject want, and the forced disintegration of family units. The tone of Spellman's poem adds a note of mysticism to the issue and suggests a spiritual and biological urgency that extends far beyond concepts of purely social well-being.

Spellman's feelings have no kinship to the Western appliances of psycho-temerity that we find in even the best (and supposedly "revolutionary") white American poets—and many black ones. These are, in some deep sense that remains unclear, African feelings. There is a totally physical aspect to these words. *Touch* and/or *reach*. If Spellman were to write a welfare program, he would probably, one suspects, include reincarnation there, too. "For My Unborn and Wretched Children" displays a decidedly non-Western conceptualization, even though the song was composed amid the continuous decomposition of New York.

Among the Umbra writers there was a similar affinity for non-Western approaches and ideas. David Henderson's early catalogues of awesome depression in the white man's twentieth-century urban America are grimly illumined by flashes of an Abyssinian metempsychosis. His figures, situated as they are in a completely recognizable urban present, turn angrily or sadly toward myth. Henderson's major concern in these poems is the concept of *atavism;* his constant wonder is whether present behavior finds its basis in a reaction to the hideousness of the black man's lot in white America or whether it is determined by atavistic traits, vaguely remembered habits from the preslavery African past. He examines all action in this light, attempting to identify the sources of each individual presentation and response.

Unlike Spellman, many of whose poems seem to take place in a timeless and unspecified contemplative space, all of Henderson's work is set in the real world, with all its shabby complexity. No one else attempting "street poetry" is able to achieve what Henderson at his best can do in a few eloquently colloquial lines and five place names. He achieves his effects almost effortlessly, as naturally as he dances, walks, and talks—and sings. In "They Look This Way and Walk That Way as Tribal as They Can Be Under the Law," Henderson wrote:

> herman the barbecue man
> famous former mayor of Harlem
> sittin   in his brand-new caddy
> aunt jemama's hat on his head
>
> in his barbecue parlor huge photos framed
> shakin hands with rockefeller
> standin next to truman
>
> and in his chain   of barbecues
> surround Harlem no
> porkchops / on the menu
> remain
> (*De Mayor of Harlem* 42)

This scene is another reality of our starvings. Our strivings. It is not, perhaps, the reality of the Nation of Islam—despite the deletion of pork chops from the menu. Sherman's badges of legitimacy in business (framed photographs of the proprietor in the presence of various "great white fathers," including the butcher of Attica and the hell giver of Hiroshima) strike Henderson's eye as glaringly reactionary. The verses outline a portrait of a sad man, shipwrecked by time, because the unspoken nuances of the poem relate to an entirely different view of the world. This canny businessman's success—and complicity with the status quo—starkly contrasts with contemporaneous events such as the Harlem community's fierce but abortive struggle to prevent construction of the Rockefeller administration's State Office Building on

125th Street (an "urban renewal" project that required demolition of Lewis Michaux's famous black nationalist bookstore—a local landmark) and a notoriously unprecedented police invasion of Muhammad's Mosque No. 7 on Lenox Avenue. Angry Harlemites asked, "Would that happen at a synagogue? Would they kick in the doors at St. Patrick's Cathedral?"

Unlike older writers like Amiri Baraka, Henderson did not feel any attraction to the early radio dramas, movies, and pulp fictions that are currently being analyzed into limbo by humorless academicians of "Popular Culture." His own radio environment was a world of Alan Freed rock 'n' roll Muzak with "News on the Hour" interruptions. No Lone Ranger, no Green Hornet and Cato. No Major Bowes with his bell. Henderson's poem "They Are Killing All the Young Men," published in his collection *Felix of the Silent Forest* (1967), is an important piece that cannot be fully understood apart from this context. While the title reproduces the agonized utterance of some elderly black man or woman, the poem itself is an accurate rendering of Henderson's response to the new aural environment. The shape and function of radio had changed with the advent of television broadcasting, and the suddenly outdated radio programming had been suitably eulogized by Baraka in his poem "In Memory of Radio" when he realized that the Lone Ranger was dead. By the 1950s, radio programming had almost completely replaced drama and live music with announcers who played records, recited commercials, and read wire service news bulletins. Radio had begun to function in a real-life Orson Welles "War of the Worlds" manner that was alarming even to people who grew up listening to it. David Henderson's poem recorded exactly what he heard and presented it in a direct ideogrammatic style reminiscent of Pound's *Cantos*.

> (THIS IS A BULLETIN!!!!)
> Malcolm X shot several times in Audubon Ballroom
> (Don't Negroes meet in the strangest places?)

Later, in his narrative voice, he added significant details of the horror that had interrupted the music:

> The thin *Times* today tells
> of three black scrubwomen
> put to work on the blood
> (just as the handymen of Harlem were put to work

after the riots—patching up)
3 scrubwomen
scrubbing up blood—their blood—in time
for a Brooklyn Social Club's dance
that night
   the Audubon must go on

just as:

the *New York Times* marches on . . .

Henderson's understanding is sound. The Audubon ballroom and the *New York Times*. The medium is the message. Ultimately, both institutions represent the same thing. They do so obviously in terms of "white ownership," but Henderson is concerned with a deeper relationship between them. The word is, of course, "commerce"—what poet Tom Weatherly called "the dark continent of the European mind." Malcolm X, spokesman for a certain idea of black independence, died in a rented hall owned by businessmen who had many other rental dates to concern them. In juxtaposing these images, the poet allows no one to forget that American slavery was nothing other than a commercial enterprise in the first place. Echoing the spiritual "Many Thousands Gone" in his poem, Henderson establishes the connection that is pinpointed by his allusion to the Audubon's unbreachable rental schedule. Commercial enterprise. The pig-meat emporiums of the Negro elite, with pictures of white politicians on their walls, are no different. Henderson said, *chains* of barbecue. You understand?

On the petty levels of enterprise to which they are limited, Negroes are more infected with commercial madness than are many whites. This fact can be observed in any ghetto grocery, ineligible for a loan from the Small Business Association; in the stores run by round-the-clock Asians whose schedules make them tense and suspicious; in any shop owned by absentee white folk, fronted by exploited and irascible black help. Confrontation is harsh here, hardly the customary performance and amusing banter of the ancient marketplace. It is an awful madness, this commercialism, and it even affects the innocently menial scrubwomen and marginally employed handymen. The psychic effect of all this might be identified in another country as colonialism, and that notion resonates through the target of consciousness illuminated by Henderson's poems in general. The socioeconomic background of these poems is horrible. Money can't change you, but money on its meanest levels corrupts care. Henderson's message in "They Are Killing All the Young Men" should be more than obvious in the simple terms of human feeling.

Simply put, the debased spirit of acquisitiveness encouraged by capitalist commercial society produces monstrous results wherever it interfaces with ordinary human concepts of feeling and care. Inhumanity and "money money money" remain America's most important products—more important than life, more important even than mourning one's dead.

In much of his work, David Henderson presents what can only be called hideous details and grotesque situations, but even a superficial reading of the poet indicates that his own sensibility is quite clearly uncontaminated by the matter he finds it so necessary to discuss. His poems about New York's skid row, "Yin Years" and "Poem for Painters," show the distance Henderson has established between his own personality and the deathly atmosphere of the American way. Without recourse to overt politics or exhortation, Henderson brings a vibrant black nationalist vision to bear on the American scenes he illumines for us in his poems.

Henderson's collection *Neo-California* (1998), containing poems written over two decades that chronicle experiences in New York and Berkeley, reveals an interesting expansion and brightening of his vision as he witnesses a cultural syncretism-in-progress that drew its energy from the 1960s. Recent demographic changes in the United States, marked by a steady increase of non-Anglo population are not—in Henderson's perception—just a matter of statistics. In "Third Eye World" he describes a nation whose people are:

third world american
english speaking with roots in ancestral lands
(like everybody else, just about)
belonging to a new world
yet of an older world
(70)

Whether the grandchildren of nineteenth-century European immigrants wish to recognize their commonality with the "new" people or not, the impact has already begun to remake American culture. "People of Color" celebrates a kaleidoscopic multiculturalism:

Black Elk and Buddha
Capoeria and Tai Chi
good lovin' jazz and oldies and goodies from R&B
tango besame mucho
getting down in the streets to survive with the people
(71)

heralding a future United States secure in "a neo national perception / beyond boundary / beyond personal history" (71).

In *'Scuse Me While I Kiss the Sky* (1981), his magnificent biography of musician Jimi Hendrix, Henderson found a topic that allowed him to trace the development of an African American aesthetic reflected in the career of an artist who was uniquely rooted in tradition while also dedicated to creative innovation. Similarly, from *De Mayor of Harlem* to *Neo-California*, Henderson gives us a poetry full of five senses, a music touched with magic learned from both Walt Whitman and Bob Kaufman, an honest document of a world he looks upon with wisdom and wonder.

What Henderson did in "They Are Killing All the Young Men" with such sardonic coolness, Askia Muhammad Touré (known as Rolland Snellings when he was member of the Umbra Workshop) accomplished with righteous passion. His Malcolm is not a victim of the news media's lopsided reality, but "Malik, the Fire prophet, God's anger cast in glowing copper, burning the wicked of the earth with his flame." Touré is probably the most popular poet to emerge from the Umbra group in that his works are known throughout black America and his poem "Tauhid," like works of Dunbar, Hughes, and Claude McKay—like Waring Cuney's "No images"—is memorized and recited by people who have forgotten or have never even known the poet's name. He has also been a tireless worker and organizer; in a speech at Columbia University's Urban Center, Ishmael Reed called Touré the "elder statesman of the Black Arts movement."

Touré is not, by any stretch of the imagination, a street poet, and he has never written in the contemporary vernacular. True enough, his poems speak of the pain that has been and is everywhere apparent in the lives of black people in America. But Touré has always managed to evoke the feeling of that reality on an almost metaphysical level that is no less affective and effective for its avoidance of the mundanely specific. Furthermore, Touré's analysis of our problems is not limited to the locus of deprivation in slum streets or imitation gilded cages. His poetry and other writings develop from a global and, indeed, cosmic perspective. Without the blinders of sentimentality—although he is a man of deep feeling—Touré asserted that Malcolm X had been marked for murder precisely because he was moving out of the slum streets into the arena of world politics.

It is one thing to exhort the curious, unemployed, and powerless throng on Harlem's 125th Street. It is not quite the same thing to confer with the ministers and statesmen of independent Africa at the Organization of African Unity, though Malcolm's message did not change. Precisely because of his consistency, Malcolm's appearance before the African politicians was extremely threatening to certain interests—specifically, the Central Intelligence Agency and the Agency for International Development (AID). Malcolm's African audience inhabited a higher level in the world's alphabet-soup rulers' fantasy value system than did the Harlemites, and Malcolm's presumption to pull their coats to what's what constituted a capital crime.

Askia Muhammad Touré saw the entire picture quite clearly. He understood why black New Yorkers rioted at the United Nations in protest of Patrice Lummumba's assassination during the 1961 Congo crisis, embarrassing U.S. ambassador Adlai Stevenson. And he understood El-Hajj Malik Shabazz. Malcolm was depicted in Touré's article "Malcolm X as International Spokesman" in a role that many have yet to fully recognize. The tone of Touré's article was eulogistic, but it suggests disciplined and insightful political analysis:

> When Brother Malcolm addressed the O.A.U. in Cairo, he was like a Ramrod, a Whiplash, a Double-edged Sword, cutting both ways; he stunned them and shocked them out of their unreality. He informed them that we were watching them and judging them as we watch and judge the Western Empire. He confronted them with the truth of our existence, why us were here, how we are treated, who abused us; and if they didn't recognize their brothers there could be no *Pan-Africa* anywhere—for how could there be *Pan-Africanism* exclusive of the people who founded it, the people of Black America? (6)

Malcolm's international role, then, was concerned with the fact that his 1964 mission to Africa was an attempt at recementing the bonds that W. E. B. Du Bois and George Padmore had forged with the European-based Pan-African movement beginning in 1919. Malcolm X, in Touré's opinion, "smashed the revisionist 'continental' *Pan-Africanism*" that had emerged after some African territories gained independent statehood or so-called associated statehood, and he "reestablished the original 'universal' *Pan-Africanism* of Garvey." At least, that's how Touré saw it.

The accuracy of these views is not the issue here. I mean only to record them as they were promulgated by Touré in the influential pages of the *Liberator* during the 1960s. It should be noted, though, that in the years since Malcolm's death, the points of Touré's argument have been widely misunderstood and seldom adequately discussed.

What *is* important is the political worldview that formed the basis of Touré's nationalism and aesthetic at the time. Even for those interested in "street poetry," such ideas contributed to the basic foundations of the new Black Arts movement. In fact, such a political conception was the only justification for the concept of "street poetry" (poetry in the vernacular of the people, specifically working-class black folks) as it was understood at that time. Such a political approach was necessary if the new genre was to be more than another bogus folklore or the songs and dances inflicted upon blacks by opportunistic white artists starting with Stephen Foster, who stole and copyrighted the creations of black slaves, and culminating in DuBose Hayward's *Porgy and Bess* and Van Vechten's *Nigger Heaven*. Futhermore, some of the confusion we face today in dealing with the political (and aesthetic) ideas of black artists like Askia Muhammad Touré is as easily traced to self-interested designs among certain critics of Black Art as it is to the ignorance that these same critics show of our true history and tradition.

Touré was politically advanced. In the early days of the Umbra Workshop, he was deeply aware of the need to liberate African peoples everywhere in the world. At a time when most of us were much more concerned with what was passing in Alabama and with the contested rights of black people to participate in American democracy, Touré had on his wall for ready reference a lecture hall–sized map of Africa (on which many nations that are now independent appeared as European colonial states). In the context of the Umbra group, Touré was an opener of directions and new fields of thought. African American popular culture, as a vital expression of ancient traditions, was unselfconsciously admitted to his poems.

Nevertheless, Touré's poetic tone begins with the Psalms and the manner of the Gospel preacher who read them to us in church. In his rhythmic language, Touré is always "lining out" a better future. His major poetic figure has always been Apocalypse—sometimes in the image of fire, always in the sense of greater knowledge being awakened in us; in other words, an enactment of the Greek word's etymology, literally an "unveiling" or "revelation." His style of presentation (closely approximated by the Last Poets), like that of the Psalms, was never "dramatic reading" but very nearly song. Touré also employs the idea of song to represent the living essence of personality, heavily emphasizing our ability to decode sound properly. In "Poem for Dionne Warwicke Aboard the Aircraft Carrier *U.S.S. Enterprise*" (1970), he protested the singer's willingness to entertain troops who, on other days, are involved with

> raining "democratic" death upon the yellow world
> of Vietnam
> (*Songhai!* 5)

The singer is "decked out in gaudy mod colors," but Touré sees the entire affair as an insulting misuse of Warwicke's radiant spirit and voice. Challenging the conscripted and misguided troops in her audience, Touré evokes other sounds:

> Where are the warriors, the young men?
> Who guards the women's quarters—the burnt-haired
>   women's quarters—
> and hears their broken sobbing in the night?
> ("Earth" 327)

In "Mississippi Concerto" he provides an answer. Addressing his woman, Touré pledges to dedicate his life and talents in a way different from that which white America usually asks of black men:

> I kiss your breast, your eyes, your hair—the
> magic night.
> And vow before your throne with solemn heartache
> To taste again your lips, reclaim your Song.
> (324)

Here life is song—and the allusion to Solomon's *Song of Songs* reinforces the political message of a poem that would otherwise be simply personal.

Touré's own voice is Rhythm and Blues second tenor, sometimes lapsing into baritone according to tradition, though one suspects that many of his poems were written in a deeper register. Touré's voice is too passionate to sustain the solemn post-Christian philosophy of Calvin Hernton, too earthily sincere to be convincing with the sly and profound flippancies of Amiri Baraka. Such tones of voice would not be appropriate to his own natural sound. There is a likeness in his sound to that of Pharoah Sanders's horn, but Touré's voice, except what he shares with some Rhythm and Blues and Gospel singers, is uniquely his own. Enchanting and determinedly instructive. Rhapsodic at times. Always reflective of African American traditional forms. In "Sunrise" he writes:

> We will rise as a pine tree, tall and proud,
>   rises under bloody
> Southern skies to kiss the moon.
> SING of our Race! SING out our Destiny
> to your sons, to your warrior-sons—in the ghettos,
>   on the tenant farms,
>   in the swelling cities by the western sea.
> ("Sunrise" 322)

The poem offers complex echoes of Jean Toomer, of Marcus Garvey, and of James Weldon Johnson's "Lift Every Voice and Sing"—all of which will resonate with most African American listeners. And the poem does privilege listeners over readers; the *song* demands precedence.

Touré's message does not change, for there is always a new reader who needs it. In the title poem of his collection *From the Pyramids to the Projects* (1990), Touré performs a griot's task, recounting 10,000 years of history, correcting the miseducated:

> These European scholars with acid pens
> attacking Black history, like the Klan attacking
> Black churches,
>   stamped out tales of Egypt, Kush;
> reclaimed our forebears as
> "dark-skinned whites"; renamed
>   Afrikans "negroes"
> (26)

His purpose is to expose the political and academic conspiracies that have promoted white supremacy—whether those of the European colonization of Africa in the nineteenth century or the continual establishment (first in fact and then, even more devastatingly, in attractive fiction) of

> new factories of oppression
> where Rhett Butler and Scarlet O'Hara

fantasized about
being New World royalty,
while millions of worn Black bodies
bent over cotton, sugar cane
(27)

In a somewhat different mode, Touré reshapes his message in "Nzingha Revisited." This is a praise poem for African American women in the collective sense, but it is phrased so that, in fact, it is perceived as a sensuous and personal love lyric:

This woman was always
yours—from the slave-
ship to the hot
cottonfields and beyond. She is your
dignity, and the only Africa you'll ever know!
(68)

Recent works such as "Dawnsong" (1997) are rich, footnoted, epic-voiced rhapsodies of ancient African history and Egyptian mythology. Touré's rhythmic line and vibrant imagery are studded with poetic devices such as his adaptation in alliterative English of the classical Arabic figure called *jinas al-mudari*—in Arabic poetry a line containing two words that differ in only a single letter but have different meanings (see Arberry 22):

Mattocks mating with
the earth
as warriors mate with
holy matriarchs, ritualizing love.

Observe, in the human dawn,
the inner dawn
break across horizons of
Nubian minds, grappling
with soil, learning
cycles of seasons;
growing crops, computing star charts,
moon charts, primordial innovation,
leading to mathematics
and solar calendars these
melanin millennia.
Moving, growing, migrating north,

gaining spiritual rhythms / original visions:
mirroring Cosmic principles
—"As Above, so Below"—
from the moon and stellar jewels
glowing against the night, like
diamonds against indigo skin.
(1877)

In the dynamic context of the Umbra workshop, Touré's African-oriented political analysis was balanced and paralleled in scope by Calvin Hernton's psychologically based examination of things closer to home.

Born in Chattanooga in 1934, Hernton attended Alabama's Talladega College, where he was known to teachers as a talented and introspective student who seemed always to be reading a book. He began publishing poems in literary quarterlies while still in college.

"Been up North!" opens Calvin Hernton's poem "Remigrant" (1954), echoing the ebullient vernacular of Langston Hughes:

Been up North!
Chicago, New York, Detroit—

The poet's mood changes dramatically in the next stanza, however:

But I'm back down home now
Back down South—to stay.
Down South:
Black man . . . unequal man,
Human freedom . . . taboo!
Down South:
I'll make my stand
As a human being, as an
Equal man.
(89)

Hernton's echo of the song "Dixie"—and the title of the reactionary 1930 manifesto by the Nashville Agrarians—adds resonance to the poem's defiant reclamation of the South as *home* to African Americans, terrain worth fighting for with the nonviolent tactics of the civil rights movement.

A year later, while a graduate student in sociology at Nashville's Fisk University, Hernton began to define a personal aesthetic—a vision of poetry as both political necessity (the authorized voice of collective struggle against economic oppression and racial discrimination) and individualized Romantic torment. His poems attacked the same targets that New York's Beat poets were assailing. Hernton knew that all was *not* well in Eisenhower's apparently placid America. In "The Underlying Strife," he declared:

> A poet is not a plaything
> A poet is a perpetual struggle . . . an eternal
> Cause-of-the-People
> Toward the self-liberation of a wilderness dream
> Deep-frozen in a profit-making civilization.
> (462)

The homophonic play on words in this tiny jeremiad is exquisite: in the 1950s as in biblical times, the complacent society calls forth truth-telling prophets.

To the younger members of the Umbra Workshop, Hernton served as mentor and model. "Hernton was *there*. He had dem fat, black, greasy deep visions," as Joe Johnson put it. Hernton's collection *Medicine Man* (1976) shows his range—from "Low Down and Sweet," a virtuoso performance of the Dozens reminiscent of Ted Joans, to the metaphysical love poem "Taurus by Aster Fire." This poetry is never abstract, however. It is a poetry of specific reference and immediacy.

"A Ballad of the Life and Times of Joe Louis, the Great Brown Bomber," an energetic collage of voices, recalls radio broadcasts of championship fights and their evocation for black listeners of all of history since 1619. Writing in a more personal mode, Hernton can be dazzling. "Burnt Sabbath. Mount Morris Park. Harlem," written in 1962, is a wrenchingly magnificent and conflicted elegy for his mother. Out of religious doubt and personal pain, Hernton rescues a defiant hope:

> Sunday is time for testimony
> I have come to the zenith to witness
> The ascension of three dead ways
> I shall never betray you, my mother
> But I am harassment in lilac bud
> Decay in order and change in law
> I am the fourth way fell from convention to know how foul
> This Sabbath called "Mother's Day."
> (53)

Hernton seldom finds hope in American society. In "Almost Sunday" he abandons both Langston Hughes's optimism and Robert Frost's grumpy grandiloquence, recognizing the brutality of the age for what it is:

If I were your poet, America!
Who walk in sun or dusklight
With black mothers of children
Betwixt eyes of white, blue
And hectic green,
Injecting easter eggs with blood
Of the assassinated fathers,
Bareboned striding footways
Of Fred Douglass—
You would hound me down, say I was
A mentally deranged Negro gone mad
Under stress of the civilized weight.
(100)

Wandering New York's Lower East Side, Hernton encounters winos, victims of domestic abuse, hopeless survivors of the Holocaust. He weeps for all of these in "The Gift Outraged," angered by what they represent—his nation's destruction of its own human potential (109).

In addition to the sonorities of the American sermon, Hernton's major stylistic influence was T. S. Eliot. But in "The Distant Drum," like Pound in his famous pact with Whitman, Hernton makes clear where he departs from his model, explicitly rejecting Eliot's self-serving demand that readers of poetry distinguish between "the man who suffers and the artist who creates":

I am not a metaphor or symbol.
This you hear is not the wind in the trees.
Nor a cat being maimed in the street.
I am being maimed in the street
It is I who weep, laugh, feel pain or joy.
Speak this because I exist.
This is my voice.
These words are my words, my mouth
Speaks them, my hand writes.
I am a poet.
It is my fist you hear beating
Against your ear.
(115)

Hernton is, in fact, making a claim for the *functional* immediacy of poetry that will be reiterated in Amiri Baraka's "Black Art."

Some of Hernton's poems are simply perfect—the strangely beautiful

"Lines for Any Woman's Birthday" or the classic masculine menace of "125th Street, Harlem USA." Poems such as these prompted people who heard Hernton's poetry readings in the 1960s to come up to the edge of the stage with requests.

All of Hernton's works—whether poetry or fiction, whether literary creation, sociological essay, or an exploration of R. D. Laing's alternative psychotherapy—are marked by a profound and logical skepticism. The racist status quo of the 1950s convinced him that a society able to rationalize such a system must also be wrong about other things. As he noted in *The Cannabis Experience* (written with Joseph Berke in 1974), that which is declared "culturally dystonic" may simply be a threat to established business and political interests (257–258). Furthermore, in any society that will destroy its citizens for short-term profit, what is considered normative may actually be toxic.

The young black writers in New York in the early 1960s were deeply inspired by Rhythm and Blues and by the new jazz forms being established and explored by John Coltrane, Eric Dolphy, Ornette Coleman (all of whom had apprenticed themselves to Rhythm and Blues bands), and Cecil Taylor (who did time in a conservatory). New York was bursting with new music. From time to time, Sun Ra brought his Solar Arkestra in from Chicago. Many of the writers had begun collecting his early recordings. Amiri Baraka and Archie Shepp were quite enthusiastically discussing the political and artistic merits of the new sound. Frank Kofsky, a controversial columnist for *Jazz* magazine, was in the thick of the intellectual fray.

A white Marxist-oriented jazz critic, Kofsky investigated the new jazz of the 1960s in terms of the sociocultural orientation of black nationalism. His work may, at first blush, resemble Askia Muhammad Touré's approach in his poems "JuJu" (for John Coltrane) and "Tauhid" (for saxophonist Pharaoh Sanders). The similarity is quite superficial. In *Black Nationalism and the Revolution in Music,* Kofsky patronizingly observed that the emergence of independent African nations in the early 1960s was important for the growth of black nationalism in this country. Kofsky's analysis precisely opposes the views Touré expressed in his article on Malcolm X. Reading Kofsky, one can only wonder whether the man remembers the 1961 United Nations riot. The riot occurred the day after Lummumba's death by assassination, which James Baldwin termed "the most sinister of recent events," and was blamed on "a handful of irresponsible, Stalinist-corrupted *provocateurs*." Baldwin did not doubt that there were, indeed, a few provocateurs in the riot. "Wherever there is great social discontent," he wrote, "these people are, sooner or later, to be found. Their presence is not as frightening as the discontent which creates their opportunity" (*Nobody* 74).

And so Frank Kofsky appeared on the "new jazz" critical scene, botching his opportunities. Speaking of the African nations that Malcolm X had taken the trouble to address, Kofsky wrote, "An especially illustrative corollary of the appearance of these new non-white nations on the world stage is that Negroes in the United States now realize, possibly by intuition, that there are other viable alternatives available to them besides that of transforming themselves into carbon copy images of the white man. The importance of this development can scarcely be overstated, because in effect it opens the door to a Negro movement of mass dimensions based on an explicit rejection of the American dream" (129–130).

Lawd! Naturally, Kofsky could never have heard of Marcus Garvey or the Universal Negro Improvement Association. Nor of Father Divine. One can only wonder again whether he understood anything at all about jazz (from Louis Armstrong on down), since he did not recognize that black rejection of fitful American phantasms has always been a practical exercise of a moral option. Kofsky's arrogance and insult notwithstanding, his statement regarding the impact of African independence is simply incorrect. The movement toward black nationalism in the United States during the 1960s did not develop by "intuition"; he misunderstands and misuses the word.

Much of the revival of the black nationalist impulse in the 1960s reflected outrage, some of it the effect of a specific political rhetoric. Many individuals, however, came to the black nationalist approach as the result of extensive intellectual analysis. Perhaps some of this analysis was as wildly off base as Touré's estimate of the ultimate significance of Malcolm X's trip to Africa. But compare that with the United States government's analysis of the situation in Vietnam. Intuition, it seems, had little to do with any of these miscalculations, so much to everyone's detriment.

There was yet another source of the revival of black nationalism in the 1960s, one that Kofsky could not be expected to know. This source was communal African American tradition. In the 1950s, the cultural expression of black nationalism was (with the exception of some prominent jazz players who embraced it) largely restricted to an underground of unknown artists—mainly sign painters and street-corner musicians—who sent their cosmic vibrations out from storefronts, basements, and brownstone stoops on a summer night. There were poets of the cell block and the corner "organ bar" lining out the grammar of our ancient language.

Marcus Garvey's Universal Negro Improvement Association mounted a militant mass movement in the 1920s, but the advance of the NAACP's legalistic approach to the struggle for civil rights had tended to push the black nationalists away from center stage. Not merely coincidentally, the Garveyite approach to culture—which had had a definite effect on the artists of the Harlem Renaissance—was purposely denigrated and misrepresented in both black and white critical media. The emphasis that Garveyites placed on the beauty (indeed superiority) of blackness did not suit the NAACP's purpose. In its journal the *Crisis,* under the editorship of W. E. B. Du Bois, the NAACP led the campaign against Garvey and his ideas. The NAACP assault on Garvey finally landed him in prison for mail fraud and effectively destroyed his UNIA organization. At the same time, Du Bois's victory established the National Association for the Advancement of Colored People as the arbiter of black political and cultural expression for almost twenty years. While the Garveyites had been black nationalists and Pan-Africanists, the NAACP at the time (Du Bois's Pan-African sympathies notwithstanding) was geared toward the integration of black people into American society on all levels. Artists of the nationalist persuasion were suppressed. After white cooptation of bebop music had been achieved in the mid-1950s, their tradition was unknown except in the black neighborhoods. Too good to quit. The arts suffered, as did the artists. In the 1950s, after twenty years of the NAACP's integrationist ethic, the black community produced its own strange echo of white folks' McCarthyism—the least connection to Garveyite groups or black nationalist ideas was enough to stamp you a bona fide nut. Nevertheless, artists who were black nationalists and Garveyites made valuable contributions that even now have been neither recognized nor properly evaluated.

While most black people were striving to acquire the outward manner and accoutrements of white middle-class America, the black nationalist artists continued doing their art and talking about the ancient glories and present sufferings of Africa. Some of them seemed maniacal in their persistence. Some appeared clownish in their embattled dignity.

Crazy or not, such people represented a vector of the community's inner dynamic. An interesting aspect of a seldom discussed communal tradition can be discerned in the outward manifestations of black nationalist ideas as they appeared in fashion concepts and the visual arts—areas where they gained a degree of popular acceptance. The wearing of dashikis and African-influenced jewelry, *geles* (head wrappings), and print dresses—which first became faddish in the late 1960s and early 1970s—indicated a familiarity with the costumes of newly emergent West African nations, but the bushy Afro hair style suggested something quite different. There is a story that the Afro originated among civil rights workers of the Student Nonviolent Coordinating Committee (SNCC) in the South who, while registering voters in rural areas, wore overalls and T-shirts and were too poor to afford regular haircuts. The tale may be true, but it does not really explain the true origin of the Afro hair style. Harlem's West Indian–dominated Garveyite organizations had been involved in promoting the fashion throughout the 1950s. Each year on 17 August, the anniversary of Marcus Garvey's birth, artist Cecil Elombe Brath (then known as Cecil Brathwaite) and his brother, photographer-designer Ronald Brathwaite, staged fashion shows featuring the Grandassa Models in Afro coiffures au naturel and African-styled gowns. These affairs were usually held at Harlem's Renaissance Ballroom on 135th Street and were sponsored by Carlos Cooks's and Jim Lawson's surviving UNIA chapters. At the time, many people found it unthinkable that a black woman would appear in public with unstraightened hair—let alone participate in a fashion show! The eventual popularity of the Afro hairdo and African patterns of hair braiding (even among whites in the 1970s) resulted from conscious and persistent promotion by the Brathwaites and other black nationalist–oriented designers.

Similarly, innumerable sign painters in black neighborhoods across the country produced works in oils, tempera, and pastels depicting black Christs, madonnas, and other popular subjects. Such works were often executed in an excellent, if corny, representational style—but the subject matter spoke of Garveyite cultural concepts. Garvey's African Orthodox Church popularized the concept of a black Jesus back in the 1920s, assisted by historian J. A. Rogers's documentation of the black Christs and madonnas among the treasured art masterpieces of Europe. These painters also developed an interesting and distinctive angular style of lettering and graphic design that persisted into the late 1950s on the album covers of records by James Brown, Sun Ra, and others. Some of these graphic forms are reminiscent of the Haitian *veves* drawn on the floor at voodoo ceremonies.

These instances and many others suggest that a self-generating group of artists and craftsmen within the black community remained dedicated to black nationalist cultural concepts from the late 1920s to the early 1960s. These men were quietly teachers and curators of cultural alternatives, and their personal frustrations must have been enormously painful when one considers the bitter shares that "recognized" black artists received in those years. Still, the manner of these men was, I imagine, like that of the Nation of Islam's legendary and revered master W. D. Fard. Fard was a Detroit junk man and a door-to-door peddler, but along with his curios he disseminated the Muslim doctrine. The sign painters were also serious, if untrained, artists—and some of them were, indeed, well trained at universities and art schools. The sign-painting shops were art schools in their own way. Abstractionist Joseph Mack, a professor at Prairie View A & M University, provided an interesting clue to the value of these shops. Mack sometimes uses gold leaf in his paintings, and the special technique used in applying it was taught him by an older man during Mack's stint as a sign painter following his graduation from art school. The technique, says Mack, "is almost a forgotten art. You have to learn it from someone, you can't pick it up by yourself" (interview with the author). And it is not taught in art schools or universities. Talk in the sign shops was not limited to the humble barbecue shop commissions the painters executed but ranged over the public WPA art of the 1930s, the Mexican muralists Rivera and Tamayo, and the design innovations of the Bauhaus. The older painters were strong men, talented and frustrated. For black men trained in the visual arts, the sign-painting shop served the same outlet that the Post Office and the Pullman coach served for those who had majored in the liberal arts. Somehow these men should be remembered. They were proud, enlightened and enlightening, and unassuming. Shunned by fame, they shone with the sincerity of their dedication—anonymous professors of magical arts and trustees of suppressed schools of wisdom. They were North American griots.

The most nearly visible members of this artistic underground group were explicitly political scholars of Marxism, leftover Garveyites, and Pan-Africanists. A less visible few were more "spiritually" oriented, adherents to various "Eastern" or "oriental" disciplines or mysteriously Christian in some form quite incomprehensible to most of us. They maintained a cultural alternative within the black community, an alternative that was investigated by the young artists of the Black Arts movement in the 1960s.

Recognition of the function of these unknowns, all of them quite literate and fluent in their arts, will demonstrate that the cultural black nationalism of the 1960s and 1970s did not spring forth from inspiration of the *New York Times* or the late news. It was a result of a continuing tradition, transmitted as naturally as possible under the circumstance of a specifically malicious and aggressive white American culture that overshadowed the integrationist ideologies of the NAACP and the Urban League.

The admittedly "literary" orientation of the Umbra circle and its location on New York's Lower East Side would seem to preclude much contact with this older underground Black Arts tradition, but such is not the case. All of the Umbra poets had questioned and conferred with these sages as part of an ordinary ghetto upbringing. Contrary to some popular and supposedly scholarly opinions, pimps and gamblers are not the only glamorous models for youngsters in the black community. I remember as a child being entranced by a chance meeting with boxer Ralph "Tiger" Jones and by seeing Shepherd Lewis of the Heartbeats (later Shep and the Limelights) on the street. Lewis and other musicians frequented Tolliver's Crystal Casino on the corner of the street where I lived, and the tavern had been a favorite relaxing spot for pianist Thomas "Fats" Waller in earlier times. In these days of media-concocted "superstars," many people are unaware of how close most black musicians and artists have been to the community. During the days when I was growing up in the neighborhood of St. Albans, it was not unusual to see James Brown on Linden Boulevard talking to friends or John Coltrane puttering around his home on Mexico Street. And the corner by Tolliver's was a friendly spot. Whether celebrities or working men, the people on the corner related to the kids on the block in the same way—talking jive and slapping five—encouraging you to think that the world was waiting for your contribution.

The Umbra writers were also in communication with Harlem poets such as Hart LeRoi Bibbs, himself a griot and (sometimes unfortunately) a true scholar of the street's traditions of strolling and rapping. Bibbs, though his orientation is not "literary," was an inventive and original poet well versed in the history and lore of Africans from here. His book *Polyrhythms to Freedom* (1962) is a rare document filled with idiosyncratically mind-jarring verse. The frighteningly intellectual poet Lloyd Addison was another influence on the Umbra writers. Addison's poems, though indebted to T. S. Eliot and Melvin B. Tolson, seemed to emerge from the black community without any foreign overtones. Other contacts with the hidden pulse of black culture came from meetings with the fabled "characters" of post–Beat Generation Greenwich Village. Joe Johnson, one of the editors of *Umbra* magazine in the mid-1960s, can still tell you all about Enrique Jorge (an obvious pseudonym), the Puerto Rican bard of Union Square, famous on the streets for his "talking coconut" and ventriloquist performances.

Some of the Umbra group (Hernton, Cannon, Dent, and others) also had a deep knowledge of black southern folk traditions that contributed to their awareness. Others had been exposed to alternative (i.e., reliable) versions of recent political history by poets such as Art Berger and Henri Percicow, an experienced trade unionist. But more than anything else, the oral tradition of the Harlem griots, and this tradition as it was reflected in black popular culture, had a major impact on the embryonic Black Arts movement in New York. The tattered but tenacious traditions of black nationalism in the streets had as much of an effect on these writers as did the literary heritage of the Harlem Renaissance and the innovations of the avant-garde.

The black nationalist approach of older men, so persistent in the face of the civil rights movement's continuing disappointments, seemed to exert a particularly powerful influence on young writers who, through the Umbra Workshop, actively sought a better understanding of the shadow world that is black life in the United States. In Harlem literary circles, Harold Cruse was beginning to acquire his well-deserved reputation as a scholar and interpreter of black history. Cruse made a special effort to include and decipher the black nationalist aspect of recent events. In Greenwich Village and the Lower East Side, the upstarts of the Umbra Workshop sponsored a series of audacious poetry readings at St. Marks Church that thrust poetry back into its original oral grandeur and reaffirmed the poet's primary role of social commentator. The poets themselves were always, as David Henderson put it, "going to Harlem" for a closer connection with the spirit of the people.

In the summer of 1964 Amiri Baraka formed an all-black group for the purpose of publishing an investigative community newspaper in the Village. At the same time, there was a noticeable estrangement between black and white artists on the Village scene, partly due to issues raised by the Harlem riots. The newspaper project never got off the ground, but Baraka's group, then called In/Formation (and including artists such as Charles Patterson of the Umbra Workshop, Steve Kent, painter Joe Overstreet, and pianist Andrew Hill), produced a well-received poetry and jazz showcase at the St. Marks Playhouse that winter. Poetry by many of the young black writers discussed here was presented in dramatic readings with complementary music by Marion Brown, Pharaoh Sanders, Dewey Johnson, and Rashied Ali.

At the beginning of 1965 In/Formation moved uptown to Harlem to establish the Black Arts Repertory Theatre/School in a brownstone on 130th Street near Lenox Avenue. The new organization openly affirmed black nationalist political and aesthetic ideas. Umbra was honored with an invitation to present the inaugural poetry reading for the May 1965 opening of the theater. The reading attracted a large community audience, including several young unknown poets. One of these was Pedro Pietri, the "people's poet" of East Harlem's barrio and of Fourteenth Street, New York's outdoor Third World bazaar.

The Black Arts Repertory Theatre/School, though it may in some ways have undermined Umbra's downtown viability, was the spark igniting a new nationwide movement more energetic and more extensive than the Harlem Renaissance of the 1920s had been, and completely controlled by black artists. The Black Arts Theatre represented a conscious decision to do art within the physical environment of the black community, using the artistic and spiritual resources of this community. The self-imposed limitation immediately came under attack, and it was suggested that the theater's orientation would preclude the presentation of white characters. Harold Cruse, in *The Crisis of the Negro Intellectual* (1967), recorded the Black Arts directors' response: "We've got actors that can play those roles in whiteface, you dig?" (536). The idea of *limiting* the theater to the resources available in the community originated primarily with Baraka, and it was so timely that it spread quickly throughout the major cities of the United States. Soon there appeared the Black Arts West in San Francisco (the theater that produced playwright Ed Bullins), the Affro-Arts Theatre in Chicago (headed by Philip Cohran, formerly a member of Sun Ra's Arkestra), the Free Southern Theatre, based in New Orleans, and the Sudan Arts South/West group at the Black Arts Center in Houston.

The Black Arts movement gave ordinary black people, particularly youngsters, a new freedom of access to the arts. It also embodied the artists' political awareness of black nationalist ideas and their determination to get back to the roots, to vindicate black unknown bards of our own time who lectured by lampposts and held in trust a knowledge that oppressive black bourgeois and white racist interests had relegated to the oblivion of slums, to shabby dwellings "across the tracks," and to burning silence.

According to Albert B. Lord, "a superior written style is the development of generations." Much black writing today deserves the epithet "superior," and I've been trying here to name some of those who contributed to that development in successive generations. What generations! Griots of Harlem streets, bedraggled saints from southern homes, "outdated" island prophets of black nationalism—all of these characters, somehow (by a process still incompletely documented) managed to transmit to the young writers of the 1960s an entirely different approach to doing art that has made contemporary black literature of the United States one of the most vibrant and beautiful human flowerings on the planet. This art is now, in its direct communicative ability, almost the equal of black music. Jazz. The turning point was the assertion of a *communal tradition* over the literary (read "white marketplace") concerns of the writers. This tradition has been invisible, in the sense that Ralph Ellison understood long ago, but its strength has been nurtured and its effects are real.

The Black Arts movement required its artists to return to the black community and to produce their art from within it. The movement encouraged a new sense of community and a new awareness of black heritage while simultaneously embracing a militantly engaged political stance. But the most important effect of the movement was the identification of artists as the spokespersons of the people and a concept of art, not as solely individualistic expression, but as the blossoming of the most ancient communal tradition of African creation.

6

Amiri Baraka

Gathering the Spirits

Coming out from New York, you suffer the Hudson Tubes on the train or else you drive through interminable marshes, the flatness broken here and there by the transmitter tower of an easy-listening New York FM radio station, onto the iron Pulaski Skyway, with its dull view and noxious swamp gas industrial fumes. I took the motor route once with Sun Ra, band members and friends jiving and doing Dozens in the car. We were going out to visit Baraka, which was really—in those days—the only sane reason to be going to Newark.

Newark, New Jersey, is, at any time, something less than you would expect. In the mid-1960s, the city was a combination of smoldering opposites. On the surface, Newark was a dull industrial city run by an exceedingly corrupt "sausage machine" (Polish and Italian Democrats), and it was also a city with a predominantly black population whose urban lifestyles continued, distorted, and disguised southern small-town folkways in an entirely predictable way. It was a town where you could always buy a half pint on Sunday if you knew where to go and whom to ask—cousin or "hometown." Even now, Newark ain't like New York City. New York has vice, indeed, but it has never developed that old-fashioned neighborhood bootlegging tradition.

Nathan Heard's *Howard Street* (1968) succinctly described Newark's hard-core inner-city ghetto in suitably hard language:

Two blocks bisected by Howard Street are bordered by Court, Broome, and West Streets, and Springfield Avenue. Dark little Mercer Street crosses Howard between Court Street and Springfield

Avenue. From Court to Mercer is a long block with two trees (birch) fighting valiantly but vainly to stay alive. . . .

The short block between Mercer Street and Springfield Avenue is something so different as to be classed almost as another world. While laborers and domestics—poor but respectable people—live in the long block, the short one is as wild and rowdy as Dodge City or Tombstone ever was, with no Hickok or Earp in evidence. It also has the strange, but familiar and inevitable, combination of religion mixed in with every conceivable vice. (20)

Heard earned his understanding of the streets. He came up hard and spent his time behind the walls before writing his novel and assuming a teaching career. Heard has been attacked by critics who, perhaps impatient with his naturalistic approach, are dismayed by his downbeat portraits of black folks, but these critics are missing an important point. Anybody who presumes to understand the dynamics of black Newark—from the good-doing black politicians on down to the junkie nodding in the balcony at RKO Proctor's—by reading Black Power essays or the militant newspaper *Unity and Struggle,* had better also read Heard. For good or ill, disrespectful of black folks though he may be, Nathan Heard tells another side of the story.

In the 1960s, Newark was still the kind of town where a white traffic cop, ridiculous in Day-glo armor, would call Ishmael Reed, Steve Cannon, and me "boys" when we asked for directions. Well. Actually, we weren't so old then. Still, the cop was but a mere whit older, so we persuaded ourselves to be indignant anyway. After you ride the Hudson Tubes, anything can make you indignant—most specially a rookie cop with international orange creeping up his neck.

Newark was also where you could listen to the futuristic fantasy music of Sun Ra's Arkestra at Art Williams's Jazz Art Study Society (JASS), a "revolutionary" cramped basement concert hall near Springfield. On another evening you could lay dead in Art's basement and hear drummer Eric Brown literally play his ass off—falling off his stool after treating the universe to a blur of hands and body, cymbals snare tom-tom and bass drum—heralding the advent of "new music." Newark, in such transcendent moments, was an exciting place.

One Christmas Eve, Reed and I went bar hopping in Newark and stopped at the Blue Note, a typical Howard Street–type bar. A sissy in slightly outdated pimpish clothes and gold dangling earrings eased Charles Brown's "Merry Christmas Baby" out of a tired piano while the assorted drinkers in the club nodded their heads and said "yessss" and drifted and drifted outward inward toward more beautiful space than the club could otherwise afford.

We broke the weird and sentimental spell and wandered down the street, on Reed's money, in a taxi. We found ourselves at the local Urban League/NAACP good-doing brothers' hangout, which was a private house catty-corner to the Father Divine hotel, with a plush red-lighted bar inside. All of the up-and-coming cats were there. In dim suits and flaming ties under the red bulbs, they were busily hustling on their level. The conversations were subdued and "significant."

—Well, just um give me a call on Chewsday. . . . um hmm . . . like that
—I'm sure we can put a little something together
—Mine host, lay another Cutty on my man here

And so forth. Same old jive. The music was canned, subtly spinning from somewhere beyond us, lacking the painful intensity and truth of the cat nodding over the Blue Note's piano.

We split from there, too. We walked through the cold quiet streets a few blocks to a union hall or community center sort of place where Amiri Baraka was reading feverish political poems to a few cheerful working-class black folks. Same kind of folks we had left in the Blue Note, but these were their mommas, sisters, little brothers, and wives. Cousins nieces nephews of the big talkers in the red-lit private bar.

Baraka was dressed in a flowing big-sleeved dashiki and a Moroccan knit cap. He was shouting and singing his poems. One of them was a severe but lyrical j'accuse aimed at the horde of colored political hacks sucking up behind Hugh Addonizio, the Newark mayor who later went to jail for extortion. The poem was cold. Baraka cynically employed images from popular literature, the doxology, and street slang in a skein of tight words stitched in acid:

> We have a nigger in a cape and cloak. Flying above the
>   shacks and whores,
> he has just won an election. A wop is his godfather. Praise
>   Wop from whom
> all blessings flow. The nigger edges sidewise in the light
>   breeze, his fingers
> scraping nervously in his palms. He has had visions. With
>   visions. With commercials. Change

6. Amiri Baraka. Photo by Roy Lewis.

rattles in his pockets. He is high up. Look, he signals.
   Turns, backup, for
cheers. He swoops. The Wop is waving. Wave Wop.
(*Black Magic Poetry* 213–214)

The audience, just like a church congregation, said "Amen" when the poem was finished.

Ishmael Reed and I sat there with our eyes bugged out, wondering if the brother was mad. Talking like that. Talking that talk. Reed at that time was editing the *Advance,* a black weekly in Newark, drawing upon his early experience as star investigative reporter on the insanely social activist Buffalo *Empire Star*. After a few weeks of Reed's bad-mouth articles on Buffalo's city government, that paper began losing most of its ads. Editor Joe Walker (later New York bureau chief for *Muhammad Speaks*) allowed Reed to continue, and by the time both of them finally quit, the *Empire Star* had lost *all* of its advertising revenue. Obviously, they'd been printing the truth (Bellamy 132–133).

The last straw had been when Mr. Walker and Mr. Reed presented an interview with Malcolm X on Buffalo's WUFO in 1960. Yes, phone calls, cards, and letters came in—many of them carrying the traditional bon voyage message: "Get outta Dodge" or words to the same effect.

Reed's constructive muckraking eventually produced much the same result in corrupt New Jersey that it had earlier in corrupt upstate New York. While the *Newark Advance* gave him an opportunity to bring some of his newfangled journalistic ideas to reality, his most notable success in the stylistic area was in inspiring art director Walter Bowart and poet Allen Katzman to publish the *East Village Other* (*EVO*) in New York City. *EVO* very quickly became the style book for the influential "counterculture/underground press" movement of the Vietnam-haunted 1960s.

As for hometown Newark, Reed ran up against the usual fat-lip small town/small mind going nowhere Negroes. From these encounters he did manage to salvage the inspiration for his bitingly satirical first novel, *The Freelance Pallbearers*. It's understandable, then, that Reed (knowing the Newark scene) was worried when Baraka returned from Harlem in 1966 and set up the Spirit House on Stirling Street in the very heart of the ghetto/saint home. And worse yet, come talking like that! Talking about the political machine.

Dig it. Christmas Eve in cracker-laced Newark, in the deeps of the Bottom. Baraka come talking that talk. As we sat in the bare hall, in the back row of folding chairs, Baraka continued reciting his new crazy poems:

> Black people!
>> What about that bad short you saw last week
> on Freylinghuysen, or those stoves and refrigerators,
>> record players
> in Sears, Bambergers, Klein's, Hahnes', Chase, and the
>> smaller joosh
> enterprises? What about that bad jewelry, on Washington
>> Street, and

> those couple of shops on Springfield? You know how to get
>   it, you can
> get it, no money down, no money never, money don't grow on
>   trees no
> way, only whitey's got it, makes it with a machine, to
> control you
> (*Black Magic Poetry* 225)

"No money down, no money never?" The people were saying "yeah, uh huh" laughing and bopping their heads. Like in church. In this undecked hall. I was amazed at what the poems were doing. Baraka was *home*.

There was, in fact, really no reason we should have worried. Newark is, of course, Baraka's hometown. You've got to figure that the brother understands the place. At the time, many of the literary folk in New York had the feeling that, following the personal disappointments and headline notoriety surrounding the closing of the Harlem Black Arts Repertory Theatre/School, Baraka had fled to Newark to lick his wounds. Far from it. If anything, his rhetoric escalated and carefully particularized his social and political concerns.

The good home folks were not, however, Baraka's only local audience. This poem, "Black People," when it was first published in *Evergreen Review* prompted a Newark judge to hand down an unusually severe prison sentence for Baraka's alleged involvement in the city's 1967 riots. The poet was later acquitted on appeal ("Poetic Justice" 24; "Jones Is Acquitted" 18; Redmond, *Drumvoices* 352–353).

Baraka's connection to this city was both practical and sentimental. In his studio at the old Lower East Side apartment on Cooper Square he had kept a large street map of Newark tacked up next to his desk. It may have served his research needs for *The System of Dante's Hell* (1965), but the map was also a sort of spiritual reminder, a yantra focusing the energies of his earliest personal awareness of the world and connecting him, at any remove, to the environs of his immediate ancestry. He possessed a profound understanding of the place and its people, which he later put to use in political organizing that helped elect Kenneth Gibson the first black mayor of Newark. Baraka also established a powerful black nationalist organization, the Committee for a Unified Newark (CFUN), which later figured prominently in both national and Pan-African politics and in the development of the Congress of African People (CAP).

The embryonic stirring of these energies rocked the bare but joyful hall that cold Christmas Eve. Baraka read on with strength and apocalyptically urgent brilliance. Though the production was humble, the people's response held intimations of power. Baraka was treading the boards of a larger stage.

It was strange, all right. And it is interesting to try to analyze the source of the energy that Baraka was then uncoiling. Most Americans tend to think of any location in the Northeast as "the big time," "the fast track." It's a national media myth. Baraka described that idea in his story "The Screamers" as heard through the grapevine of touring musicians: "Newark had a bad reputation. I mean, everybody could pop their fingers. Was hip. Had walks. Knew all about the Apple" (*Tales* 77). Sure they did. But there are small towns up that way, too. There are even parts of the major cities that breed the drives and sensibilities that we have so long associated with growing up in Nebraska. In a certain sense, Baraka suffered such urges. Like any ambitious midwesterner, he also went to New York—just across the river on the Hudson Tubes—and conquered it; a young "literary lion" in Greenwich Village, he had a full-length play, *A Recent Killing,* scheduled for Broadway when he blew it all off and headed for Harlem and the Black Arts notion.

In a very real sense, Baraka's return to Newark was the return of a prodigal son grown wiser for his sojourn in the cruelest core of the Big Apple. He'd seen the fast tracks both uptown and down. Returning home, he was one up on his neighbors. He knew exactly who and what they were, and he knew also what was going to happen elsewhere. Baraka returned to Newark with ideas that were incredibly advanced by any standards but definitely far beyond the Newark he had left in the 1950s. Or even the city of turmoil to which he had returned.

These energies of ambition and social consciousness were intensified by Baraka's peculiar racial alienation. From his earliest days, Baraka had nurtured a desire to "fit in" with the black community. He chronicled the frustration of this desire in his youth in *The System of Dante's Hell,* the earlier stories in *Tales* (1967), and poems such as "Letter to E. Franklin Frazier" (written in 1963). The trouble was that Baraka was attracted to the dark and desperate glamor of Howard Street–style Negroes, in whom he detected an urgency of life and genuine feeling that was denied by both white society and its black "middle-class" shadow. A grandchild of the Great Migration, recognizing the mythic potential of Newark's location somewhere between the mecca of Harlem and the down-home

South, Baraka never stopped writing about the city. More important, the outline of his sophisticated social analysis in later years—Marxist or otherwise—can be found in his earliest perceptions of his hometown.

William J. Harris has explained precisely how the move to Harlem in 1965 changed Baraka's aesthetic orientation. "Citizen Cain" and other works of that period, says Harris, demonstrate the author's "realization that if he is going to be a black revolutionary artist he cannot be like his white friends. Unlike them, he cannot work out his problems on a psychiatrist's couch because his problems are more than personal in nature—they are political and, therefore, communal" (*Poetry and Poetics* 82). In a moving and important poem, "Letter to E. Franklin Frazier," Baraka looks back almost twenty years to his high school days.

> Those days I rose through the smoke of chilling Saturdays
> hiding my eyes from the shine boys, my mouth and my flesh
> from their sisters. I walked quickly and always alone
> watching the cheap city like I thought it would swell
> and explode, and only my crooked breath could put it together
> again.
> (*Reader* 212)

Certainly, the poem expresses a universal adolescent anxiety; it is a touchingly accurate memoir of the awkward period during which one is aware of the world's apparently unlimited options and also acutely feels one's own paralyzing sense of inadequacy. This poem is particularly interesting because of Baraka's keen understanding of intraracial class differences—a gulf between "a postman's son" and those who live in the public housing projects, measured not merely in family income but also in cultural expectations and future opportunity. Even in dimly industrial 1940s Newark, such differences worked to complicate all imagined possibilities.

The collective aspirations and concepts of racial progress shared by African Americans are simple enough to understand, even if—as documented by Kevin K. Gaines in his thorough and thoughtful study *Uplifting the Race* (1996)—diverse and sometimes conflicting strategies have been employed in the effort to achieve the goal. "Reflecting both their desire for social mobility and the economic and racial barriers to it," writes Gaines, "African Americans have described themselves since the post-Reconstruction era as middle class through their ideals of racial uplift, espousing a vision of racial solidarity uniting black elites with the masses. For many black elites, uplift came to mean an emphasis on self-help, racial solidarity, temperance, thrift, chastity, social purity, patriarchal authority, and the accumulation of wealth" (2). The occupations and income of this group did not, however, equal that enjoyed by the white middle class (14–16).

By midcentury, *The Black Bourgeoisie* (1957) by sociologist E. Franklin Frazier offered a stinging critique of this orientation, pointing out the self-delusionary character of "achievements" that were still circumscribed by segregation and persistent racial discrimination. Worse yet, Frazier attacked the hypocrisy of the leadership class. "When the opportunity has been present," he charged, "the black bourgeoisie has exploited the Negro masses as ruthlessly as have whites" (236).

In "Hymn for Lanie Poo" (1961), Baraka chose to present himself as an angry and doubly alienated young hipster—a hopelessly self-critical "schwartzer Bohemien." Sarcastically rejecting the role of self-serving social awareness he and his peers were expected to embrace, he writes, with deliberate ingratitude:

> (O, generation revered
> above all others.
> O, generation of fictitious
> Ofays
>   . . . . .
> my sister drives a green jaguar
> my sister has her hair done twice a month
> my sister is a school teacher
> my sister took ballet lessons
> my sister has a fine figure: never diets
> my sister doesn't like to teach in Newark
>   because there are too many colored
>   in her classes
> (9–10)

While the speaker's rejection of such shallow self-centeredness is justified, this poem—and others such as "Notes for a Speech"—also registers a sense of guilt for having failed to live up to others' expectations.

It is important, however, to be aware of the actual parameters of this rebellion. "Hymn for Lanie Poo" can be read as Cullen's "Heritage" irreverently revisited, its speaker even further "removed / from the scenes his fathers loved" in a mythical ancestral Africa. In fact, there is no

Africa in this poem at all, except for images remembered from Tarzan movies. This poem suggests that the grandchildren of the Talented Tenth were as uncomfortable in their world as Cullen had been.

Though Baraka saw the black middle class in the 1950s as merely an imitation of the morally bankrupt white American mainstream, it is clear that he did not completely abandon the "vision of racial solidarity" inculcated by his parents. This vision reemerges as a primary motive of the Black Arts movement—whose participants were, of course, an intellectual elite in search of what Larry Neal and others termed "a black value system" to supersede bourgeois ideals. In this sense, the didacticism that emerges in Baraka's work during the period of the Black Arts movement is no anomaly. A decade of unflinching poetic self-examination earned him the right to lecture a new generation of "half-white college students" sternly.

Having himself come from that shadow "middle class" (which still does *not* share economic parity with the white middle class), there was no place for Baraka on Howard Street, and his yearning for an impossible involvement there made him suspect in his own environs. In *Tales*, he wrote: "Our house sat lonely and large on a half-Italian street, filled with important Negroes, (Though it is rumored they had a son, thin with big eyes, they killed because he was crazy.)" And he admits his contempt for the "carefully scrubbed children of my parents' friends," his own peers who "fattened" on washed-out imitations of real jazz and blues music, studiously imbibing the white value system "until they could join the Urban League or Household Finance and hound the poor for their honesty" (*Tales* 74). The irony of contempt, of course, comes from the writer's knowledge that he is much like these others. "Hymn for Lanie Poo" complains that his own sister, a government social worker in those days, had fallen into such bourgeois wrongheadedness. The portrait he draws of her is strikingly reminiscent of daughter Beneatha in Lorraine Hansberry's *A Raisin in the Sun* (1959). Indeed, the social identity problem that beset aspiring young blacks in the 1950s is central to both Hansberry's and Baraka's writings; the difference is that, while Hansberry (after carefully exposing Beneatha's naive illusions) reconciled herself—and her characters—to the expected behavior and long-faced hair-trigger patience demanded of her class, Baraka persisted in his love affair with the hard streets. "You see," he wrote in *Tales*, "I left America on the first fast boat."

Obviously, as James Baldwin learned in Europe, one does not flee America quite so easily. Baraka did not actually vanish into the ghetto;

rather, he assumed the role of an intellectual, though he tempered it with the rebellion of bohemianism. But he did not completely abandon his yearning to find a place in a vital black community, away from the tawdry void of white society. The same desire, with which he experimented on a higher and more meaningful level, again finding himself frustrated by the Harlem experience, was succeeded by Baraka's perception and acceptance of a leadership role in Newark's black community.

He wasted little time. Spirit House, established at 33 Stirling Street, was a direct application of the new ideas about art and society that he had attempted to work out in Harlem, but activities here were consciously structured to avoid the tensions and conflicts that had destroyed that Black Arts group. Spirit House was a happy place, decorated in a bright neo-African color scheme, full of neighborhood children. The order of the house seemed to be a disciplined determination, a desperate survival motion. In "Stirling Street September," Baraka wrote:

We are strange in a way because we know
who we are. Black beings passing through
a tortured passage of flesh
(Black Magic Poetry 177)

Clearly, the way through was to be accomplished by the exercise of a higher spiritual consciousness. Revitalization began with a self-knowledge that would lead to actual, tangible power in the sense of self-determination. Meaningful art and useful instruction. Organization. And a black mayor!

The resident company, called the Spirit House Movers and Shakers, was to be a sort of model of cooperation on which, later, the United Brothers and its successor the Committee for a Unified Newark would be based. The entire program was designed as an exercise in organization to achieve clearly defined goals.

Poet Sonia Sanchez, visiting the house, was impressed by the healthy energy there and wrote a lovely poem comparing the place to the depressed ghetto environment recorded by Nathan Heard:

if each one of us moved to a
howard street
and worked hard like they do on
stirling street
wudn't be no mo howard sts at all
(Sanchez, "A Ballad for Stirling Street" 147)

Spirit House was much more than a theater. It was also a social and political movement, and what began to happen there in 1966 changed the municipal government of Newark and changed the entire aesthetic of Amiri Baraka's work.

The first work to emerge from Spirit House was the play *Black Mass* (1967). Based on the Honorable Elijah Muhammad's teaching about the mythical scientist Yacub's creation of the white race, *Black Mass* was an important and disturbing production that provides a key to understanding Baraka's subsequent directions. "Yacub's creation," wrote critic Larry Neal, "is not merely a scientific exercise. More fundamentally, it is the aesthetic impulse gone astray. The Beast is created merely for the sake of creation. Some artists assert a similar claim about the nature of art. They argue that art need not have a function. It is against this decadent attitude toward art—ramified throughout most of Western society—that the play militates" (*Visions* 73). Baraka's art, from the very first, certainly had a function—social change in its most mundane and immediate form, *and* the higher spiritual development of black people. Later he realized that even artists who claimed to work purely "for art's sake" invariably produced work marked with its own social utility. "Poetry," Baraka wrote in *Hard Facts* (1975), "is apologia for one particular class or another and that class' views, needs and visions."

Baraka's own early alienation amid the conflicting motives of the black bourgeoisie, his later religious searching, and the self-assumed "hopped-up witch doctor" phase in which he accomplished the work of "gathering the spirits" for the Black Arts movement in Newark and elsewhere led, eventually, to a new stance in which he seemingly abandoned these spirits in favor of "scientific socialism." He's been quite straightfoward about it. His own earlier militant poems, Baraka said, "came from an enraptured patriotism that screamed against whites as the eternal enemies of Black people, as the sole cause of our disorder + oppression. The same subjective mystification led to mysticism, metaphysics, spookism, etc., rather than dealing with reality." Reality, he feels, would have been the recognition of his movement's innocent adherence to "an ultimately reactionary nationalism that served no interests but our newly emerging Black bureaucratic elite and petit bourgeois, so that they could have control over their Black market." Baraka's later disenchantment with mainline black municipal politics, marked by a highly publicized split with Mayor Gibson and the National Black Political Caucus, reflected his dismay with the continuing influence of the same black middle-class consciousness that his earliest poems and stories had satirized (introduction, *Hard Facts*).

It may sound like the consolation of hindsight to the blind but, in my opinion, all of these developments could have been read in the roots of Baraka's lifelong involvement with Newark, in the social reality of the city itself, or in the casual experience of anyone who has ever been there.

Baraka's critics and readers have to deal with *all* of this "motley of experience." Poems such as "Remembering Malcolm" (1977) represent Baraka's own attempt, from his new "scientific socialist" viewpoint, to grasp the actual meaning of the turnings of his road, and the new tone is much more humble than the confession in *The Dead Lecturer:*

> I am a man
> who is loud
> on the birth
> of his ways.
> ("The Liar," *Reader* 74)

Humility has not necessarily diminished his power—his purpose may even be stronger—but the close reader of Baraka's earliest Marxist-oriented work may sense a certain diffusion. The flame is still burning "full up," but the damper may not be all the way down. Some of Baraka's readers may feel a draft either from excessively extraliterary concerns or from "new" political influences that have more than once proven to be inappropriate to the real issues of black people in the United States. While the works of Lenin and Amilcar Cabral are still essential reading, I'm certain that Baraka's 1975 apotheosis of Josef Stalin was more than distasteful to black activists of an earlier generation who suffered firsthand from the expediencies of Soviet politics as filtered through the pre–World War II American Communist Party. With Stalin, I'm afraid, Baraka was temporarily taken in by the mystique of "the man of action" without carefully scrutinizing what those actions were. The socialist ideology may be different, but the rhetorical mannerisms of *Hard Facts* (1975) seem repetitious of earlier (and often better written) works. Even so, the polemical invective of poems like "Gibson"—in which, after the united front "honeymoon," Newark mayor Kenneth Gibson was bitterly satirized in the dramatic monologue mode perfected by Robert Browning—is effective and arrestingly entertaining. No one can doubt that Baraka remains a grand master at Dozens. When he gets on somebody's case he can be as cuttingly funny as Oliphant or Gary Trudeau, and his rhetoric can be as outrageous as the "double punishment" so-called diplomatic notes that Mao's emissaries used to hand carry to Khrushchev and Ike. Baraka's talent for clever signifying is impressive in the poem "History on Wheels":

> negroes world wide, joined
> knees, and shuffled heroically
> into congress, city hall, the
> anti-p progam, and a thousand
> penetrable traps of cookstove
> america. a class of exploiters,
> in black face, collaborators,
> not puppets, pulling their own
> strings, and ours too, in the
> poor people's buck dance, w/o
> the bux.
>
> (*Transbluesency* 151)

As the beboppers of my daddy's Harlem days would say: "Take it easy, greasy . . . you got a long way to slide." Such black bourgeois complicity became almost redundant in the 1980s and 1990s, however, as policies devised by the Republican Party ensured the disempowerment of workers and the continued immiseration of the underclass (Rifkin, *The End of Work* 74–78, 250–256).

My point is that Baraka's sense of balance (which, in his early Greenwich Village days, he claimed to have learned from Charles Olson and others of the William Carlos Williams school) seldom reduces even his most ideological pronouncements into mere didacticism. Moreover, his earlier training in "talking that talk" guarantees that, no matter what the matter is, Baraka's statements will never be boring. Annoying, perhaps—when you disagree with him, or when it is painfully obvious that he has gotten caught up in one of his own fashions and is not thinking—but never irrelevant or boring.

Amiri Baraka's work—the work he has been able to accomplish in a varied career during a troubled time—repays a reader's interest with its tantalizing complexity. Toni Cade Bambara complained that, ideologically, Baraka seems to believe that he must personally relive every historical moment. "If you can read," she said, "seems like you could learn something out of a book . . . like, you don't have to do *everything* yourself!" (interview with the author).

Others might say that African Americans must be sophisticated enough today to do without self-appointed pioneers and martyrs. It was not always so, and this might be a point of foolish pride. Still, too many other men done gone. We really do need to hold on to what we got. This is not specifically a literary concern, but then, Baraka's own works and personality make purely literary questions seem small.

Baraka has, through all his personal and ideological changes, achieved a lasting place in the history of the African American struggle and has influenced that struggle with his own concerns. It was he, Calvin Hernton wrote, "who first assaulted the white world with what he called the Black Arts, The Black Theater of Cruelty." ("Blood of the Lamb" 218). In those turbulent days, Baraka declared:

We are the witchdoctors and the assassins
But we will make a path for the true scientists

Many are not always convinced by his notion of science. For good and bad reasons. Baraka, as critic Ezekiel Mphalele (otherwise one of our most alert readers) has consistently failed to understand, is best as a poet of intense personal reflection, which is exactly why he always appears to us in the prophet's sackcloth of social activism. Literally, he does not have time to be himself. But were he given the time, who (as he himself eloquently ponders in his poems) would that self be? In this way he speaks to us in our lostness, striving, and misery, and we are habituated now to the eager anticipation of his own subsequent interpretations of each current guise. For all his complexity, however, Baraka's work reveals a fundamental consistency.

"In the Tradition" (1982) is a 300-line poem that draws on the popular Beat trope of list making and repetition (similar to the Homeric catalogue) and the standard Black History Month catechism. The strategy is essentially the same as that informing Tolson's "Dark Symphony," but Baraka singles out the musicians, writers, and visual artists whose efforts both created and documented African American expressive culture in its most glittering form. In a boldly confrontational manner, "In the Tradition" repeats and updates James Weldon Johnson's view of the African American cultural contribution:

We are the composers, racists & gunbearers
We are the artists
Dont tell me shit about a tradition of deadness & capitulation
of slavemasters sipping tea in the parlor
while we bleed to death in fields

tradition of cc rider
see what you done done
. . . .

get out of europe
come out of europe if you can
cancel on the english depts this is america
north, this is america
where's yr american music
gwashington won the war

where's yr american culture southernagrarians
      academic aryans
      penwarrens & wilburs
   say something american if you dare
    if you
    can
       where's yr american
       music
        Nigger music?

(*Reader* 307–308)

Baraka's most recent poetic project brings him directly into the tradition represented by Melvin Tolson. "Why's/Wise" is a long series of poems that Baraka feels is similar to Tolson's *Libretto*, Williams's *Paterson*, and Olson's *Maximus*—all of which, of course, are modeled on Pound's *Cantos* to a certain extent (*Reader* 480). Unlike those poems, this one is written with almost transparent lucidity. There is an absence of Baraka's usually lush and signifying allusion and a focus on his considerable ability to create a diction as precise as Creeley's. Or, for that matter, Williams or Pound. "Wise 9" reports:

our war
was for
liberation
to end
slave times
now war
is over
we free
they say

but in the next stanza, he asks:

> who they
> who say
> what free
> gone be?
> (*Reader* 489)

It is not, really, a rhetorical question.

The large volume of poetry that Baraka has created in the past forty years is among the most significant poetry ever written in the United States partly because of the poet's own excellence of technique, partly because his sensibility led him to suffer as the public conscience of his society—reporting, as he puts it in one poem, "each change in my soul, as if I had predicted / them" ("The Liar," *Reader* 74). With Baraka, such introspective anxiety leads to an insight that, while intended for particular utility, offers readers a wisdom that is ultimately universal:

> The nation is like our selves, together
> seen in our various scenes, sets where ever we are
> what ever we are doing, is what the nation
> is
> doing
> or
> not doing
> is what the nation
> is
> being
> or
> not being
> ("The Nation" 265)

PART THREE

Songs for the People

7

A Change Is Gonna Come

Black Voices of Louisiana

To discuss a number of poets and identify them as voices of the South is not necessarily to revive the controversies of 1930s regionalism. Such a localized focus can, in fact, help to demonstrate that the Black Arts movement grew out of ideas that enjoyed wide currency throughout the nation. It is, of course, also a fact that the South enjoys a continuing mythic presence in African American thought and culture that is most directly engaged by writers who live there. But the hold that the South has on the African American imagination is problematic. As Calvin C. Hernton noted in *White Papers for White Americans* (1966), many African Americans in northern cities "never really leave the South. They migrate physically but do not migrate spiritually or culturally" (7). Hernton did not think that this was necessarily a good thing. "The South," he wrote, "is a psychocultural region of mixed personality determinants whose conflicting vectors completely immobilize the flexibility and continued growth of the psyche" (8). Certainly, the history of the region—not to mention the essays in *I'll Take My Stand* (1930)—offers ample evidence that anyone's attachment to the South might be as easily assumed to be haunted as fondly nostalgic.

I think it has something to do with the territory. The entire southwestern United States suffers from a violent legacy of hatred, colonialism, and slavery. The Deep South shares a similar heritage—though the colonialism is more metaphorical than actual. Louisiana is unique but shares with the rest of the region the problem of race. In Louisiana, however, the coils of racism and miscegenation have made the question of identity into a conundrum.

In the nineteenth century some people of color thought they were both Frenchmen and poets. The talented Armande Lanusse edited an anthology entitled *Les cenelles* (1845), which showcased these writers. Langston Hughes and Arna Bontemps included Lanusse and Pierre Dalcour in their anthology *The Poetry of the Negro* but complained that there was little racial consciousness in the poetry of this group. They "had not been taught to link themselves personally with the conditions of the slaves," Hughes and Bontemps complained (xxii–xxiii). In his excellent study *Drumvoices: The Mission of Afro-American Poetry* (1976), Eugene B. Redmond reiterates this charge, but it is not entirely true. The 1840s in Louisiana were a far cry from the 1940s in New York when Hughes and Bontemps made their assessment. Lanusse and his group did, in fact, have a racial consciousness. Lanusse himself served as chief administrator of the colored orphan home and school in New Orleans for many years—a position that, in his day, required both political sensitivity and moral commitment. The school itself was endowed by one wealthy Madame C., a freed African slave. To grasp the situation in those days, one might recall that Bienville's *Code Noir* and the Deep South's Nat Turner–inspired ordinances prohibiting black literacy were still in effect in the 1830s. As principal of his school, Lanusse literally went around New Orleans begging and got mixed up politically with the wrong side in the Civil War yet managed to survive. And his school survived as well. Literary historian E. M. Coleman noted that Lanusse was white enough in appearance to "pass" but, like Adam Clayton Powell, chose to identify himself with the oppressed.

Again, to gain a proper perspective on Lanusse, we should note that many free Negroes of Louisiana, known as the *gens de couleur,* owned considerable property, held slaves, and dominated the crafts in the area. They were also notorious culture mavens. Free Negroes, some of them "whiter than white" in appearance, established a symphony orchestra in New Orleans that perpetuated the airs of continental European culture. At the same time the music of Louis Moreau Gottschalk, a Creole composer (whose racial background is disputed by music scholars), created symphonic settings for the African and African American melodies of Louisiana, achieving great fame in Europe and South America. Gottschalk played the international planter (read "slave-holder") circuit that, at the time, constituted the "cultured world."

In recent years, of course, the question of African American cultural contributions in Louisiana has not been as ambiguous as in the cases of Lanusse and Gottschalk. Indeed, the state can claim to have produced a number of extraordinary writers: N. R. Davidson, author of the popular play *El Hajj Malik;* poets Pinkie Gordon Lane and Brenda Marie Osbey; Ernest J. Gaines, author of *The Autobiography of Miss Jane Pittman;* and many others. Four of Louisiana's most powerful poetic voices—Ahmos Zu-Bolton II, Kalamu ya Salaam, Tom Dent, and Alvin Aubert—through correspondence and travel during the 1970s were particularly influential in creating a climate in the region that encouraged the growth of African American cultural activity.

Ahmos Zu-Bolton's poems in *A Niggered Amen* (1975) are concerned with people and places. The places are remembered from the poet's actual physical and spiritual wanderings, while the people are folks he grew up with in DeRidder, Louisiana. Born in 1935, Zu-Bolton held a number of jobs as a youth to help support his family. Later, in the early 1950s he played professional baseball for the Shreveport Twins of the American Negro League. After serving as an army medic in Vietnam, he attended California State Polytechnic University, where he edited a poetry magazine called *The Last Cookie.* Working at Howard University in the early 1970s he came into contact with Stephen E. Henderson, E. Ethelbert Miller, and others, resulting in his involvement in a number of literary projects of national scope. One of these, in collaboration with Alan Austin, was the innovative *Black Box*—a poetry magazine issued on audio cassettes that allowed subscribers to hear the poets recite their work. Zu-Bolton also edited a small magazine called *Hoo Doo,* which, after 1977, expanded into a series of Hoo Doo Festivals that presented poets and musicians in various cities.

In his own poems, Zu-Bolton's open yet precise form displays the full, booming voice of the blues (as opposed to the equally authentic whining tone that Jelly Roll Morton first recorded):

> the fool
> you know him
> he once told you the secrets
> of his life
> there's a file on him
> at the pentagon
> he ain't no myth
> him for real baby,
>
> he calls
> to the great firegods:
> *daddy-o-blues, where*
> *you at, where*
> *y'all at . . .*

Zu-Bolton's poems recreate ritual. As people transcend place, these poems transcend their instigations, but the mysteries here are not linguistic conundrums. His poetic language is a tense mixture of common speech and sense. There are no obvious verbal acrobatics, yet the economical precision of Zu-Bolton's usage of the daily tongue raises language to a rare and functional beauty that conveys the intricate depth of his personal—but hardly private—vision.

Zu-Bolton draws his sanity from knowledge of self and of those around him. The characters in his poems are interesting and deftly depicted. Besides Blackjack Moses and "the governor of Ollie Street," there is Livewire Davis, basketball scholar looking toward a million-dollar future in the pro leagues:

> except for the terrible puzzle of books
> he was free
> (30)

Sure, except for one other thing. You know what. Zu-Bolton brings us close to Livewire's woman, Sister Blues, who is not at all proud of his desperate freedom:

> did not know his place:
> much too loud in a prayerful
> kingdom, too uncontrollable
> in a world of controls
> (31)

One may think that Sister Blues, following recent sociological "archetypes" of black womanhood, fears for her man's safety in the hostile environment of socially straitjacketed southern race relations. In fact, Sister Blues is dismayed because she cannot follow in her mother's footsteps and "domesticate" her man:

> This tore at her as if to cripple,
> this loss of face.

> So she made him babies
> in the image of other men
> (31)

not being able to make the proper kind of baby out of him. What Zu-Bolton accomplishes in such portraits, more often than not, says what we ordinarily would like to leave unsaid. His insight is sometimes startling. It also becomes clear that part of the effect comes from the fact that Zu-Bolton has deliberately chosen a language that is quite un-remarkable—shared by ordinary everyday people at bus stops, pool halls, in church. His poems, then, literally illuminate this language for us, revealing both the depth of insight and the casually brilliant im-agery of ordinary African American vernacular.

Recent works in *Ain't No Spring Chicken: Selected Poems* (1998) affirm that "there is a cure / for the blues" (91). "Moments: for Ywenboui," one of a series of playful love poems, conjures a crossroads where the poet pledges his true love in words that echo the extravagant "fancy talk" required by the etiquette of courting in antebellum times:

I could wish it a blues
or jazz it up, I could play it
with violins

I could make it zydeco,
or give it a caribbean beat
shout it the gospel truth
and make it hum

could mix it up with opera
and tom-toms,
give it a latino guitar,
a sugarcane banjo,
and a big band horn section
upfront

as each music sings its own, lingers,
translates a sweet moment
where we are now.
(89)

Zu-Bolton's point, of course, is the timelessness of this affectionate mo-ment. Just as the specifics of a language indicate the speaker's philo-sophical positioning, this elaborate catalogue of African diaspora musi-cal forms persuades us to reconceptualize the richness of what should be construed not merely as "cultural survivals" but also as an un-quenchable vitality that defines what linguists who study our Creolized vernacular have termed "the continuous present." But this present is filled with anxiety, and there is no nostalgic glorification in Zu-Bolton's work. Much like Countee Cullen in "Heritage," Zu-Bolton shows that diasporic time—a vortex of intercultural contradictions—is troubling.

One of Zu-Bolton's poems, "By the Fifth Generation," deserves to be quoted in full because it is so honestly true about the place many young black people find themselves in today—the very same place young black people found themselves in during the 1920s and the 1870s:

> it had gotten so bad
> that they hated
> sugarcane, though
> they needed a good crop
> to get them thru the winter
> (hating that which gave
> some prayer to life.
>
> the young ones hated
> the most. they blamed the land
> for what was not the
> land's fault.
>
> they hated the church
> for not giving them hope
> in this life
>
> *o hope, blessed hope*
> *now now now*
>
> until they discovered
> that their hatred
> was hopeless
> (46)

The story, as they used to say on *Dragnet*, is true—Zu-Bolton himself worked in the cane fields in his youth. Though the poem thrashes through some clumsy prosody in the second stanza, there is something powerful and plain about the language, something so profound in its insight that one cannot but insist that Zu-Bolton be read and reread.

There is neither hatred nor hopelessness in the poems of Kalamu ya Salaam. His theme is black love, but there is sometimes an atmosphere of desperation about his affirmations. "Look at our conditions," Salaam has written. "No one can truthfully deny that we need to unify, that we need self-determination." And he has been careful in outlining the process of such self-determination: "In order to better ourselves; in order to teach, preach and practice our values; in order to create symbols and ceremonies, it is not necessary to lie about or to demean anyone or anything." Nevertheless, everyone knows that such desires must confront a powerful nemesis—regardless of whether or not we want to demean or even name it.

In *Ibura* (1976), Salaam seemed unwilling to acknowledge that desperation is itself the nemesis of hope and joy, that symbols and ceremonies are games within real crises, that poems are not needed, but are gifts to those in need. The trouble with *Ibura* (a Kiswahili term meaning "something wonderful or miraculous") is that the poetry was overwhelmed by the poet's sense of political and social necessity.

The poems and short stories in the book are arranged, like Baraka's *Home,* Dante's *La vita nuova,* or a programmed instruction manual, in a sequence designed to suggest the expanding consciousness of a sane, mutually supportive, nonexploitative, and loving relationship between a man and a woman. Thankfully, it avoids the excessive "O Black Woman" gyno-idolatry that characterized many neo-Negritude effusions of the late 1960s. Warmly illustrated by Dallas-based artist Arthello Beck, *Ibura* is frankly political in the sense that both artists view the spiritual reorganization of the black family as a crucial necessity. *Ibura,* however, is not as successful in communicating this idea as was Salaam's earlier *Hofu Ni Kwenu* (1973). Still, *Ibura* contains passages of almost irridescent lyricism and pertinence:

> black man is, black man is, black man is, is
> you my love listening to a radio in the
>> 20th century preparing
> now to deal on these devils
> riding round in aeroplanes
>> who have brazenly stolen our rhythms
> and use them to sell
> trinkets cross the airwaves
>> where music and greetings, blessings
> and salutations
> once flowed in unbroken chains
>> from the lips of our people

It would be a mistake, however, to read this complaint about misappropriation and the distortion of values as an antitechnological affirmation of tradition. Kalamu ya Salaam's thinking—even in the early

1970s—avoids the simplistically formulaic notions put forward by Maulana Ron Karenga and other doctrinaire black nationalists.

Throughout the 1980s and 1990s, Salaam remained a passionate social activist and prolific writer. Developing into a perceptive music critic, he also explored how the aesthetic choices implicit in African American musical performance could be applied to literature. The poems and essays in *What Is Life?* (1994) extend these concerns toward the articulation of a moral philosophy that is both practical and personal. In his essay "The Blues Aesthetic," Salaam declares: "The blues ain't slave music. didn't no slaves sing the blues. we didn't become blue until after reconstruction, after freedom day and the dashing of all hopes of receiving/attaining our promised 40 acres & 1 mule" (*What Is Life?* 7). This statement—in language that simultaneously evokes myth and streetwise signifying—is historically accurate in placing the origin of blues music in the period between 1890 and 1915, which historian Rayford W. Logan called "the nadir of race relations." Salaam's statement also follows the outline of African American cultural development proposed in Baraka's *Blues People: Negro Music in White America* (1963).

One of the elements that Salaam sees as central to this blues aesthetic is "an optimistic faith in the ultimate triumph of justice in the form of karma." This term, borrowed from Hindu philosophy and popularized by the 1960s counterculture, also represents a convenient way to express a concept of retribution for evil that is found throughout African American folklore. In this sense,

> what is wrong will be righted, what is last will be first. balance will be brought back into the world. this faith was often co-opted by christianity, but is essential even to the most down-trodden of the blues songs. (14)

The "balance" described here needs to be understood not in the sense of a Manichaean dualism of good and evil but rather as a kind of Hegelian process. In more concrete terms, Salaam alludes to a political struggle fraught with dangers and deceptions. "We have bought into mainstream Americanism so deeply," he writes, "that we do not even realize the great American secret: we have made America a democracy. Left to Whites, the ideal of American democracy would have remained a patriarchal, racist, and sexist ideal." Where Langston Hughes, in the 1930s, eloquently pleaded

Let America be America again.
Let it be the dream it used to be

Salaam updates the message. Throughout this century, he argues, "The struggles of our people gave real definition to freedom and democracy. We forced America to be America" (*What Is Life?* 181; Hughes, *Collected Poems* 189).

The fullest realization of this blues aesthetic is found in Salaam's recent poetry and, in his case, the most complete experience of that poetry is to be found in his audio recordings. "My Story, My Song" (1996) presents Kalamu ya Salaam at the height of his powers. The poem's opening phrase evokes a hymn made familiar to millions through Reverend Billy Graham's evangelical "Bible Crusades" and then proceeds to knock the props out from under it. Instead of a praise song for a Southern Baptist conception of Jesus Christ, Salaam's song is a twenty-minute epic exploration of history aimed at the redemption of maligned African selfhood. If the poem evokes George Beverly Shea's familiar anthem, it also echoes the profoundly meaningful and ancient spiritual "I Been 'Buked and I Been Scorned." In a trope that recalls controversial poems by Countee Cullen and Langston Hughes, Salaam replaces Christ with the enslaved African:

after the whiplash fever,
I rose

The black and unknown bards who created the spiritual did not know the word "karma," but they trusted in a sort of careful compensation nonetheless. They sang

Talk about me as much as you please
Gonna talk about you when I get on my knees

but Salaam is more boldly outspoken. For Salaam, Christianity and slavery represent complementary forces that have *both* oppressed African peoples for 500 years, while black folk music generates resistance and constitutes a mechanism of cultural and actual survival:

the Blues is our literature
our rights, our wrongs

As with the blues songs themselves, of course, such a statement is not intended to be merely metaphorical.

In his liner notes for the AFO Records compact disc, Salaam describes "My Story, My Song" as "a performance poem in the manner of Baptist preachers" and reveals that it is a genuinely spontaneous collaboration with blues guitarist Walter "Wolfman" Washington. "For twenty minutes," writes Salaam, "he fed me variation after variation, responding to my changes and me responding to his musical inventiveness." Alluding to concepts of spirit possession, Salaam views the musicians he works with as something more than just artistic collaborators: "This is some dangerous vibrations. The shit be so dangerous, all I got to do is stand there and open my mouth. The spirit will jump out and make it sound like I 'know' what I'm doing, when all I know is nothing compared to what this music opens me to imagine" (quoted from the liner notes).

My Story, My Song, then, is a communal project—like the jazz created through collective improvisation by the marching band ensembles in early New Orleans. Each man, knowing the song and knowing his part, sounds like he knows what he's doing, yet what emerges from the band is far greater than the sum of its parts. Listening to Kalamu ya Salaam's poetic performance, it is clear that both his aesthetic and his political ideals emanate from this practice.

It is clear also that, for Salaam, communal health—in the black community or the nation at large—ultimately depends upon individual sanity and freedom of the imagination—an extension of the message worked out earlier in *Ibura.* Kalamu ya Salaam's vision, his undistracted attention to his community's most profound need, is concisely stated in "Sun Song XIII":

> be about beauty
> as strong as a flower is
> yet as soft too
> as an open petal
> receiving the mist
> of a midnight raindrop,
> be about beauty
> no matter life's dirt
> be about beauty
> (*What Is Life* 223)

Kalamu ya Salaam's concern with the social struggle toward genuine naturalness, described in *Hofu Ni Kwenu* as a twenty-four-hour job, is shared but differently approached by Tom Dent in his first collection of poems, *Magnolia Street* (1976). Dent, founder of New York's influential

Umbra Workshop in the early 1960s, shared the activist role assumed by Salaam (with whom he worked in the Free Southern Theatre and in several poetry and drama workshops), but his poetic concern is less a project of moral development than an attempt to find and exhibit the spiritual strengths that already exist in African American people. Like Ahmos Zu-Bolton, Dent draws our attention to qualities possessed by ordinary people but often ignored. "Magic," Dent writes, "clothes our people":

> like a great god had rode in from the lake
> & said peace, peace unto you my people
> be beautiful

So it is that on a Sunday afternoon, Roberts the bus driver reconnects his African spirit to the gods via an outing to the shores of Lake Pontchartrain. This atavistic moment finds expression in a determined realization of a deeper identity than is recognized by the daily status quo—an identity that is both spiritual and nascently political:

> let me be free
>   which you can't take away from me
>   . . . .
> yea, white man when i go to the lakefront
> the city can wait
> yr bus can wait. . . .
> goin nowhere nohow.

Like a tree, standing by the water. The spectral echo of that old Civil Rights campaign song is evident, and the bus driver's holiday becomes significantly emblematic of a larger determination of black selfhood. "Goin nowhere nohow," like the slogan "We shall not be moved," does not mean that Roberts has no destination, rather that his peaceful moment of self-realization is itself a *moving* place. A place in motion, like a planet. He's sure he's right, and there he makes his stand.

Dent's poems resonate with a very specific sense of place, no matter how ambitious their project. New Orleans is both vibrantly present tense and aggressively nostalgic—from the literary ghosts who haunt Pirate's Alley to the Dixieland band passing the hat in Jackson Square where the driver of a horse carriage may "sit in" for a soft-shoe solo. Yet for all the city's famed joie de vivre, its poorer neighborhoods are not charming, and living in them is not easy. This ever-present, if overlooked, New Orleans appears in Dent's poems.

No writer captured this reality more poignantly than did Marcus B. Christian (1900–1976), a poet who achieved some notice beginning in the 1930s and who was something of a mentor to Dent (Bryan 100–102, 112–114). Christian's "McDonogh Day in New Orleans," published in the Urban League journal *Opportunity,* describes a little girl dressed beautifully for the annual public school pilgrimage to Lafayette Square. Christian's sonnet, however, also focuses attention on the sacrifices required of the girl's mother:

> But few would know—or even guess this fact:
> How dear comes beauty when a skin is black.
> (171)

McDonogh Day, when schoolchildren traditionally carried flowers to the statue of the nineteenth-century philanthropist who had made public education in the city possible, was also a notorious reminder of segregation: white children made their pilgrimage in the morning, black children in the afternoon (Delehanty 260–261). Many of Tom Dent's poems about the city and its people might be viewed as a perceptive continuation of Christian's elegantly understated critique. Dent's family encouraged both civic engagement and the arts—his father was president of the city's Dillard University, and his mother had been a concert pianist and the first African American student admitted to the Juilliard School of Music (K. Rogers, *Righteous Lives* 120–121). Dent himself, from his student days at Atlanta's Morehouse College in the early 1950s, had been involved in the growing civil rights movement.

In a poem such as "Roberts the New Orleans Busdriver," Dent's choice of such an apparently inconsequential incident, told in a faithful rendering of the character's everyday speech, effectively accomplishes both a poetic purpose and a political one. Indeed, many of Dent's poems are studies of similarly "magical" atavistic transformations, pictures of a world filled with extremely efficient spirits who inform the music that Dent loves and revitalize people for the continuing struggle to be free of the artificial degradations devised by their oppressors.

Black history in Louisiana is, in this sense, continuous and present, a strange mixture of reality and myth. Like Dunbar before him, Dent understands the mysteries of the mask. In his poem "For Lil Louis," Dent points out that Satchmo did not grin offstage because he knew only too well the dark places "where the frustration of our people / boiled into daily slaughter" under the blood-burning moons of desperately ludic Saturday nights. As one imagines Louis Armstrong himself must have done, as novelist Ishmael Reed did in *The Last Days of Lou-*

isiana Red (1974), Dent wrestles with the incongruity of black people killing each other within earshot of the music that literally calls the names of the African gods. He wrote an excellent play, *Ritual Murder* (brilliantly staged by the Ethiopian Players under Chakula Cha Jua's direction at the 1976 festival of the Southern Black Cultural Alliance), which proposed that an answer might be found in more extensive analysis of the ways in which the systems and patterns of slavery persist in American society.

Let me step back a minute and show some slides. Turn the lights down low and gaze into the magic cauldron's glow. I know a place in New Orleans, an elegant jardin restaurant in the Vieux Carré where stunningly beautiful young white men dine, chatting about the latest novels and art books. About January vacations to Yucatán to view the ruins. Expensive watches, rings and things flashing in the afternoon sunlight as they assay filets.

There are no colored people there. And, indeed, no one at all of any more than contrived substance.

The magic cauldron glows. Blue music floods in from the long, deep Mississippi. Another voice:

That's not the only place I know. When I lost my baby, during Mardi Gras, it was because I almost lost my mind in literati glee paying homage to the streetcar named DESIRE that is enshrined quite suspiciously and ignobly in the run-down produce market.

When I look up from my reveries, there are no other Negroes there but me (communing with Great American Literachaw)—and my impatient lady. She has her hands on her hips. Toe tapping.

As my eyes refocus, I can see some black dudes in the background. Working. Hosing down the stalls, trashing empty crates. Suddenly all of them frozen in slooooooow motion, looking my way. She, still, has her hands on her hips.

"Cultured," she calls me sarcastic. "Well, you're *colored!*"

She turns in determined disgust, arms swinging and frowned-up pretty face, off toward the hotel. The brothers in the freeze go back to work because it's coming quitting time and they are tired, too.

At this point, sweat on fevered brow, I wake up.

Slavery.

The problem, as Zu-Bolton pointed out in "By the Fifth Generation," did not end with the abolition of physical slavery, because a psychological and cultural slave structure persists. In his poem "Secret Messages," Dent contrasts the hangouts of the musical in-crowd with the vestiges of slavery (historical and mythical) represented by tourist rip-off praline shops in the Vieux Carré, where, instead of the old-time tobacconist's wooden Indian, doorways feature imitation life-sized stuffed black mammies straight out of *Gone with the Wind* or Edward Weston Kemble's grotesque nineteenth-century caricatures. Finally, against the contradictions of what passes for everyday life in tourist-ridden New Orleans, Dent is pressed to invoke the death-ruling *guedes* and zombies of the Voodoo tradition (which has a much deeper involvement with jazz music than the Dixieland bands at Shakey's Pizza may ever know):

maybe someday when nobody
is checking it out the drummers will come to life in
St. Louis No. 1 at midnight
beating out the secret messages
& all the masks will drop.
(*Magnolia Street* 29)

Faucheaux, Tom Dent's St. Louis No. 1—the city's ancient graveyard on Basin Street—is a far cry from French impressionist cemeteries by the sea, and "Secret Messages," whether you believe in magic or not, is heavy traffic.

Magnolia Street, besides such brilliant short poems, is distinguished by a Faulknerian vignette, "Report from New Orleans," which explores the desperation of the city's young blacks. There is also a major poem, "Return to English Turn" (30–36), that explains why the deferred dreams of young black people in New Orleans sometimes explode. English Turn is a bend in the Mississippi River that, for Dent, conjures up the region's history of successive colonizers, all of whom have stamped their mark on the culture and language of the people. The poem is epic in its intentions and its accomplishment.

Capturing both the accent and unseemly pride of French-speaking Louisianians (both black and supposed-to-be white), Dent identifies the place:

it is here bienville
convinced english
this land french
in 1699
sign say.
(30)

But also, more important for black people:

it is here
chained to the hulls of ships
we begin our neo-european forced journey
(30)

Dent has understood, for all the false pride of the creole's French or Spanish "heritage," that—for the identifiably black—this journey leads to constant economic exploitation and, for many, ends in the depressing environs of a funky run-down housing project (read "plantation slave quarters") in the neighborhoods of Algiers or Desire. It's no wonder that Dent—not to mention my Mardi Gras companion—might find Tennessee Williams's concept of "human suffering" a bitter joke.

The wormwood turnings of 400 years in the wildernesses of North America are brilliantly catalogued in "Return to English Turn," and Dent emphatically declares that he will settle for no more colonialism, not even the "USA version" that conveniently and greedily absorbs all others:

let us return to english turn
rip up the signs
wipe out the legacies
pledge no more forced journies

no more english turns
no more spanish turns
no more french turns, portugese
or german turns

rip the markers of neo-european conquest from
    their roots
plant a new one marking:

our turn
(*Magnolia Street* 35)

It's hard to say how generous Dent is in his use of the word "our." That's up to each reader to ponder. "Return to English Turn" is musical and thoughtful rather than inflammatory, yet it is clearly and strongly a cultural and political statement, persuasive in its eloquence.

A later collection, *Blue Lights and River Songs* (1982), offers political commentary that avoids stridency through a carefully scaled personal perception. In "St. Helena Island," Dent notes the obligatory care with which the tourist records a visit to the Gullah country later made fashionable in Julie Dash's film *Daughters of the Dust.* For the tourist, even slavery is contemplated at a discreet remove:

> the stately museums of Beaufort
> the arsenals and ports of the english
> built above Native remains:
> the romance of American history
> (*Blue Lights* 40)

On further reflection, however, this romance contains more than a tinge of gothic horror. The more attentive visitor will learn that

> this land has been stolen and stolen
> again. . . .
> made into cotton & rice riches
> off strong brown backs . . .
> the blowing sand and the palmettoes
> know much of these things
> but speak only at night speak
> their silent mysterious language
> only to themselves.
> (*Blue Lights* 40)

Similarly, "Third Avenue, Near Fourteenth Street" reports that the reality of American history and its present-day consequences is not limited to problems that might disturb our perceptions of an otherwise picturesque Southland. The problems are everywhere to be found and this poem identifies objective correlatives for the frustrations of living in poverty in New York City. Here is a neighborhood of "Hoarse, tough laughter / the tear suppressed"—a crowded kaleidoscope reminiscent of Archibald Motley's urban street scenes:

> Food shop arm-in-arm with Fuck shop
> Whisperin suggestive noise to
>   Pawn shop
> Pawn shop holds secret of
> Starvation Army blue-clad trumpet
>
> Starvation army trumpet say hello to Miles Davis
>   then drown in gurgle of faded purple
> Silver parking meter. . . . .expiring
> Dented gold chain. . . . .dangling
> (18)

In the poem's second section Dent playfully parodies Allen Ginsberg, Bob Kaufman, and Frank O'Hara as the city's streets become magically animated:

> Third Ave. is a slide trombone immobilized
>   by 40,000 transistor
> radios blasting a call for surrender . . . on
>   the rocks
> (*Blue Lights* 19)

This wild personification, Dent's surrealistic confusion of setting and actor, masks a deeper concern that informs his Afrocentric aesthetic. Other poems, however, make the point much more directly. Praise songs for African American sports heroes such as "Poem for Willie Mays" and "Cool Papa Bell" join "Coltrane's Alabama" and "Ray Charles at Mississippi State" in celebrating an idea of artistry that demands audience participation as much as virtuosity. "Ray Charles at Mississippi State," an often anthologized work, is particularly interesting. The poem foregrounds issues that focused Dent's aesthetic ideas: the interface of tradition and innovation, artistic expression and "mainstream" resistance or cooptation, and the relationship of individual effort (whether artistry or activism) to group consciousness. A litany in the form made familiar by Margaret Walker's "For My People," the poem explores the expectations of the young concertgoers, while the geographical location and the music itself echo with "the clang of sounds of battling lives" (46). Here the question that informed "For Lil Louis"—how people can fight and kill each other while listening to music that affirms life—is taken even further. Do white listeners hear the same thing that black folks do? What eventually assumes the greatest importance for Dent, however, is that the music provides a nexus for the confluence of past, present, and future.

As early as 1969, Dent had called for "functional poems" in an editorial in *Nkombo,* the journal he edited with Kalamu ya Salaam. As Jerry W. Ward, Jr., has noted, Dent was primarily interested in "the features of performance that activate aesthetic dialogue between performers and audiences: orality and visual movement. In Dent's prose [and poems] one hears the longing for the communion generated by the work of the Free Southern Theater" (147). Beyond this concern, of course, is the communion that is supposed to be enacted in primeval African ritual—compared to which the impoverished zones of American cities, however animated, produce only chaos. Nowhere in Dent's work will one find even a shadow of the Romantic notion that material dilapidation somehow enhances spirituality; indeed, in the play *Ritual Murder* and his poems, Dent seems to indicate quite the reverse. It is a continuing struggle for the spirit to prevail over the conditions of poverty and oppression, and part of the struggle is the kind of communion ideally produced by art—which might then serve as a model for more directly political and social activism. In Dent's poems this desire for communion is often expressed through rhetorical figures that imply or even elicit *call and response.* "The Seventies: A Poem for Blacks of the Sixties" is such a poem, a litany of cynicism and disappointment that remains timely because it is a reminder that life is a *process,* not an event:

> if you thought the Fifties were gone forever and white men could
>   not ride in on a white horse and tell us they had to qualify us
>   the right to live like human beings in america, if you thought it
>   had progressed to that . . .
> if you hoped the Seventies were not the Fifties in drag . . .
> if you thought just because seven follows six the Seventies
> would be
>   better than the Sixties
> (*Blue Lights* 51)

Among his prose works, Dent's *Southern Journey: A Return to the Civil Rights Movement* (1997) can be read as an eloquent history that names the brave black people of the South's small towns who were the true soldiers of the movement. It is, in a way, the last word in his quarrel with historical markers that—from the Sea Islands to the banks of the Mississippi—misrepresent who we are. *Southern Journey* also tells what happened in those small towns after the federal marshals and the media went home. Dent's implicit warning, echoing an earlier intellectual activist, reminds us that vigilance is required to protect the rights so dearly won. This poet's personal choice was, of course, to remain a literary and community activist season after season. Dent, who died unexpectedly in 1998, will be remembered for his energy and perception and a living legacy made manifest in the many younger writers—from New York's Umbra Workshop to many college classrooms and community centers—whose development he never ceased to encourage.

Alvin Aubert, the founding editor of *Obsidian: Black Literature in Review* and a professor at several universities, including Wayne State University and the State University of New York at Fredonia, is well traveled. Unlike Dent, Salaam, and Zu-Bolton, Alvin Aubert has not lived in Louisiana for many years, but many of his poems record experiences of rural Louisiana in another time, teach us what he learned there, and bring a practiced sensitivity to bear on the little incidents of racism that occur everywhere in this country.

Born in Lutcher, Louisiana, in 1930, Aubert dropped out of school in his teens but continued his education during a seven-year stint in the army. Discharged, in 1955 he enrolled at Southern University and almost immediately began to publish poems. It was an interesting time to begin writing. In the mid-1950s—when the war in Korea was over and the Supreme Court had declared racial integration "the law of the land"—things looked peaceful and optimistic enough to make critic Arthur P. Davis express concern that the absence of something to protest had "dealt the Negro writer a crushing blow" ("Integration and Race Literature" 141). A young poet and former GI, Aubert was not quite so optimistic about the "precarious pledge" that the world's leaders had made to keep peace and prosperity. An early poem appearing in *Phylon* reports Aubert's visit to the impressive new United Nations building (opened in New York in 1952). In it Aubert wonders whether the promising and peaceful future represented by the towering glass edifice exists only in

a place near heaven
Where there alone your hymn rings true
And even then only as a dream
("On Seeing" 146)

Aubert's later work would be much more interiorized, his contemplated world mediated by the structures of memory or by other art forms.

Aubert's first book, *Against the Blues* (1972), was impressive. The title referred not to a cultural prejudice but to a personal commitment to freedom and joy. *Feeling Through* (1975) brought him closer to the goal. In these works, Aubert spends words with an almost stingy economy, yet he always communicates. He has a meticulous sense of form and detail, and his perceptions possess a cutting edge. He also speaks with knowledge of the country's regions and people. During the riots of the 1960s when cities were burning, a southern city like Houston was spared simply because its ghetto areas were too spread out. Similarly, a riot could never happen in New Orleans because the police are past masters of crowd control. Aubert's elegy for Mark Essex (a black Vietnam veteran who went berserk and died Bonnie-and-Clyde style in a hail of police bullets) makes this point with grim clarity. The police, under siege from Essex's sniper fire at a Howard Johnson's motel, are:

> thinking
> order and mardi gras. of clearing
> the streets and air for the annual
> festivity.

They'll never need a SWAT team in the Crescent City. After a couple of Carnival tours of duty, any copper on the beat can handle such minor unpleasantness. Reasons for the disturbance? What reasons? As poet David Henderson wrote in his "Ruckus Poem," "The police protect the stores" (*De Mayor of Harlem* 68). Business as usual is what matters. People? What people?

But there are people, of course. And people have feelings. In other poems, Aubert suggests some of the frustrations that set off a man like Mark Essex. Little things, as in the poem "The Opposite of Green":

> the blonde neighbor lady tells my wife
> looking square past her dark skin
> into her deep black eyes,
>
> "i can't make a thing grow.
> i even kill weeds.
> i have a black thumb."
> (*If Winter Come* 25)

Such is suburban friendliness in a "color blind" society where racism is not even noticed. On the facing page Aubert placed a clever and beautiful little poem that expressed the anger of black people of his generation, posing an existential question that each person of African descent in the United States has somehow had to face. The poem, quoted in full, is titled "My Name Is Arrow":

> my old man bent down
> so long so low
> he turned into a bow.
> (*If Winter Come* 26)

The message is fully comprehended when one reads Aubert's "Fall of '43," which tells of Italian prisoners of war brought to Louisiana to cut cane who, in spite of their status, "went places / my old man could not" because they were white. And of course, black boys from Louisiana were facing hostile fire overseas.

In "Local Color in Western New York," we get a cuttingly provocative meditation on the little jockey statues that tasteless people inflict on their lawns:

> they're flowering all over
> those little black caricatures
> red lipped and liveried
> in gaudy child colors, hand
> perpetually extended for the
> thoroughbred that never comes.
> (*If Winter Come* 29)

Graciously, Aubert did not paint into the landscape his boorish neighbor lady's station wagon, but surely we know what he means. It doesn't soothe the pain he feels to know that these statues, monstrosities of *kitsch* that they are, commemorate the 1880s Kentucky Derby hero Isaac Murphy (or to notice that black jockeys have been conspicuously absent from the run for the roses since then).

As a poet, Alvin Aubert is a lapidarian of verbal delights. One is constrained to quote his work directly because his poems defy paraphrase or redaction. He writes not only of race but also of private things that every man shares: advice to his children, dreams of his father, instructions for killing chickens for Sunday supper, his failures as a fisherman. Aubert touches an uncommon moment of love and mystery in "Spring 1937," a moving memoir of the day his grandfather died:

> the fullmoon night   hog maws
> fell from heaven and pig knuckles exploded
> like bombed crackers in the bloom
> of our prized magnolia
> (*If Winter Come* 32)

These lines, a child's confused recollections of a wake, only set the scene as something unexplained—perhaps a spirit, or a soul in the ancient Egyptian sense of the Ka—exposes its presence in the house:

> shattering the plugged fireplace
> unmasking the hooded piano
> scattering mourners like sootwinged swifts
> (*If Winter Come* 32)

This writing is intended to recall not stories of old-timey bayou haints but something that is spiritual, more real, and older. All of us share a knowledge of sadness as surely as we also share an almost complete ignorance of where the boundary really lies between life and death.

Aubert has continued to polish his poems to quiet perfection. *Harlem Wrestler and Other Poems* (1995) contains works of total confidence and maturity. "Migration Scene c. 1939" is a dramatic monologue on southern etiquette that begins

> boy, that old cracker said to me, what the hell
> you doin' sitting down in my shade?
> i was real young and must not've known
> any better so i said to him,
> your shade, bossman? i wasn't
> so young as not to know i was
> supposed to call him bossman though.
> yeah, nigger, he said, my shade.
> that's my trees you sittin' under
> on my land so that makes it my shade.
> now once i got started it seemed
> i couldn't stop so i asked him
> what makes the shade, the sun or the tree?
> i must've caught him off guard 'cause
> he answered me almost civil like
> he said, the sun's got a part in it
> but his civilness didn't last all
> > that long.
> ("Harlem Wrestler" 16)

As might be expected, the story gets better. As they say down South, it gets real exciting as a matter of fact.

These poems, and most of those written in the 1990s, show Aubert following the pattern set by Sterling A. Brown, exploring the possibilities of vernacular language with an understanding that its real strength is found in its speakers—that, in fact, a philosophy or worldview shapes these phrases. In "The Rally," Aubert commiserates with an ineffective public speaker while contemplating the true meaning of power:

> she had nothing but a woefully diminished
> voice which might have made a better show
> if somebody backstage hadn't kept messing with the power.
>
> she could have been my sisters my wife my daughters
> my grandmothers my mother all three of my

living aunts all rolled into one if only we'd had that
to turn loose on the bastard
give him a run for his money.
(*Harlem Wrestler* 35)

If Winter Come: Collected Poems, 1967–1992 (1994) suggests that
Aubert usually writes about what inspires his eye (paintings, landscapes
at change of season) or intrigues his mind. There are also praise poems
for African American heroes such as Nat Turner, Miles Davis, and
dancer Judith Jamison. Yet Aubert's own precise music and careful attention to the subtle sounds of words unfailingly bring us the greatest
pleasure. "Just a Photograph" is a fine example of Aubert at his understated best:

in Aram Saroyan's book
Genesis Angels

Gary Snyder's
holding Lew Welch's arm

while thru horn rimmed
glasses drink in hand
Philip Whalen looks on.
I am wrong. Snyder's
holding on to his own arm.
And Whalen isn't looking on
he's looking out
(60–61)

One might easily say that this poem is as much about the poetry of
Snyder and Whalen as it is about the snapshot, a kind of quiet semiotic
exercise. Aubert—a man who relaxes by "Diggin' Northrop Frye / And
reading the Blues" (26)—nudges us gently toward sharing his realization that sense cannot be separated from the senses, that they work
together or not at all.

Despite the variety of their subject matter and the differences in
their approach, one word that applies to all of the poets we have been
discussing here is *power*. Taken to any number of places, power multi-
plies—as European slavers should have known when they decided to
bring Africa to Louisiana. Alvin Aubert is most certainly a modern
American poet, yet the spiritual mysteries that his best poems explore
are consistently clothed in traditions with African roots. He does not

even have to insist on being African, as Kalamu ya Salaam has done; the power and sensibility come from Africa. While his work does not provide the human surprise of Ahmos Zu-Bolton's, the social urgency of Salaam's, nor the all-encompassing mythic vision of Tom Dent's, Aubert's poetry is rewarding in its flawless craftsmanship and mature choosings. When critics complain that Aubert has no "cause," he replies: "I have voices." And when they ask about his vision, he says: "I have vexed myself enough to write a poem."

8

Neon Griot

The Functional Role of Poetry Readings

> the gift and ministry of Song
> Have something in them so divinely sweet,
> It can assuage the bitterness of wrong
> —Henry Wadsworth Longfellow

The poetry reading has a long history as a social occasion for aficionados and has also often been considered a marginalized activity by those who participate. Thousands of people may, in fact, participate in reading circles or in poetry workshops that meet weekly at branch libraries or in members' homes, but none of them thinks that their chosen leisure activity carries the same level of societal acceptance as, say, bowling. Most of these people, of course, would be disappointed if it did.

On their most pretentious levels such gatherings are called salons, but all of them function as the gardens that nourish the readers of books and those who eventually produce both popular and great literature. Saturday night gatherings at Georgia Douglas Johnson's home in Washington, D.C., in the early 1920s, brought together a number of Harlem Renaissance figures: Jean Toomer, Alain Locke, William Stanley Braithwaite, Langston Hughes, and many others. The discussion centered on poetry and politics. In another time and place, poet Kent Taylor recalled a poetry workshop organized in the early 1960s by Russell Atkins, editor of the long-running little magazine *Free Lance:*

Adelaide Simon (Martin, her husband, played cello with the Cleveland Symphony) hosted the workshop in her comfortable Shaker Heights home. The locale was notable for being racially mixed, an almost singular occurrence in the Cleveland area. The Free Lance Workshop served a vital social function. Many of my first contacts with fellow poets took place there.

The ambiance was more leftbank coffeehouse than traditional literary workshop. While there was some informal criticism, most of the time passed in animated discussion that ran the gamut from politics to philosophy to the locally neglected status of contemporary poetry. (levy 224)

A hundred similar examples could be offered, and each reader would be able to contribute one more.

In another of its aspects—more prominent in some historical periods than in others—the poetry reading is an intellectual form of public entertainment. Before the twentieth century the two most widely known African American poets were Frances Ellen Watkins Harper (1825–1911) and Paul Laurence Dunbar. Harper was an accomplished elocutionist. Her programs—like those of Ralph Waldo Emerson—were not what we would call "poetry readings" per se. Her audiences could expect an abolitionist or feminist speech accompanied by poems composed on appropriate topics. Harper's practice was aimed at the harmonious alignment of head and heart. Unlike Emerson's "Self-Reliance" and other lyceum circuit lectures that are now classic texts of American literature, it is Harper's widely circulated *Poems on Miscellaneous Subjects* (first published in 1854 and reprinted for several decades thereafter) that still commands attention. While much of her work, like the eloquent poem "The Slave Mother," resembled Harriet Beecher Stowe's campaign to persuade white Americans that slavery must be seen as intolerable, some of her writing was intended very specifically for African Americans. In a recent biography of Harper, Melba Joyce Boyd comments: "Because most black folks were illiterate or in the process of pursuing literacy, the invention of a characteristic voice was needed to carry Harper's message and to bridge the cultural distance between standard English and black dialect. Hence *Sketches of Southern Life* [1872] was composed in the language of the people as reflected in the slave narrative of a newly literate woman with similar experiences and a familiar voice" (*Discarded Legacy* 150). Harper, intending this book for use in adult literacy programs, employed standard spelling to avoid the "overapostrophied" conventions of dialect fiction, depending instead on word order and syntax that would "assure a folk pronunciation" of the poems (Boyd 156).

Writing teachers know that students tend to write just as they speak, and Harper believed—according to Boyd—that beginning readers would benefit from a primer that, when actually read aloud, sounded like their own accustomed style of speech. After identifying this early attempt to demystify the mechanics of literacy, Boyd formulates a more generalized statement about dialect that raises many questions: "The dialectics of dialect poetry operates within a cultural and a linguistic framework, and the nineteenth-century American writer who strove to authenticate indigenous speech had to abandon imperialist perceptions of the English language and consider the American language as a departure in cultural values and expression" (151–152).

While Boyd imputes this view to Harper, many would also see it operative in Mark Twain's celebration of regional speech. It has also been suggested by Margaret Walker and others that a similar motive underlies the more apparently "entertaining" dialect poems of Paul Laurence Dunbar. While Boyd's understanding of Frances E. W. Harper's attempt at capturing the vernacular is contextualized by Boyd's own apprenticeship as a poet of the Black Arts movement, it is not at all the sort of ahistorical reading that mars some recent postmodernist criticism. The point is that we cannot assume—even with nineteenth-century texts—that the use of dialect is necessarily humorous or meant to ridicule its speakers.

That we should tread upon this ground with care is suggested also by Paul H. Gray's investigation of the "poet-performer movement" that lasted from 1870 to 1930 and shaped the careers of Will Carleton, Ella Wheeler Wilcox, James Whitcomb Riley, Vachel Lindsay, and others. This "movement," writes Gray, was self-consciously and deliberately "low-brow," seeking a following among neither the readers nor the writers of traditional poetry. Instead, it aimed unerringly at the petite bourgeoisie—farmers, merchants, salesmen, and housewives—people who claimed they hated poetry but flocked by the thousands to hear these poets perform and then bought their books. Gray makes two important points about this movement that may, in fact, also tell us something about the popular arts in general. First, success "depended as much on the poet's ability to perform his work as to write it"; second, "the kind of poetry the movement produced and the poetic careers it shaped were remarkably homogeneous." It is important to understand precisely what success meant in this context. Detroit newspaperman Will Carleton, for example, was earning almost $500 a week in 1871 for nightly readings of his dialect monologues in rhymed couplets, and in 1873 his collection *Farm Ballads* sold 40,000 copies. Carleton himself saw his work as a commodity and believed that his success depended upon "a keen sense of the public taste" and his ability to satisfy it (Gray 2–3).

Gray refuses to dismiss Carleton's position as merely crass, noting that one reason for his popularity was that midwestern audiences "were amazed and delighted to discover through Carleton's verses that their own lives and region could be a fit topic for poetry" (4). Furthermore, Carleton's poems dealt with realistic incidents of American life. But while Carleton was able to offer rhymes on divorce, frustration in business, and destitution in old age (albeit with happy endings), his most successful competitors were less probing about society.

James Whitcomb Riley, for example, was the master of a type of homespun sentimentalized nostalgia that owed some of its popularity to the fact that it could be easily copied. "The Old Swimmin' Hole" (1883) became something of a classic:

> But the lost joy is past! Let your tears in sorrow roll
> Like the rain that ust to dapple up the old swimmin' hole.
> (II, 471)

Riley's poetry celebrates itself as pure nostalgia:

> The simple, soul-reposing glad belief in everything,—
> When life was like a story, holding neither sob nor sigh,
> In the golden olden glory of the days gone by.
> (II, 472)

It is worth noting that Riley spent several years touring as a salesman with medicine shows and that his Hoosier dialect poems were published in the fictitious guise of unsolicited contributions from a rural subscriber. In a sense he took F. E. W. Harper's conceit in *Sketches of Southern Life* a step further. While her poems are written in a voice closely approximating that of her protagonist Aunt Chloe, Riley's impersonation of his reader's voice extended to the reputed authorship of the poems themselves. In any case, Riley was the most widely read poet in the United States in the 1880s, and his influence can readily be seen in the work of Paul Laurence Dunbar and others. Dunbar's publishers, for example, emulated Riley's habit of issuing collections in December to accommodate Christmas shoppers. Beginning with *Candle-Lightin' Time*

(1902), Dunbar published several beautifully illustrated volumes clearly intended as gift books. Whatever contemporary readers may think of their poetry, which is not comparable in skill or message to Emerson's or Mrs. Harper's, Will Carleton and James Whitcomb Riley were indeed consummate performers who—in an age before radio and television—used the skills of oratory and dramatic presentation to fashion evenings of satisfying entertainment that were advertised to the public as poetry readings (Gray 9).

Dunbar's performances were of a quite different nature. Though he was opinionated and outspoken on social and political issues, Dunbar's readings were straightforward recitals of his poems—written in dialect and standard traditional stanzaic forms. Because he was a talented humorist, Dunbar's recitals were above all entertaining, but his was clearly always entertainment with a message. In choosing to write in dialect, Dunbar was certainly attempting to reach a large public. When he was growing up in the 1880s, Joel Chandler Harris's Uncle Remus books were best-sellers. Negro dialect was also part of poet James Whitcomb Riley's popular repertoire. But those who thought Dunbar's dialect poems somehow glorified slavery days or the antebellum South were mistaken. His message, made explicit in his journalistic pieces, was a celebration of African American kinship and strong, morally upstanding families and communities. If the communal joy depicted in such poems had been possible for unsophisticated rural blacks, certainly Dunbar's audiences would be led to think that an educated, empowered people could do as well or better. Dunbar's was a double-coded message, but it said the same thing to everybody.

Dunbar achieved fame with white audiences and was beloved in the black community. Fraternal lodges and cultural organizations were named for him during his lifetime. He was proud, also, that African American high school and college students earned funds for themselves and their school organizations by presenting recitals of his poems. Dunbar authored some eloquent and lasting protest poems such as "Sympathy" and "We Wear the Mask," but he was most often concerned with drawing attention to the minor hypocrisies of daily life, the moments when

> As you breathe some pretty sentence,
> though she hates you all the while,
> She is very apt to stun you with a made to order smile
> (*Majors and Minors* 126)

There is little doubt that such poems were suitable for the audiences—whether black or white—and venues of Dunbar's national tours. Dunbar had not only made a careful study of the literary marketplace but knew his listeners and understood the most effective way to communicate his message.

If the reception given to Langston Hughes in Houston in 1932 is any indication, his celebrity in the African American community equaled Dunbar's. Sponsored by the local YMCA and YWCA branches, Hughes's appearance was highly publicized for weeks in advance. The city's Pilgrim Auditorium attracted a capacity crowd. Audiences responded to Hughes's urbanity and good looks as much as to his poetry. After the reading, Carter Wesley editorialized in the *Houston Informer:* "There was a purposefulness about the man and his work that gave us the key to his success. He had been to Africa and to parts of the West Indies, where Negroes live. He went because he wanted to know the black man everywhere" ("Langston Hughes" 2). "Perhaps," wrote reporter Bernice Johnson, "Langston Hughes cannot be called great now. He lacks that maturity, that ripening, that tolerance that comes with age. But he understands his people" (1).

Hughes understood what his audience wanted. Fashionable and debonair, employing a slightly sardonic tone, he read his poems with precise and elegant diction—even those written in the blues stanza form. His purpose was not to impersonate the unlettered but to elevate their idiom to a plane on which its poetic qualities would be recognized. While many of his poems are in his own male voice, the blues poems often present a female persona, and Hughes also wrote dramatic monologues with specific social types as speakers. Individually these poems resemble Robert Browning's "My Last Duchess," but together, as in the 1931 collection *The Negro Mother and Other Dramatic Recitations* (intended for the use of schoolchildren), they depict a cross section of the African American community. Very few of these monologues, however, are as perfectly crafted as Hughes's memorable "Mother to Son" (1922). In all of his poetry, and in his performance style, the character and experience of his personae are revealed by the words that Langston Hughes has chosen for them, not by a stage accent.

Readings and personal appearances provided Hughes with much of his income throughout his life, and he never deviated from the mode he had established on his first national tour in 1932. In any case, his audiences would not have allowed him to do so. Recalling a visit Hughes made to Detroit in 1961, Woodie King, Jr., noted that the poet was a

7. Langston Hughes's national tour in 1932 was front-page news in the African American press. *Houston Informer,* Saturday, 2 April 1932.

genuine celebrity among ordinary people, "the factory workers, the car washers, the day workers, domestics, bartenders. . . . They knew one of his poems or one of his short stories or one of his plays or some of Simple they had read in the *Chicago Defender.*" King and his circle of local artists (including Margaret Danner and Ron Milner) wanted to meet Hughes but worried that he might be so much a celebrity that "the new mayor and the middle-class Negro doctors and lawyers [had] cornered him" (21). Of course, that wasn't the case; Hughes welcomed the young poets into his hotel suite as if they had been the real purpose of his visit.

Dynamic interactive relationships—formal and informal—between artist and audience define the heritage of the poetry reading; yet to the extent that poetry readings have been perceived as entirely secondary to the existence of poems as printed texts, very little attention has been directed to the possible impact of performance contexts on poetic composition. As Kristin M. Langellier has shown, "even scholarship in the discipline of speech communication is only slowly beginning to concern itself with this question" (65). Literary critics who see themselves as activists for innovation sometimes claim more for the contemporary practice of the oral presentation of poetry than they should. Reporting on "the scene" in the early 1960s, art critic John Gruen was noticeably underwhelmed by the Monday night open poetry readings in New York's East Village: "At the Metro, located on Second Avenue at East Tenth Street, you sip coffee and are treated to hours of poetic verbiage, most of it of the therapeutic, pretentiously self-purging variety. As for performance there are very few nascent Dylan Thomases. Frequently they know not when to stop, and then an aura of impatience and frustration makes itself felt" (69). In his *Tales of Beatnik Glory*, Ed Sanders also wickedly lampooned the staged solipsism likely to be exhibited on such evenings (12–25). When the coffeehouse poetry readings first reemerged in the 1950s, however, the aura was much more electric.

II

What we have suffered from, is manuscript, press, the removal of verse from its producer and its reproducer, the voice . . .
—Charles Olson, *Projective Verse*

And we were there, lost in the sound of a beat
—Bob Kaufman

What Werner Sollors has described as the "centrality" of African Americans in the avant-garde movement called the Beat Generation was partly metaphoric, because the Beats had chosen to move to the margins of *mainstream* society and to adopt the aesthetic of African

American music as the principle of their artistic efforts. It was also true that the Beats were probably the first group of so-called white people who—past the age of puberty—actually knew some black people as individuals, equals, and sometimes even lovers. By the same token, young black people involved in the movement would have to be the most completely "integrated" African Americans of that era. To appreciate the historical context, one might recall that integration of the U.S. Army did not occur until 1948 following an executive order from President Harry Truman.

That the United States at midcentury should have produced poets who did not regard their work as "high art" is not surprising; the notion can be traced to Emerson's rejection of European "cultivation" in favor of an indigenous and energetic American inventiveness. In the late 1940s, John A. Kouwenhoven pointed out that cinema and jazz—the twentieth-century art forms that most fascinated young poets—were both "products of the interaction of the vernacular and cultivated tradition" that are nonetheless perceived primarily as vernacular forms "suitable for mass participation and enjoyment and so universally acceptable" (222). African American poets, particularly because of their interest in jazz, found it easy to develop similar ideas. Indeed, as Amiri Baraka suggested in a speech at the 1994 National Black Arts Festival, one of the goals of the Black Arts movement was the creation of a mass art. Similarly, as far as the general public was concerned, the Beat Generation was Jack Kerouac, Allen Ginsberg, and the mediagenic Ted Joans.

It is not negative criticism to say that Ted Joans's masterpiece was the creation of Ted Joans; after all, carefully orchestrated eccentricity in the pursuit of publicity is no vice. Joans was a welcome incarnation of an ancient Greenwich Village lineage, the postwar equivalent of Guido Bruno (1914's entrepreneurial "mayor of Greenwich Village" who commuted from Yonkers); his genial rebellion perfectly suited the Eisenhower era—which fact explains why his photo wound up in *Life* magazine. Joans's persona looked like Bobby Troup under ultraviolet light. Even so, he was ahead of his time; the rest of us didn't get black light until the 1960s. Many of Joans's poems from the 1950s seem like material for standup comedy—lacking the manic quality of Hugh Romney or the subtlety of Dick Gregory but a pretty good warm-up act (if anyone had been paying attention) for Richard Pryor.

Although journalists described the movement as apolitical, demanding the freedom to pursue interracial relationships (including romances) was clearly part of Beat nonconformity—as can be seen in Joans's poetry and in Kerouac's little masterpiece *The Subterraneans* (1958).

The Beats were also interested in restructuring the poetry reading as something other than a genteel diversion. In New York, with the help of a young lawyer named Ed Koch, they fought City Hall and won a campaign to exempt Greenwich Village coffeehouses from the city's post-Prohibition cabaret license law. Sure, poetry readings should be entertaining, but the poets argued that they were also "art." The coffeehouse owners supplied energy and funds, of course, but the successful crusade represents the full measure of Beat political activism in the 1950s (McDarrah 286, 306–307).

In California Kenneth Rexroth ecstatically recalled the Six Gallery reading in October 1955 where Allen Ginsberg first recited "Howl": "What happened in San Francisco first and spread from there across the world was public poetry, the return of a tribal, preliterate relationship between poet and audience" (*American Poetry* 141). The Beat innovation perhaps consisted in returning poetry to the bacchanalian atmosphere of saloons, coffeehouses, and low-rent Friday night house parties. The mainstream press in the late 1950s titillated readers with accounts of poets disrobing and engaging in other improprieties. Charles Bukowski—the last bonafide bum "poet"—turned this aspect of the Beat legend into a vaudeville act, appearing in saloons across the country in the late 1970s. At one such appearance in Tallahassee, the "poetry reading" degenerated into little more than Bukowski trading chugalugs and insults with the fraternity boys who filled the ringside tables. Here, the relationship between poet and audience was decidedly subliterate.

But even genuine Beat poets sometimes had to participate in the poetry reading as "cultural event." When Ginsberg, Gregory Corso, and Peter Orlovsky gave a reading at Columbia University, Diana Trilling's account of the evening in *Partisan Review* might have had a greater impact than the reading itself. Trilling coyly admitted knowing Ginsberg only as a "troublesome student" from a decade earlier but also managed to interpret his appearance on the platform where T. S. Eliot had stood as meaning "that Ginsberg had always desperately wanted to be respectable, or respected, like his teachers at Columbia" (145). What Trilling's article demonstrates most profoundly is that audiences hear what they want to hear.

One would hardly expect to find in a jazz nightclub the decorum built into an Ivy League university auditorium, but the idea of respectability that Diana Trilling pulled out of a hat was elaborated by Kenneth Rexroth in the pages of *Esquire.* On the one hand, Rexroth stressed an antiacademic theme. "Jazz poetry reading," he declared, "puts poetry back in the entertainment business where it was with Homer and the troubadours. Even Victorian epics like *Idylls of the King* and *Evangeline* were written to be read to the whole family around the fire in the evening by papa—not, certainly, to be studied for their ambiguities by a seminar." On the other hand, as a jazz poet himself, Rexroth wanted respect. "Rehearsals," he assured his readers, "are pretty elaborate, far more finicky than the average band rehearsal." In fact, he noted with pride, "jazz poetry is an exacting, co-operative, precision effort, like mountaineering" ("Jazz and Poetry" 61–62). Despite such efforts at precision, Rexroth's week at the 5 Spot was nowhere near as memorable as Thelonious Monk's wordless and continually extended residency or July 1961's intricately spontaneous Eric Dolphy/Booker Little performances, which yielded four LPs that still amaze even those who long ago memorized every note. As one critic put it, Rexroth "knocked out the poetry fans" but left jazz fans unimpressed. One of the reasons might have been that there was jazz in the room but not in his poems.

Perhaps the most influential experiment of this kind was Charles Mingus's 1960 recording *A Modern Jazz Symposium of Music and Poetry.* Despite the pretentious title, it was a well-realized and swinging piece of work. As Ross Russell wrote in *Jazz Review:* "The script for 'Scenes in the City' was conceived and written by actor Lonne Elder in collaboration with Langston Hughes and is narrated by Melvin Stewart. It is a rambling, introspective monologue of a young man of the city, any city, whose thoughts and dreams have been influenced by jazz, and it is a skillful amalgam of Harlem vernacular, Tin Pan Alley references, and believable bits of everyday speech" (31). If Russell makes the performance seem a bit like an audio version of Hughes's *The Sweet Flypaper of Life* (1955), the comparison is not at all inappropriate. What is most important about Elder's "Scenes in the City," however, is that the narrative structure follows the logical collage of a jazz solo. Mingus's musical setting brilliantly complements and underscores both the spoken cadences and the meaning of the monologue. Though this was an enormously influential work, most poets who later attempted to capture the mood of jazz or to work with musicians chose to employ a more declamatory style—even with similarly personal material.

Bob Kaufman exemplifies the Beat commitment to an oral poetry. Capable of extemporizing astonishing poems, he not only memorized his own compositions but was fond of reciting the works of Federico García Lorca and other poets at length. Kaufman was an electrifying performer even in his declining years, as poet Kaye McDonough reported:

The dynamite volcano is not extinct
We heard you at Vesuvio's
singing Hart Crane
You blew America from your mouth
and smiled your ancient vision
round a shocked barroom
(78)

There is a direct line between the Beat poets and the Black Arts movement. Amiri Baraka—whose enduring stylistic influence on younger American poets is matched only by John Ashbery's—was a key figure in both movements, and the document that expressed the poetic theory of both movements was Charles Olson's 1950 essay "Projective Verse," which Baraka resurrected from the pages of Rolfe Feldje's *Poetry New York* magazine and published in his Totem Press chapbook series in 1959. Speaking for the poets included in Donald Allen's *The New American Poetry, 1945–1960,* Baraka stated: "We want to go into a quantitative verse . . . the 'irregular foot' of Williams . . . , the 'Projective Verse' of Olson. Accentual verse, the regular metric of rumbling iambics, is dry as slivers of sand" ("How You Sound" 17). By the end of the decade this view would also be seconded by young African American poets across the country (see Madhubuti 85–86).

Because it mimics Ezra Pound's authoritarian tone, Olson's essay strikes many recent readers as windy and offensively "patriarchal," but Olson's ideas had an undeniably widespread impact. Since every young writer in the United States goes through an e. e. cummings period and a Carl Sandburg and/or Gertrude Stein phase, *any* perceived affinity between Olson's prosody and those models (even if mistaken) couldn't hurt. Certainly the most significant and unimpeachable idea in Olson's essay—essentially a reiteration of a point made in Pound's edition of Ernest Fenollosa's *The Chinese Written Character as a Medium for Poetry* (first published in 1936 and reprinted by Lawrence Ferlinghetti's City Lights in 1958)—is that poetry is an act of speech, that its element is breath, and that writing it down is a skill. Simplistic as that statement may first appear, it was soon shown to have far-reaching philosophical and—as redefined by African American poets—political implications.

In 1964 Amiri Baraka, Steve Kent, Larry Neal, Askia Muhammad Touré, and several others established an arts center in a Harlem brownstone. The Black Arts Repertory Theatre/School (BARTS) collapsed in clouds of notoriety in less than a year, but by 1968 there was a nationwide network of similar theater groups, poetry workshops, and groups organized by musicians and visual artists. The Black Arts movement embraced many divergent tendencies. Perhaps the one thing that all of its participants agreed on was that art was—and should be—a political act. In his 1968 essay "The Black Arts Movement," Larry Neal declared: "the political values inherent in the Black Power concept are now finding concrete expression in the aesthetics of Afro-American dramatists, poets, choreographers, musicians, and novelists. A main tenet of Black Power is the necessity for black people to define the world in their own terms. The black artist has made the same point in the context of aesthetics" (62).

Black Power political gestures disrupted many preconceptions, and one aspect of radical self-determination seemed, surprisingly, to be a rejection of the decades-long struggle for racial integration. It would simplify the literary historian's task if we could say that the theme of "separation" employed by Black Arts writers was, like the "newness" of the verse published in Harriet Monroe's *Poetry* magazine, merely a polemical conceit. It wasn't. In the case of the activities associated with the Black Arts movement, rhetoric often conformed to reality. Nor was this only the fault of the poets: even now, except for a sentence in the biographical note on Amiri Baraka, you probably won't find the Black Arts movement mentioned in college texts that supposedly introduce students to twentieth-century American literature.

While the movement rejected mainstream America's ideology, deeming it inimical to black people, Black Arts poets maintained and developed the prosody that they had acquired from Black Mountain and the Beats. Even this fact, however, tended to cause dismay and some anxiety in literary circles. Ted Berrigan recalled an afternoon that he spent at Frank O'Hara's apartment talking poetry and "art world" gossip. Suddenly another friend of O'Hara's bounded up the stairs and burst into the room, heart-attack-if-you-don't-slow-down written across his face.

"Amiri Baraka's on the radio," the man gasped, red with alarm, "and he's talking about killing white people!"

"Well," said Frank consolingly, "I don't think he will begin with you or me. Now sit down and have some wine."

Not everyone is blessed with Frank's gift for nonchalance. The efforts made by Baraka and others to distance themselves from the Beats and downtown avant-garde created resentments and hurt feelings in many relationships. Some suffered through strained or ruined friendships; a few welcomed hatred. Many succumbed to the bad American idea that mutual mistrust is the same thing as civility, that optimism is a sign of deviancy or brain damage. Dudley Randall summarized the inner turmoil of the era with remarkable objectivity. Black poets, he wrote in 1971: "have absorbed the techniques of the masters, have rejected them, and have gone in new directions. Perhaps this rejection had its roots in the [Civil Rights] movement of the fifties and sixties. When the poets saw the contorted faces of the mobs, saw officers of the law commit murder, and "respectable" people scheme to break the law (there was no cry for law and order then), perhaps they asked themselves, Why should we seek to be integrated with such a society?" (xxv).

Race relations in the United States deteriorated badly during the 1960s. A series of spectacular urban disturbances forced President Lyndon Johnson to appoint a commission headed by former Michigan governor Otto Kerner. After a year of investigation and hearings, the published *Report of the National Advisory Commission on Civil Disorders* (1968) became a best-selling book with a grim message. In terms of race and opportunity, the Kerner Commission concluded, the United States was becoming "two nations—separate and unequal." In an important chapter, the commission compared the economic upward mobility of European immigrants and urban African Americans and concluded that "segregation denied Negroes access to good jobs and the opportunity to leave the ghetto. For them, the future seemed to lead only to a dead end" (15). While certain cultural traits were cited as possible factors contributing to the relative success of white ethnic groups, there is no mention in the report of anything indicating African American cultural distinctiveness. It was precisely this vacant area that the explorations of the Black Arts movement—through poetry, music, and the development of communal celebrations such as Kwanzaa (the external manifestation of "a Black value system")—were intended to fill, either by discovery or invention.

With self-anointed missionary fervor, Black Arts poets extended the venues for their performances beyond storefront theaters to neighborhood community centers, church basements, taverns, and the streets. Not surprisingly, the poetry that proved effective in such settings drew upon the rhetorical conventions of the black church, the matrix of

African American culture. Exhortation and easily accessible satire, as appropriate and time-honored techniques of street-corner orators, also became a notable element of this poetry. While these are natural developments, the idea that form is never more than an extension of content came under fire during the Black Arts movement. As the poets moved toward the African American vernacular, it also became necessary to find ideological rationalizations for employing forms that came from the same black church that the poets were otherwise fond of denouncing.

As Henry Louis Gates, Jr., eloquently and succinctly puts it, "the Church is at once a culture and a black cultural event, a weekly unfolding of ritual and theater, oratory and spectacle, the most sublime music, and even dance" (7). Indeed, whether or not one is religious, the influence of the black church within the African American community is basic and unavoidable. One can hear the rich, emphatic voice that distinguishes much Black Arts poetry in the speeches of Martin Luther King, Jr. Listening to a recorded sermon such as *I'm into Something I Can't Shake Loose* by W. C. Thomas, Jr., of the Canaan Baptist Church in Dayton, Ohio—Paul Laurence Dunbar's hometown—we can experience the full power of the African American sermonic tradition. You hear the speaking voice that trespasses into song and an antiphonal interaction with the congregation revealing the same structures that inform the early "collective improvisation" of New Orleans jazz, bebop, and the avant-garde jazz of the 1960s.

The factors that influenced the developmental direction of Black Arts poetry included (1) the model of African American music—particularly jazz; (2) an interest in finding and legitimizing an "authentic" African American vernacular speech; and (3) the material and physical context of Black Arts poetry readings. In her useful study of African American theater, Geneviève Fabre has pointed out that in the work of poets such as Baraka, Sonia Sanchez, and Marvin X, "theatre and poetry exchange customary structures and images." After noting that the neighborhood Black Arts theaters were most usually the site of readings rather than fully staged dramatic productions, Fabre adds: "The dramatization drawn from poetry and the use of lyrical modes on the stage are evident in the public reading. Read aloud, poetry becomes theatre. Black theatre thus embraces both dramatic poems and 'pure' plays. Which form is used will be determined by the message the theatre wants to communicate" (66). Perhaps even more important, the poetry reading as a characteristic mode of publication reinforced poets' tendency to employ "dramatic" structures and direct first-person address. The apostrophic mode was made obsolete by the presence of an audience prepared (and encouraged) to play the role of "amen corner."

The link between poetry and drama was not only evident in the way some poets wrote plays—Baraka's *Dutchman* (1964) and Sanchez's *Sister Son/ji* (1969) were both composed in night-long bursts of creativity, not in actors' workshops and rehearsals—but in commercially successful plays such as Ntozake Shanges's *For Colored Girls Who Have Considered Suicide When the Rainbow Is Enuf* (1976) and Melvin Van Peebles's *Ain't Supposed to Die a Natural Death* (1973), both of which are actually staged poetry readings, collections of dramatic monologues assigned for recitation to "different characters."

Generic definitions were not the only boundaries challenged by Black Arts writers. Dunbar's poetic production was cannily and problematically divided between dialect poems and lyrics in standard English. The poetry of Amiri Baraka also occupies two modes: intensely personal lyrics and incisively political social comment. The persona of Baraka's lyrics, however, is always clearly in this world now. The result is that the poems have both a universality and a dimension of social comment. It is not surprising that Baraka brought something of his ideas—as expressed in his bifurcated poetic output—to the developing Black Arts aesthetic. Baraka had expressed his position forcefully in 1970. "There is no such thing as Art and Politics, there is only life," he wrote. "If the artist is the raised consciousness, then all that he touches, all that impinges on his consciousness, must be raised. We must be the will of the race toward evolution. We must demand the spiritual by being spiritual. THE LARGEST WORK OF ART IS THE WORLD ITSELF" ("Black Nationalism" 11).

The practical application of such ideas was not quite as chimerical as some readers might expect. In a 1973 article on Miami's Theatre of Afro Arts (TAA)—one of more than 150 such organizations then in operation—Eddie Osborne stated that Black Arts activists understood that "art definitely is not the revolution": "The founders of the TAA acknowledged this fact from the start, but they were also aware that art could, nevertheless, play a decisive role in the revolution; that art was an excellent means of interpreting the black experience to the masses, while at the same time fostering the principles of work, struggle, and self-determination" (38).

Transforming the poetry reading from an event suited to a genteel parlor or even a rowdy night out for bohemian artists and models soon became an important goal of the movement and was rationalized by the political thrust of the developing "Black Aesthetic." Readings in nontraditional venues were now invested with a strategic value. It is worthwhile to understand why.

The antibourgeois stance of the Black Arts movement and its dismissal of the Harlem Renaissance as a failure was not merely an expression of generational revolt but was also a considered political position. Robert A. Bone, author of *The Negro Novel in America,* had stated: "The early novelists were loyal members of the middle-class who desired only equal rights within the status quo. The younger writers of the 1920s were the second generation of educated Negroes: they were the wayward sons of the rising middle class." Bone points out that "the parents of the Renaissance novelists were 55 per cent professionals and 45 per cent white collar" and concludes that Langston Hughes, Jean Toomer, and Countee Cullen "were rebelling against their fathers and their fathers' way of life" (412). At this point Bone invokes psychology, but it might have been more appropriate to compare these writers with contemporaries who faced similar decisions: Hart Crane, for example, or even Wallace Stevens.

In New York, however, when Baraka and his group abandoned Greenwich Village for Harlem, they also rejected the bohemian option in favor of a unique position that, however quixotically, denied the notion of avant-garde marginality. In recalling the early activities of the Black Arts group, Baraka stated:

> But that one glorious summer of 1965, we did, even with all that internal warfare, bring advanced Black art to Harlem. We *organized,* as part of HARYOU/ACT, the nation's 1st anti-poverty program, a summer arts program called Operation Boot Strap (under the overall direction of Adam Clayton Powell's point cadre, Judge Livingston Wingate). For eight weeks, we brought Drama, Poetry, Painting, Music, Dance, night after night all across Harlem. We had a fleet of five trucks and stages created with banquet tables. And each night our five units would go out in playgrounds, street corners, vacant lots, play streets, parks, bringing Black Art directly to the people. ("The Black Arts Movement" 6–7)

In spite of Baraka's retrospective inventory of BARTS's brief period of success, the artists and the funding agency never had an easy relationship. Harold Cruse assessed that situation in *The Crisis of the Negro Intellectual* (1967): "The institution established was not economic or political, but cultural [and] was forced to enter an uneven struggle with a federal agency over the dispensation of funds, without having prepared for such an eventuality with a grassroots economic institution of its own in the community." For Cruse, the issue of aesthetics and/or ideology was irrelevant by comparison with realistic political issues. Cruse argues that if the theater group had begun with its own endowment or even an "economics planning group," it "would have been able to wage a more effective political struggle with the HARYOU administration and the Federal government over the funding of anti-poverty programs" (367).

The directors of the Black Arts Repertory Theatre, fully cognizant of the contradictions inherent in using government funds to support "revolutionary" art, were not lax in creatively exploring alternative resources. One afternoon's brainstorming session resulted in a staff pilgrimage to the movie set where Sammy Davis, Jr., was shooting *A Man Called Adam* (1966) on location in Harlem. The film crew's presence was the neighborhood's big news, and the movie itself—the story of a jazz musician's confrontation with racism, economic exploitation, and despair—set a pattern for the black action films of the 1970s not only in terms of content but also in establishing a commercial strategy that "became the dominant mode of producing and distributing major studio films on African American life" (Reid 72).

When Baraka and his colleagues arrived to beg the star for a contribution of time or (preferably) money to support the Black Arts theater, they found Davis completing a scene that had him on his knees abjectly begging a white villain to let him live. The poets immediately realized how ludicrous the coincidence was but not that it might be instructively prophetic. Of course, once they did get a moment to discuss the purpose of their mission in detail, Davis turned down their request.

The kind of patronage that many Black Arts movement groups did manage to secure was, to say the least, perilous—and sometimes extravagantly Byzantine in nature. The unusual relationship of art and politics in the movement created peculiar problems, especially because the word "politics" embraced both the poets' "revolutionary" theories and local municipal reality. If Black Arts poetry readings sometimes resembled political rallies, there were also cases—as in the successful 1970 mayoral election campaign of Newark's Kenneth Gibson—when political rallies *were* poetry readings. After Gibson's election, however, the poets' self-defined role as social critics and urban griots caused serious friction with the politicians they had previously supported.

In Cleveland, Ohio, during the same period poet Norman Jordan complained that involvement with Mayor Carl Stokes's Summer Arts Festival actually destroyed the Muntu Poets group. "We had been meeting about a year," Jordan writes, "when, in the summer of nineteen sixty-eight, about nine of us began making plans to read on street corners and a few other places. We knew we could attract a Black audience. When the 'man' heard this, he sent word that they would pay us to read in the park, plus give us a mobile stage with lights, a new P.A. system and publicity" (61). The resulting $2,400 contract with the city not only compromised the Muntu Poets' original "revolutionary" intent but also divided the members in terms of whether the windfall should be shared or reinvested in various community projects. "That," Jordan says, "was the end of the MUNTU POETS." It wasn't the end of the story. Several months later, Jordan adds, "when the UNITED BLACK ARTISTS held their first announced meeting, a policeman, disguised as a Black artist, was in attendance. So before we had a chance to really organize, the Man sent word for us to submit a proposal for six-hundred thousand dollars, assuring us that he would see to it that we would be granted the money" (62). In this instance, arguments over the offer itself were enough to destroy the organization before any programs were ever produced.

While municipal antipoverty agencies were sometimes willing—for whatever reasons—to accept the idea that artists could help relieve the resentments that led to urban violence, some Black Arts poets were not unwilling to align themselves with the campus protests of the period. "Like students burning down buildings that lie to them," wrote one poet, "our poems aim ultimately to help deliver the capitalist oppressive system to some museum of time, to leave it 'out there' somewhere as a relic of western space" (Major 17).

What was required to accomplish this, wrote Geneva Smitherman, was that the poet should not "be set apart from his ghetto brethren by using the 'standard' dialect (known as 'talkin proper,' or 'tryin to talk white' in the Black community)" (81). According to Baraka: "We wanted a mass popular art, distinct from the tedious abstractions our oppressors and their negroes bamboozled the 'few' as Art. We thought it was Ain't! White Ain't. And we wanted Black Art" ("Black Arts Movement" 7–8). Whether they used the proper "improper" idiom or not, the artistic offerings were uncompromisingly avant-garde and surprisingly well-received by the audiences.

If Langston Hughes's triumphal 1932 tour epitomizes the national impact of the Harlem Renaissance, then two events might indicate the scope of the Black Arts movement. One of these was "Black Spirits: A Festival of New Black Poets." This well-attended three-day festival held at New York's New Federal Theatre in 1971 was produced by Woodie King, Jr., and featured readings by a cross section of Black Arts poets including Baraka, Ed Bullins, Mari Evans, the original Last Poets (reading together and individually), and many others. King also amplified the impact of the event by producing a record album issued by a division of Motown Records and an anthology published under the Vintage paperback imprint of Random House. The other event was a reading by Amiri Baraka at a community center in Newark on Christmas Eve 1966, a cold night. This reading was attended by neighborhood residents—teenagers, women with small children, a number of senior citizens. It was a small crowd but not disappointingly so, about the number of folks who regularly turn up at Twelve Step meetings or county commissioner's hearings. Both of these events were notable for the enthusiasm of the audiences, and the huge New York poetry festival was actually only a media-visible manifestation of many grassroots events like the Newark reading.

At the grassroots level the Black Arts movement was a genuinely national movement. Chicago's Affro-Arts, housed in a refurbished movie theater, was directed by jazz musician Philip Cohran. A veteran of Sun Ra's Arkestra, Cohran was also connected with the avant-garde Association for the Advancement of Creative Musicians (AACM), whose performing unit was known as the Art Ensemble of Chicago. The young people who benefited from the Affro-Arts music workshops included Maurice White and others who later achieved popular success as Earth, Wind and Fire—a band that, without issuing manifestos, subtly disseminated Black Arts ideas more widely (Semmes 452–454, 458). In some ways Earth, Wind and Fire's musical approach achieved the synthesis of Rhythm and Blues and avant-garde jazz for which music critics of the Black Arts movement had begun calling in the late 1960s. Songs such as "Shining Star" and "Keep Your Head to the Sky" represent the positive (and sometimes numbingly didactic) community message that was de rigueur among grassroots Black Arts organizations. The iconography and costumes associated with the band served, as Paul Gilroy has perceived, "as an important means for communicating pan-African ideas in an inferential populist manner" (*Small Acts* 241).

In Brooklyn's Bedford-Stuyvesant neighborhood a coffeehouse called The East often featured poet Yusuf Rahman and filled every evening of the week with concerts, plays, poetry readings, lectures on history, and community organizing on local political issues. The East also published a magazine called *Black News* and was a center for visual artists.

Located in two renovated movie theaters and a warehouse building, Houston's Black Arts Center (BAC) was an artists' collective and a school: Loretta Devine and Mikell Pinckney taught drama; at various times Rahsaan Connell Linson, Thomas Meloncon, Harvey King, and I taught creative writing or organized literary events. In addition to music and dance workshops there was also Robert Gossett—a dauntingly versatile art teacher with an M.F.A. in painting who was an excellent woodcarver and also a competent ceramicist. Other people involved were Lloyd Choice, Neva Deary, Robert Becnel, and Mickey Leland (who started out as a poet and was later elected to Congress). Houston's BAC depended upon arts patronage and funding from antipoverty agencies. The result was a fragile, if not unwieldly, structure. As with similar groups in other southern cities, there was no real antagonism between the BAC and other local arts groups. Although the Black Arts Center stood firm in its aesthetic philosophy, it was simply another part of the city's cultural variety.

In Houston in the early 1970s, bars such as Sand Mountain and the Hard Thymes Soup Kitchen were venues for weekly poetry readings. These were extremely democratic events attended by a crowd that included a few settled southern beatniks (folks who knew Jon and "Gypsy" Lou Webb and the old school New Orleans bohemians), members of the Poetry Society of Texas, and kids who had missed the Summer of Love but were doing their damnedest to make up for it. Attending such an evening, one could hear a wide variety of oral presentation styles—and some of the most riveting were the performances of African American poets such as Edgar Jones.

A teenager who wandered into Houston's Black Arts Center in the early 1970s, Jarbari Aziz Ra was interested in poetry and music. He left Texas on a basketball scholarship and found his vocation in Chicago's Organization of Black American Culture (OBAC) poetry workshops.

Jarbari Aziz Ra's "A Writer's Statement" self-reflexively touches on the idea of "taking the poem off the page" as well as issues of censorship, the social utility of art, and the function of poetry itself:

unable to cry poems the broke
have no time, no ears, only eyes which become weary to glitter
seeing no merit in ink on poems i color black,

so if obscene today is also absurd, then let these pulse-beats be
hieroglyphic notes for your momma, i need not leave too many
hostile reasons for tomorrow's Black world as they shall have
    more
than enough, i will only tell them my words were Black Dancing
    Trees
sprouting branches dancing skyward hope filled to touch God's
    face
(*Vision* 22)

This poem perfectly demonstrates the method used in creating works
expressly designed for oral presentation. The poem's technique is, to
use Ra's own terminology, hieroglyphic. It is analogous to a jazz solo:
Ra's glossolalic rush of rhythm contains a bidialectal alternation of
slang and archly formal English as a vehicle for allusions and phrases
that invite several differing but simultaneous interpretations. Like the
musical ideas in a solo by Eric Dolphy or John Coltrane—as likely to
include eastern motifs or snatches of Tin Pan Alley standards—allusions slide one upon the other in a glissando, "faster than a bible shooting blanks / from a preacher's machine gun mouth," echoing the Dozens and Langston Hughes, Joyce Kilmer, and a motif that appears in
Harlem Renaissance poems such as Waring Cuney's "No Images" and
Gwendolyn Bennett's "To a Brown Girl." As his earlier references to the
stereotypical preacher and to "casper the ghost" indicate, Jarbari Aziz
Ra is concerned with managing audience response and is undoubtedly
aware of both the accessibility and possible triteness of these allusions.
Indeed, this performance may usefully illustrate Stephen E. Henderson's
suggestion that, in the "New Black poetry" as in jazz, "the use of stock
phrases, lines, and other elements is not limited . . . to Black folk song,
but the practice is so widespread in Black song that it must be considered an important part of the process of composition" ("Cliché" 534).

An instructive documentation of what some of these readings were
like is provided by Stanley Crouch's *Ain't No Ambulances for No Nigguhs
Tonight* (1972), issued as a long-playing record by Flying Dutchman, the
label that also featured albums by many avant-garde jazz musicians.
Recorded live on a college campus, most of the program consists of a
lengthy and tendentious lecture on black history, didactically espousing the same Afrocentricity which Crouch now rails against on network television. The whole performance is actually an energetic call-
and-response "teach-in" that includes Crouch's recitation of a few of

his poems. By the standards of the period, Crouch's poems are respectable products though not outstanding, and his polemics were precisely what the age (and audience) demanded. During these years even James Brown "interrupted" his concert to sit on the edge of the stage at the Apollo Theatre and rap for about ten minutes on self-esteem and civic responsibility. Afterward he would spring to his feet and electric slide into "There Was a Time." It is telling, though, that the proportion of polemical prose to poetry in Crouch's performance is almost exactly the reverse of what one experienced at a reading by Sonia Sanchez or Amiri Baraka.

Crouch's revolutionary rap is, literally, all talk. His performance should not be considered typical of all Black Arts poetry readings. Crouch has none of the ecstatic oracular sonority of Askia Muhammad Touré and none of the swooping lyrical invention of Kalamu ya Salaam, who does both words and music in his own voice in the manner of a cappella Delta blues.

In "Black Poetry—Where It's At" (1969) and other essays published in *Negro Digest* and widely discussed among poets, Carolyn Rodgers proposed new prosodic categories specific to black poetry. Her ideas were based on what Jerry W. Ward, Jr., has called "culturally anchored SPEECH ACTS and Reader/Hearer Response" ("Literacy and Criticism" 65). Stephen E. Henderson elaborated upon this work in his *Understanding the New Black Poetry* (1973). Henderson spends little time on the typographical strategies that poets devised. Instead he attempts to identify carefully the vernacular rhetorical devices that became more central to their work as the poets began to depend more and more on oral presentation in the ubiquitous and popular poetry readings of the Black Arts movement.

Typography, however, was important. In the work of the best poets, typography showed readers the mechanism of "taking the poem off the page." To anyone familiar with Olson's *Projective Verse,* the text of Sonia Sanchez's "Queens of the Universe" functions precisely as a *score.* The poem as printed indicates exactly how Sanchez performed it and how it should be read:

Sisters.
      i saw it to
               day. with
My own eyes.
         i mean like i

got on this bus
                      this cracker wuz
driving saw him look/
                            sniff a certain
smell and
                  turn his head in disgust.
sisters.
          that queen of sheba
                          perfume wuz
doooooooooing it.
                      strong/
                          blk/
                              smell that it
be. i mean
                it ain't delicate/stuff
sisters.
            when you put it on
                              u be knowing it on.
(186)

Similarly, Johari Amini's text (justified left and right, set in lower case) instructs and allows the reader to reproduce her breathless, exasperated voice:

we will be no generashuns to cum for blks r
killing r.selves did u hear bros. did u hear the
killings did u hear the sounds of the killing
the rapine of the urgency of r soil consuming
r own babies burned n the acid dri configura-
shuns of the cycles balancing did u hear. did u
hear. hear the sounds of the balancing &
checking off checking off erasing r existence
(4)

A poem such as Askia Muhammad Touré's "Transcendental Vision: Indigo" indicates through typography a sense of how the poet intends it to sound. The typographical method employed functions as punctuation and reveals the poem's grammatical structure:

And
          there
                      are
                          Whirlwinds embodied

in
   the
      minds of
Visionary griots/singing:
                  Tomorrow!
                     Tomorrow!) Language of
transcendental passion-flame
                  (spirit-tongue. Surreal
                        Saint-
inflected solo) motivating warrior
                  generations
            venerating liberation
                     in
         primary language of
                     forever.
(55)

Here Touré describes the aesthetic goal of Black Arts music and poetry: an attempt to recreate in modern modes the ancestral role of the African griots, the poets, musicians, and dancers whose songs record genealogies and the cosmologies of societies such as the Wolof and Mandinka. It is worth noting that most of those who have heard Touré read compare his style of declamation with that of the traditional black southern preachers, who also inspired James Weldon Johnson's *God's Trombones* (1927), one of the true masterpieces of the Harlem Renaissance and a pioneering attempt to present African American vernacular speech using the techniques of Modernist poetry.

Similar connections are illumined by Ugo Rubeo's analysis of Etheridge Knight's style. Attempting to decipher precisely how Knight's use of orality works, Rubeo identifies the poet's employment of biblical parataxis and folkloristic motifs in a manner that establishes a "double dialogue with past and present" working to reinforce African American folk traditions while also creating a "mutual, dialogical pattern of oral communication" with the audience present (278). A similar process has been identified in the traditional style of African American preaching. In a brilliant discussion of Johnson's *God's Trombones*, Dolan Hubbard has demonstrated the political implications of this type of speech performance:

As the freestanding spokesperson in the community, the preacher was one of the few members of the African American community who was permitted by the politically powerful white community

> to be educated, self-determined, and successful. The preacher is
> the transformational agent who walks the critical tightrope be-
> tween the sacred and the secular; his speech act (sermon) is the
> agent for historical location. As the tap root of black American
> discourse, the sermon historicizes the experience of blacks in
> America. The sermon as agent provides a link between genera-
> tions of black families and makes it possible for the culture of
> black America to be transmitted over time. (14)

Hubbard is clearly referring not merely to the *content* of the traditional
black sermon but to the performance as well. What Touré calls "Saint- /
inflected solo) motivating warrior / generations" identifies the interwoven allusions of the traditional sermon that moves from biblical
events to current events as if they were all occurring in the same moment, as indeed they are in the preacher's performative act. African
American artists did not need Bakhtinian terminology to understand
any of this performance, and the musicians admired by the Black Arts
poets were skilled practitioners of this technique. The bands of Charles
Mingus and Sun Ra—which included some of the most innovative so-
loists of the 1960s and 1970s—frequently quoted or evoked earlier jazz
styles ranging from Ferdinand "Jelly Roll" Morton to swing and bebop.
Mingus, in compositions titled "Folk Forms" and "Wednesday Night
Prayer Meeting," also created advanced jazz based on the choral music
of the black church.

One of the arguments for the African American writer's continuing
interest in the folk tradition is concisely stated by Calvin C. Hernton
in *The Sexual Mountain and Black Women Writers* (1990):

> Because people talk and sing before they write, poetry is the pro-
> toplasm of all literature and culture, it is the blood of all life. The
> folk always produce, preserve and transmit an entire [culture]
> based on speech and song. The oral culture of the folk is the foun-
> dation from which all writing springs. Poetry is the primal hu-
> man form, the instinctive response to human existence. The aes-
> thetics and the concerns of the written literature are contained in
> the oral nonliterate foundations of a people. (153)

This perception was central to the Black Arts movement and is, of course,
entirely consistent with a Herderian strategy—also employed by Alain
Locke during the 1920s Harlem Renaissance—based on the idea that

celebrating the folk tradition simultaneously builds group solidarity and protects the artist from the aesthetic distractions of novelty.

The German philosopher Johann Gottfried von Herder maintained that a national literature must be grounded in the characteristics of the folk. His influential thesis found adherents in Ralph Waldo Emerson and Walt Whitman and was much discussed by African American writers during both the Harlem Renaissance and the Black Arts movement. Bernard W. Bell's discussion of Herder in *The Folk Roots of Contemporary Afro-American Poetry* (1974)—first published in *Negro Digest*—helped stimulate a vigorous debate among the poets themselves concerning the use of folklore elements. A similar debate regarding Herderian concepts focused on Richard Wright's view of folk culture in *White Man, Listen!* (1957) and Baraka's essay "The Myth of a Negro Literature," published in his collection *Home: Social Essays* (1966). All of these conversations touched on the ideas that Locke had carefully put forward in *The New Negro* (1925).

In other words, the Black Arts movement's interest in African American vernacular was not a return to Dunbar's use of dialect. Dunbar, as William Stanley Braithwaite wrote in 1925, "expressed a folk temperament but not a race soul. Dunbar was the end of a regime and not the beginning of a tradition" ("The Negro in American Literature" 38). At work in the Black Arts movement, rather, was an extension of Langston Hughes's Modernist idiom and a similarly Modernist determination to avoid the clumsy artifice of traditional "poetic diction." Black Arts poets were in fact attempting to find the "race soul" and to set it singing.

The impulse toward what, in political terms, was called self-determination is evident in all aspects of this poetry. Linguist Geneva Smitherman notes that "it is in style, rather than in language *per se,* that the cultural distinctiveness of the Black idiom can be located." There were many attempts to capture this distinctiveness in sound and on paper. For example, writes Smitherman, "The phonological items employed by the poets represent their attempts to spell according to Black America's pronunciation" (86). As with nineteenth-century attempts to write dialect, similarly approached without formal linguistic study, Smitherman concludes that this effort and its orthographic renderings achieved "uneven success," but she adds, "We can certainly applaud their success in oral performance for here is where the full range of Black intonation patterns, tonal qualities, and other aspects of Black phonology in the poetry spring to life" (86). Short of employing the International Phonetic Alphabet or the musical stave, the most efficient way of indicating these phonological features in written discourse would be to discuss the *generic* modes most readily associated with them. This approach has been taken by insightful critics such as Smitherman, Carolyn Rodgers, and Stephen E. Henderson.

Citing traditional African American folk forms such as "the Dozens" and "Call-and-Response," Smitherman concludes, "The linguistic/stylistic machinery of this poetry is firmly located in the Black oral tradition, and the Black poet of today is forging a new art form steeped in the uniqueness of Black expressive style" (86). Smitherman's claim was certainly reasonable at the time that she composed her essay. Even if more modestly framed, it remains true: the Black Arts movement expanded the American poetic vocabulary, adding new, useful, and effective free verse options to those already available in American English.

III

If you could hear it you would make music too.
—Gwendolyn Brooks

Some critics have raised the legitimate issue of whether poetry that is so oral/performance oriented is properly represented in the literary canon offered to high school and college students. The approach taken by these critics to the question, however, often seems like special pleading. Sheet music is not a symphony; indeed, according to the protocols of jazz and the practice of an artist such as James Brown, even an audio recording of a "live" performance is not an adequate representation of the art; the art can properly be found only in the next concert.

We should also be careful about how we historicize such performance-oriented art, and in this instance Dunbar's poem "The Party" provides a useful pedagogical cue. While the narrator tells us you "ought to have been" there (Dunbar, *Complete Poems* 86), what listeners are really enjoying is the narrator's generous, delightful inventory and delicious recollection of what went on. The fun is in the present narrative, not in the past event. We all remember similar experiences. As kids, the schoolyard retelling of the Saturday matinee could often excite us as much as the movie itself had done. A kid who was really inventive not only told you the plot but impersonated the actors and simulated all the sound effects as well. Some of us, perhaps overly nostalgic, may argue that—for some movies—the schoolyard version is better than the director's cut.

We must eventually confront the different types of artistic reproduction that can be called "poetry" and a concern to identify the different skills they engage in both performer and audience. It is true, as Steven A. Athanases reports, that experiencing the voice and person of Gwendolyn Brooks allows one to grasp fully the artistry of her "Ballad of Pearlie Mae" (118). Yet he also notes that much the same effect can be achieved from a student's carefully prepared recitation of poems by Langston Hughes. To use a technological metaphor, we should be concerned equally with the technical quality of both *recording* and *playback*.

In the tradition of Carl Sandburg and Vachel Lindsay, Gwendolyn Brooks prefers a style of recitation based on the premise that poetry transcends ordinary speech. Her reading style is musical and carefully paced with subtle emphasis, but it does not resemble the fervent prayer style of the black church. Though the intervallic relationships of her words are less fluid than singing or chanting, Brooks does not read her poems in the rhythm or timbre of everyday speech. The relationship of her poems to these other forms of utterance is like the relationship of Tai Chi Chuan (a sort of aerobic exercise in slow motion) to the ordinary movement of our limbs. At the podium Gwendolyn Brooks is herself the "teller" she asks for in "The Womanhood" (1949)—the voice that recounts the world's realities but does so in a tone that ultimately confirms:

Behold,
Love's true, and triumphs; and God's actual
(*Selected Poems* 64)

"The audiences for black poetry of the sixties and seventies were already conditioned to the style and delivery that the poets exploited," noted Stephen E. Henderson ("Worrying the Line" 63). But while it became clear that, as Smitherman put it, "the people's lingo is the poet's lingo, too" (81), it may be suggested that the reason the poets chose to adopt the vernacular is multifaceted.

The poetry of the Black Arts movement was shaped by the context of oral presentation precisely because the highly politicized aesthetic devised by the poets decreed that it should be. Fully cognizant of the implications of this decision, the poets must ultimately be held responsible for their written texts as well as their performances. Either the poems on paper succeed or they don't—and if they don't, it is the poet's fault. To suggest, as some critics have, that the Black Arts poets—as an entire school—were necessarily inadequate in the written transcription of their own work is both inaccurate and insulting. The alphabetic conventions according to which poetry in English is recorded on paper are not imposed externally but have been subject to continuous revision by the poets themselves for centuries. As a result, the properly trained reader should be able to handle the typeset transcriptions of George Herbert and Johari Amini, or Will Carleton and Haki R. Madhubuti, with equal facility.

All poetry is incomplete until it is read aloud. The idea that sophisticated readers can simulate this experience mentally is, of course, a long-standing article of faith that has been systematically assaulted by subsequent technological efforts to construct "virtual" realities. Nevertheless, the poem printed on the page is effective when it (1) functions as a memorandum to excite the reader's recall of a previous performance or (2) serves as a score for future vocal reproduction. If the poet has done the job of preparing that alphabetic transcription well, she can be sure that the poem will live.

During a period when much American poetry seemed the limited province of apprentices in writing workshops, or a type of specialized do-it-yourself psychotherapy, one indisputable fact is that the poetry of the Black Arts movement was *popular*. It reached a visible and enthusiastic audience even if the movement's leaders tended to exaggerate the proletarian profile of their mostly collegiate following. "Granted," Mance Williams wrote, "many of these radicalized college students came from grass-roots environments; but the degree to which they epitomized 'the people' is somewhat minimal" (154). If, however, one looks backward to consider the hopeful strivings of those audiences' foreparents, it is hard to imagine that Frances E. W. Harper, for one, would have had a problem with that.

9

At the Edge of the Twenty-first Century

A free mind has no need to scream
A free mind is ready for other things
—Mari Evans

"May you live in interesting times" is an ancient and unremovable curse. The poet whose times provide something important to write about is fortunate; one who finds an audience willing to listen, even more so. African American poets have long enjoyed—or been cursed by—the role of spokesperson for a race. There is no indication, however, that this situation will change. Writing in the *New York Age* in 1918, James Weldon Johnson declared that only great literature makes the world recognize that a race is great. This redemptive idea powered both the Harlem Renaissance of the 1920s and the Black Arts movement of the 1960s.

Both movements—and the major writers who found voice in the 1930s and 1940s—erased all doubt of African American agency, but the integrationist thrust of one effort balanced the separatist impulses of the other and, coupled with the nation's persistent view of African Americans as *Other,* forces contemporary poets to address many of the same issues that confronted Dunbar at the turn of the century. And as Dunbar well understood, there is also the challenge of avoiding despair in the struggle with the American racial dilemma.

The younger writers of the 1990s demonstrate a keen awareness of their role as inheritors of a historic and literary legacy. "We are the lost-found generation; the children of Malcolm and Martin and Fannie Lou and Ella," write Kevin Powell and Ras Baraka in their introduction to *In the Tradition: An Anthology of Young Black Writers* (xiv). While it is clear that a century of African American struggle for respect and rights is important, these writers also find that the very success of the civil rights movement—and an energetic right-wing reaction to this success—resulted in new personal and societal anxieties that have yet to be as efficiently diagnosed as the "double consciousness" about which W. E. B. Du Bois first wrote in 1897. Kevin Powell, in his poem "Mental Terrorism," describes a society in which conspicuous brand-name consumption becomes the sole index of upward mobility while government statistics document an alarmingly widening gap between income groups. Facing this postmodern American dilemma, Powell cries:

all i want is the opportunity to have an
    opportunity
where does one run to when stuck in the
    promised land?
(263)

Erica Hunt views even the promise with skepticism and has, in both prose and poetry, issued an eloquent Marxist-based critique of the omnivorous "New World Order." "Dominant modes of discourse," Hunt writes, "the language of ordinary life or of rationality, of moral management of the science of the state, the hectoring threats of the press and the media, use convention and label to bind and organize us" (199). She argues for a radical reorganization because the effects of society's conventional definitions can be devastating: "We act in an echo chamber of the features ascribed to us, Black woman, daughter, mother, writer, worker and so on. And the social roles and the appropriate actions are similarly inscribed, dwell with us as statistical likelihoods, cast us as queen or servant, heroic or silent, doer or done unto" (200). Hunt insists that a useful function of innovative fiction and poetry would be to undermine demeaning stereotypes and to disrupt the dominating language of oppressive social control by "creating opinion and critique to supply a multiple focus and means of opposition" (211).

Hunt's poetry is a brilliant enactment of what she knows, not theory or polemic chopped up into lines. *Arcade* (1996), beautifully illustrated with Alison Saar's woodcuts, underscores the points that Hunt has made in her critical essays. In a democratic society addled by advertising, where the public good is secondary to access to consumer goods, "we have the illusion of doing what we want" (28). Reality, however, is undone:

> To be sure snacks kill the appetite.
> The feeling of drama kills the feeling of action.
> The feeling of the surreal sells perfume.
> (22)

Even our personal and collective attempts at serious discourse are derailed:

> race talk
> erases race
> chases thought
> down disowned
> alleys of envied
> sports figures
> divides eros from
> commotion where
> narcissus sits
> cooling his heels
> (24)

Hunt's allusion links the pop psychology understanding of narcissism with the Greek myth, thus carefully reinscribing the word's etymology: we live in a society narcotized by the disintegration of linguistic precision. We certainly cannot solve a problem if we are unable to say what it is.

Hunt's poetry is neither primarily focused on race nor limited to complaint; often she employs a personalized surrealism and deceptively simplified vocabulary to explain how we can heal ourselves—individually and as a community. As she puts it in "Science of the Concrete":

> people "make"
> the people around us
> and they write
> to write
> the reader
> out of retreat
> out of distant austerity
> concealing this same
> fragile activity

people make
each other
part by part
then whole
into whole
(32)

While Hunt's analysis is important, it is not shared by many of those involved in the strong communities of poets that have appeared in various parts of the country. These groups included the Carolina African American Writers' Collective in Durham, the Dark Room Collective in Boston, the Eugene B. Redmond Writers Club in East St. Louis, and writers associated with the Nuyorican Poets Café and the St. Marks Poetry Project in New York. Some of these writers and groups adhere to theoretical ideas explored during the Black Arts movement; others seem more directly involved with trends seen in 1990s popular culture. Unlike the nationwide artistic activity inspired by the "New Negro" Renaissance in the 1920s, all of this talent and energy has not been either a directed movement or a unified one.

There was a similarly widespread and mostly innovative swell of activity in the late 1940s and 1950s, documented in Eugene B. Redmond's *Drumvoices* and more recently in Aldon Lynn Nielsen's *Black Chant: Languages of African American Postmodernism*. In some ways, though, this activity was "invisible"—when the writers did achieve visibility, they did so under the name of the Black Arts movement or as "the New Black poetry"—a more neutral term employed in anthologies edited by Clarence Major and Stephen E. Henderson.

In fact, I would suggest that this level of creative activity is the natural order of things, as is its invisibility to academic critics. Visibility depends upon the emergence of an aesthetic or political program that provides a convenient *rubric* or perhaps a fortunate commercial interest. The emergence of the Black Arts movement manifestos in 1965 and at the 1966 Fisk University Writers' Conference provided such a rubric. And it is also clear that those writers became visible in part because of *Negro Digest* (later titled *Black World*), a journal published by Johnson Publications and edited by Hoyt Fuller, which enjoyed a huge national circulation in the mid-1960s.

It is interesting to explore the extent to which the more commercialized productions of popular culture in the 1990s are reflected in the writing and artistic perspective of the younger writers, not to mention, of course, the philosophical outlook presented. As long ago as 1988, critic Greg Tate pointed to rap music's postmodern "cross-referential complexity" and demanded critical respect for what the style represents. "Hiphop being more than a cargo cult of the microchip," he argued, "it deserves being debated on more elevated terms than as jazz's burden or successor" (Tate 123). A recording industry novelty that has lasted two decades, rap unfortunately became stuck in postures of adolescent fury and—too often—a defiant definition of race consciousness absurdly based on lumpenproletariat stereotypes. Nevertheless, its vibrant energy—and perhaps also its cynicism—has impacted all of the nation's artists in the past decade.

If an almost immediate and phenomenally successful commercialization explains hiphop music's failure to fulfill the political and aesthetic expectations of early commentators, it is important to understand why—especially because, as Askia Muhammad Touré asserted in 1969, music is "the root or core of African American culture" ("Crisis in Black Culture" 31). During the Harlem Renaissance, as Winston Napier reminds us, Alain Locke "focused on black artistic culture as the means by which black self-image was to be reinterpreted and reshaped." Promoting the debut of Countee Cullen, Langston Hughes, and others in *The New Negro* (1925), Locke declared: "Here we have Negro youth with arresting visions and vibrant prophecies; forecasting in the mirror of art what we must see and recognize in the streets of reality tomorrow" (Napier 94–95).

Black Arts theorists in the 1960s vociferously distanced themselves from the integrationist motives of the Harlem Renaissance, but Larry Neal's call for a movement based on "the useable elements of Third World culture" that would also "address itself to the mythology and the life-style of the Black community" is basically a more militant restatement of Locke's aesthetic position (Neal 30, 39). The run-of-the-mill hiphop productions of the mid-1990s, however, reversed the ideas of Alain Locke and Larry Neal. Replacing artistic vision with an unimaginative notion of racial and class authenticity—"keeping it real"—many of these performers could say at best, if they were honest, "Look what I found in the street."

If the more creative "hiphop aesthetic" promoted by Greg Tate—described to some extent in Dick Hebdige's *Cut 'n Mix* (1987) and Tricia Rose's informative *Black Noise* (1993)—does exist, its most fully realized literary application may be found in Paul Beatty's work. Writing in open form that follows the principles described in Charles Olson's *Pro-*

jective Verse, in poems that recall Allen Ginsberg's bardic manner, Beatty captures the vibes of his rap music contemporaries on the printed page. "Big Bowls of Cereal" in Beatty's collection *Joker, Joker, Deuce* (1994) is a gently self-mocking B-boy's autobiography:

> with absolutely no regrets
> i spent the summer of my discontent
> in the corner arcade
>
> bent over the pinball machine
> nine extra balls and a line of niggas
>> sucking they teeth
>>> waitin for me to get off
>
> (83)

Such quotidian details of inner-city or suburban teenage life may not seem important to many readers, but Beatty's depiction is certainly accurate. Such accuracy makes Beatty's picture authentic, not attitude. "That's Not in My Job Description," on the other hand, is a cleverly signifying commentary on the one group in America that—until recently—eluded categorization as "ethnic":

> cross my sneakers on the desk
> threaten to call my union rep
> if these fools
>
>> dont stop lookin at me crazy
>> whisperin lazy
>> under their breath
>
> but during my siesta
> i eavesdrop on societys best
>
>> imagine im a distinguished ethnographer
>
> on the black pbs
> talkin with a british lisp
> in front of a bookshelf
>
> welcome to *In Search of*
> today we pursue The Elusive True Nature of Whitey
>
>> notice as
>> our cameras
>> zoom in on

a pin-striped pack of business school well groomed brooks brother
     smoothies
   encamped around a water cooler jostling for room in their
natural
     habitat
(11)

The good news is that Paul Beatty refuses to take himself too seriously; the bad news is that you know what this means in terms of his opinion of other people. His novel *The White Boy Shuffle* (1996) shows him to be a fine social satirist. The book is a postmodern bildungsroman, a witty account of learning the unspoken protocol of race and navigating the shoals of identity. Beatty's protagonist, an inner-city basketball star improbably named Gunnar Kaufman, must continually rediscover himself among "white kids who were embarrassingly like myself but with whom somehow I had nothing in common" (179).

In *The White Boy Shuffle,* Afrocentricity and self-identity are a helically plaited lifeline. Here "authenticity" is less important than simple sanity—which must be rescued from a living legacy of societal hostility and self-hatred, from a lopsidedly affluent society's debris of stereotypes and brand names. A funny book with a grim message, Beatty's view of how Martin Luther King's dream has become a nightmare offers an ultimately frightening discussion of how "black America has relinquished its needs in a world where expectations are illusion" (225). American society as depicted in Beatty's novel is not much different from the society shown in Ralph Ellison's *Invisible Man* (1952); it is filled with the same prejudices, dangers, toils, and snares. The protagonists of these novels are, however, quite different—perhaps because Beatty's Gunnar Kaufman has read Ellison's book. Who knows what strengths may be discovered by those who read Beatty's.

Somewhat different explorations of the hip-hop vocabulary have been pursued by poets such as Tracie Morris and Willie Perdomo. Morris has performed on the nationwide Lollapalooza concert tour, and one of her recordings has been chosen as a score for a ballet by choreographer Trey McIntyre. The more literary-oriented Perdomo is also an effective performance artist, but that fact does not diminish the strength of his work on the printed page.

A serious and eloquent elegist, Willie Perdomo employs bright rhythmic language to depict the harsh poverty and spiritual despair that can be found in the inner city—a Harlem neighborhood where he finds numerous examples of love and sacrifice, meanness and opportunism. Willie Perdomo's 1990s Harlem is much more dangerous than Langston's; in fact, it's lethal; Fenton Johnson's street peddler's cry has been replaced by the pseudo-Rap "hustler's song" of the streetcorner drug slinger. Perdomo knows the difference between an alert political consciousness and the compensatory nostalgia for degradation that—from Zora Neale Hurston to Clifton L. Taulbert to the stand-up comedians on cable television—too often substitutes for ethnic "authenticity." The *barrio* is a site of struggle on many levels, but the experience of living in a ghetto is only useful if it is clearly understood. Perdomo's work aims at achieving such clarity by undoing the code of nostalgia. In "Nuyorican School of Poetry," he writes:

> Looking for happy endings
> we came
> over-extended familias
> with secrets named
> sofrito y salsa
> that made broken homes smell
> good from the outside
> (*Where a Nickel* 41)

Perdomo's collection *Where a Nickel Costs a Dime* (1996) suggests that even if racism and alienation are endurable, the illegal narcotics traffic is the neighborhood's true curse. Perdomo is quite aware of the brutal ironies generated by a hypocritical society where the "underground economy" mirrors the rapaciousness of Wall Street (where the drug money is laundered). As he puts it in "Save the Youth":

> I can only speak about
> the youth
> growing on the corners
> of my block
> like weeds in an
> abandoned lot
>
> They stay up
> way past bed time
> selling brand-name poison
> keeping the economy healthy
> and making new rules

Just like the men
who built
this country
(*Where a Nickel* 48)

Tuned by the fiery competition of Nuyorican Poets Café "open mike" nights, Perdomo's performance—a brilliantly musical bilingual vernacular fully rooted in the syncopated tradition of Langston Hughes, Calvin C. Hernton, and David Henderson—is such an important aspect of his work that his book is accompanied by an hour-long compact disc including his recitation of all thirty-three poems. The CD vividly demonstrates Perdomo's ability to "go from a hip-hop strut to a blues rut" (27) without missing a beat.

Although the two artists never actually met, Kevin Young's ekphrastic poems achieve an unusually vibrant collaboration with Jean-Michel Basquiat's paintings. *Two Cents: Works on Paper by Jean-Michel Basquiat and Poetry by Kevin Young,* an extraordinary museum exhibit organized by Amy Cappellazzo at Miami's Wolfson Galleries, offered two young black men's reflections on the need to articulate their presence. Young's ventriloquial "Jack Johnson" delineates the inner dimensions of an iconic figure—a heavyweight champion who found life in a racist society his toughest challenger. As a poet, Young is as dazzlingly agile and as hard-hitting as Jack Johnson in his prime and surer. In one powerful sequence, hated and harassed by the law for his militancy, Johnson agrees to take a dive in a Havana bout. It is the price he must pay:

Down, I counted too, blessings
instead of bets. Stretched
there on the canvas

—a masterpiece—stripped
of my title, primed
to return to the States.
("Jack Johnson" 42)

In another example of what Tate called "cross-referential complexity," Young also responds to African American music in a refreshing way. The inventive irreverence Young shares with Basquiat is evident as well in "Everywhere Is Out of Town," a clever and gentle lampoon of the jazz hagiographies churned out by poets during the 1960s and the over-extended culinary metaphors favored by pop music journalists as far back as the 1940s. The poem is cuttingly hilarious as Young describes a "leftover band" still out on the road:

Afros. Horns slung
round necks like giant
ladles. Dressing. Uptempo
blessing: *Good God*

everywhere! We bow our
heads before the band
lets loose. Drummer unknown
as a hymn's third verse.
(12)

Similarly, Thomas Sayers Ellis has found subject matter and structure in the dadaistic revisionism of George Clinton's Parliament/Funkadelics—a band that ludicrously extends, celebrates, and plays havoc with the most hallowed traditions of African American music. It is not possible to appreciate Clinton's music fully without a knowledge of those traditions, and the same is true regarding the collages of Romare Bearden or the writings of Ralph Ellison or August Wilson. Ellis, of course, knows the key. His poems, while he starts with Clinton, extend the useful referentiality of the Sorrow Songs still further. This music is not John Coltrane's, yet Ellis finds a similar depth of meaning in it:

Legs for rockets, bones separating like boosters.
Guitar: a lover, slanted in a hug, plucked,
Scratched, strummed. You will raise
One finger, on the one, for the one,
Then lift like a chorus of neck veins,
All six strings offering redemption.
(Ellis 72)

That poets have not, of course, abandoned jazz is evident in works such as Hermine Pinson's *Mama Yetta* (1999); Bill Harris's *Yardbird Suite* (1997), a dramatic Tolson-influenced "biopoem" on saxophonist Charles Parker; and Nathaniel Mackey's multivolume *Song of the Andoumboulou*, the most recent installments of which include *Whatsaid Serif* (1998) and the compact disc *Strick: Song of the Andoumboulou 16–25* (1995), on which Mackey's recitation is splendidly accompanied by flutist Hafez Modirzadeh and percussionist Royal Hartigan.

Patricia Spears Jones is a poet whose work also developed structurally from the music's foundational traditions. Armed with the brightness of a "down home" Arkansas childhood, a top-notch education, and an apprenticeship in the vortex of the St. Marks Poetry Project, Jones boasted a distinctive and excitingly personal style that earned her a fellowship from the National Endowment for the Arts. In her collection *The Weather That Kills* (1995), her observations are both urbane and compassionate. A daughter's loving memory—the calculus of closeness and estrangement that none of us can ever quite master—informs "In My Father's House." The poem begins:

> There was little conversation and too much
> store-bought food. Across the dull green carpet,
> my father and I tried to make a language
> as common to us as our names
> (9)

Each tenderly unfolded detail in this poem amplifies its predecessor as carefully and precisely as a blues lyric and with the same deceptively casual tone. Unlike some of the experiments of the 1960s, or even the earlier explorations of Langston Hughes and Sterling A. Brown, Jones does not attempt to mimic the sound or rhythms of African American music. Instead, she builds her work on a perfect understanding of the logic of black music and reshapes this structure to carry her own exquisite melodies. The closing lines of "Rhythm and Blues Two" display Jones at her best, her voice carrying a soulful complexity learned from Billie Holiday and Dinah Washington:

> If I toss my tears across the pillow
> or call my girlfriends and complain
> how will I accept the beauty of this pain?
> I sit and drink my coffee and realize
> that just like Otis Redding what I want is
> "Security." But fool for wanton kisses
> leaves me waiting out the morning.
> Angry with the light.
> (65)

The power of the poem lies in Jones's perfect sense of the line and its possibilities, her control of consonance that is subtle but effective. As with the meaningful pause created by the line break in "There was too little conversation and too much / store-bought food," an enjambment that immediately falls apart on the second reading of the poem, Jones creates unexpected tension by balancing the rhymes "complain," "pain," and "what I want is": "wanton kisses" with an aural precision that grows more delightful each time one reads her work.

As attractive as her prosodic versatility is, Patricia Spears Jones's soft-spoken wisdom makes her poetry most memorable. She knows that, on some days, "The oops of life like a stadium wave / wraps the planet" (59). As she puts it in "A Question of the Weather":

We humans sweat. We try
to make contact.

She adds—just to keep things in perspective—

And every dance I know itches my feet.
(40)

Harryette Mullen's early poems reveal an extraordinary attentiveness to the way words work: their power to soothe or hurt, to encourage, or to deny the sharing of thoughts and emotions. Like Curtis Mayfield and Marvin Gaye, Mullen was able to set overheard everyday phrases into a music that reminds us of just how beautifully clever, and sometimes profound, ordinary language can be. "Momma Sayings," a deservedly much anthologized poem, achieves universality through specificity:

she trained us not to leave lights on

"all over the house,"
because "electricity costs money—
so please turn the light off when you leave a room
and take the white man's hand out of my pocket."
. . . .
Momma had lots of words for us,
her never quite perfect daughters,
the two brown pennies
she wanted to polish
so we'd shine like dimes.
(531–532)

Raised in Fort Worth, Texas, Mullen participated in Austin's vibrant and tentatively multicultural artistic scene during her college years. Later, she fine-tuned her art while working in the state's Poets-in-the-Schools program and producing the works collected in her first book *Tree Tall Woman* (1981). A fellowship from the Texas Institute of Letters

8. Harryette Mullen. Photograph by Judy Natal.

allowed her time to write uninterruptedly while living at the isolated Dobie Paisano ranch. Mullen's subsequent work in *Trimmings* (1991) and *S*PeRM**K*T* (1992) included prose poems and prosodic experiments that reflect a serious study of Gertrude Stein and other Modernists. *Muse and Drudge* (1995), an impressive book-length poem written in sparkling quatrains, proclaims a feminist challenge, immediately disturbing our notions regarding poetry and 2,000 years of civilization.

While the title *Muse and Drudge* refers to the seemingly contradictory stereotypes that limit female self-expression, the phrase's dramatically polarized vowel sounds form the keynote of Mullen's delightfully complex and carefully controlled poetic diction. Everything is open to creative questioning here, even English syntax. Allusions to popular culture, African American folklore, and poststructuralist philosophy are handled with the fluent rapidity of jazz improvisation, yet one is aware—as in listening to jazz—that the text has an author, a ventriloquist adept at reproducing a collectivity of voices in each deceptively simple statement. This is the art of Billie Holiday, at once intimate and impossibly distant. Holiday was a consummate jazz artist, writes Robert O'Meally, because "she listened with intimate understanding to the other players. When her turn came, she improvised comments (with her music) on their musical statements, weaving into a piece's fabric her own musical colors and rhythms." The effect of this charged, intense level of communication was that Holiday "lured the listener into her tight emotional orbit" (O'Meally 27, 30, 33).

If Frank O'Hara's impeccably understated elegy "The Day Lady Died" (1959) allows Holiday to win her own immortality, Mullen's evocation of her in *Muse and Drudge* employs a kind of cinematic cubism that simultaneously insists on Holiday's materiality and recites transcendent attributes in the manner of West African oriki:

dark-eyed flower
knuckling under
lift a finger for her
give the lady a hand

not her hard life
cramped hot stages
only her approach
ahead of the beat

live in easy virtue
where days behaving send
her dance and her body
forward to a new air dress
(*Muse and Drudge* 20)

Speaking to Calvin Bedient about *Muse and Drudge,* Mullen acknowledged her use of conventions derived from the blues: "Any time 'I' is used in this poem, it's practically always quotation: it comes from a blues song, or it comes from a line of Sappho; it comes from—wherever it comes from. The 'I' in the poem is almost always someone other than myself, and often it's an anonymous 'I,' a generic 'I,' a traditional 'I,' the 'I' of the blues, that person who in reference to any individual experience also speaks for the tradition, speaks for the community" (Bedient 653). Yet she also insists that the poem veers away from the orality seen by some critics as the signal characteristic of recent African American poetry. Mullen states that "the written tradition is a rich reservoir of possibility. I feel myself wanting, especially in this poem, to use both possibilities" (Bedient 667).

Tolson's *Harlem Gallery* (1965) is one of Mullen's models because of what she calls its "dense allusiveness"—a hint to readers about how to approach *Muse and Drudge*. As she puts it, "one of the questions or problems for me is the kind of aesthetic turf that exists for black writers, and how black writers who do not fit into the notion of what black turf is can sometimes be overlooked or forgotten or go unread, because people require interpretive strategies related to their notion of the black canon, or what it means to be outside of the black canon" (Bedient 667).

Mullen's work—brilliant and bluesy, demanding (like Tolson's) to be read aloud by anyone who wants really to appreciate it or even to understand it—is a forceful gesture intended to encourage a more serious investigation of the diverse linguistic strategies that have always been part of African American expression. Mullen's methods include Joycean wordplay, Oulipo structures, and strategies of folk wit. A recent poem recalls an antebellum African American courting game that was often lampooned on the minstrel stage. "Any Lit" (1998) explores tradition through improvisation:

> You are a ukulele beyond my microphone
> You are a Yukon beyond my Micronesia
> You are a union beyond my meiosis
> You are a unicycle beyond my migration
> (48)

and so on—until we recognize that what had been dismissed as malapropism was, in fact, playful invention. In Mullen's work even silliness might serve a serious purpose.

The wordplay in her title "Any Lit" offers a diagrammatic clue to Mullen's methods of composition, while the poem itself subtly recalls the acrostics of the slave poet George Moses Horton (1797–1883). Is Mullen's poem an avant-garde gesture infused with tradition or an ancient gambit that seems new because it has been forgotten for so long? In the 1830s Horton created what Joan R. Sherman calls "formulaic" productions made to order for the young white gentlemen of Chapel Hill; love poems that illustrated, she says, "the flaws of nineteenth-century poetry: intellectual and emotional banality" (*The Black Bard* 43, 38). But that was what his customers wanted. While nodding to Horton's acrostics, Mullen's poem actually explores another tradition of "courtship's ways and games," improvising on a folkloric theme that fascinated Zora Neale Hurston (Hemenway 154–156; see also Hurston and Hughes, *Mule Bone*). Hurston viewed such fancy talk as an expression of an innate African American élan vital that she termed "the will to adorn" ("Characteristics" 50–51). What Hurston presented as folklore had, in Horton's day, also inspired derisive minstrel skits.

Mullen was aware of this complex history. Her parodic performance in "Any Lit" highlights the *agency* of speech and illumines J. Saunders Redding's explanation of why even black audiences tolerated the comedic defamation in minstrelsy. "This audience's amusement," contended Redding, "derived from its knowledge that whites were incapable of perceiving the essence and the spirit which underlay the dialect" ("James Weldon Johnson" 206). Her unique poetic stance allows Mullen to explore what Redding called a peculiarly African American "ironic perception" and, at the same time, to demonstrate its continuing relevance.

In *Negro Slave Songs in the United States* (1953), Miles Mark Fisher recounted the genesis of one of the most beautiful of the Sorrow Songs: "In a song called 'Deep River' that originated in Guilford County, North Carolina . . . a conservative slave told his Quaker benefactor that he wanted to 'cross over' to Africa, the home of camp meetings. He said this more than the usual three times because the Quakers, as they said, had difficulty in placing confidence in the ambiguous speech of Negroes" (41). Of course, one can never be certain how much even a sympathetic listener understands. It may, in fact, be true that the singer who sang, "Deep river, my home is over Jordan," was referring to his longing for an African birthplace. It is also quite obvious, as Amiri Baraka pointed out in *Blues People* (1963), that this song—which Fisher dates to 1825—and all of the other spirituals and blues songs, could not have existed until English had become the language of the African people in North America. Yet as we know, this is not the entire story. The dilemma that has faced the African American artist was poignantly expressed in Countee Cullen's magnificent lines

> Yet do I marvel at this curious thing:
> To make a poet black, and bid him sing!
> (915)

As we have seen in our discussion of poets who have devised and employed a Modernist idiom, there is another way to ask Cullen's question. What does one do with a flawed language—especially if it is your own?

In some ways, this question is posed to those who attempt criticism of the contribution of any African American artist to American culture. For example, should the insights afforded us by postcolonial studies be applied to these artists or to the United States? Or both? Would such an inquiry be more distracting than useful?

If this remains a problem for the critic, it is one that African American artists—especially poets and musicians—seem to have confronted and sometimes to have resolved. Clearly, though, the process of resolution is complex. The task facing the artists has involved more than assimilation of the trends of American society or resistance to them—whether this society was viciously segregated, nominally integrated, or a maelstrom of conflicting values and interests. The African American poet in the twentieth century has maintained a vision rooted in an Afrocentric knowledge of self and community. In *Does Your House Have Lions?* (1997), a breathtakingly elegant long poem written in rime royal, Sonia Sanchez presents the voice of an ancestor asking

> have you prepared a place of honor for me?
> have you recalled us from death?
> where is the mmenson to state our history?
> (45)

The answer, one hopes, is that the mmenson—Africa's ceremonial ivory horns, called oliphants by European traders in the Renaissance—have been crafted anew in the words of poets as careful of their ancient racial heritage as of the possibilities offered by their mastery of modern skills.

African American poets have, above all, been conscious of a mission and have been convinced that poetry can, in fact, make things happen. In the best instances, however, the effort has entailed more than facile pronouncement. These poets have understood that gauging the space between symbol and reality is not always easy but is always crucial.

The parallel and sometimes interflowing streams of Modernism and Afrocentric thought have nourished—and sometimes overwhelmed—twentieth-century African American poets. The Afrocentric perspective has supplied the poets with a sense of mission—awareness of "a new day"—while Modernism suggested a certain skepticism. Yet the poets have shared an ambition toward prophetic statement best and most boldly expressed in Tolson's *Libretto for the Republic of Liberia*, the capstone of a 150-year-old tradition. The acceptance of poetry as a vocation was eloquently phrased, in her characteristically modest majesty, by Margaret Walker. The African American poet's task, she told Joanne V. Gabbin, is "to write about the future that you do not see, but that is evident in everything you do and hear" (Gabbin, "Margaret Walker" vi).

The Afrocentric sense of identity and diasporic consciousness, of perseverance during almost four centuries of catastrophe, of resistance to despair, continues to inform the poets' vision. A recent work by Sekou Sundiata illustrates this continuing tradition. The poem recounts taking children to view the Harlem entourage of Nelson Mandela, an activist lawyer who spent two decades as a political prisoner and who later became the first black to be elected president of South Africa. An iconic figure and source of pride for people of African descent around the world, Mandela focuses Sundiata's attention and also allows him to impart a vital lesson:

See, there he is, we point you out for the children
but all they see is us
pointing through the crowd to a place they have to
    reach up to.
See see and see, the look on our faces the only vision
that finally counts.
(282–283)

The variety of African American poetic voices suggests that critics should approach their temptation toward systematic philosophy and prescriptive sociology warily. While we must attend to the fact that—as far as the poets themselves are concerned—the complex oeuvre of Melvin B. Tolson makes him the grand precursor of this era, it is also clear that younger poets demonstrate an energetic diversity within the African American intellectual tradition that has often been ignored or suppressed in earlier decades. Furthermore, we are long past the day of the quota system that limited African American literature to *the* one black writer of the decade. Whether in the genre of poetry—serious or popular—the novel, or the deeply contemplated and finely written social analysis, the numbers of talented writers at work now (and the availability of various means of publication and distribution) preclude a return to that situation.

Whether any of these writers—or any writers—have something to say that will save us is, of course, a matter that *you* alone can decide.

Bibliography

Abbott, Craig S. "Magazine Verse and Modernism: Braithwaite's Anthologies." *Journal of Modern Literature* 19 (Summer 1994): 151–159.

"Aboriginal Poetry." *Poetry: A Magazine of Verse* 9 (February 1917): 251–256.

Adas, Michael. *Machines as the Measure of Men: Science Technology and Ideologies of Western Dominance*. Ithaca: Cornell University Press, 1989.

Advertisement for the *Champion Magazine. Champion Magazine: A Monthly Survey of Negro Achievement* 1 (April 1917): 420.

Advertisement for the *Champion Magazine. Crisis* 13 (January 1917): 152.

Agar, Herbert, and Allen Tate, eds. *Who Owns America?* Boston: Houghton Mifflin, 1936.

Aiken, Conrad. "Prizes and Anthologies." *Poetry Journal* 4 (November 1915): 95–100.

——. *Skepticisms: Notes on Contemporary Poetry*. 1919. Freeport, N.Y.: Books for Libraries Press, 1967.

——, ed. *Modern American Poets*. London: Martin Secker, 1922.

Aly, Lucile F. *John G. Neihardt: A Critical Biography*. Amsterdam: Rodopi, 1977.

American Poetry: The Nineteenth Century. 2 vols. New York: Library of America, 1993.

Amini, Johari. "Untitled (in Commemoration of the Blk/Family)." In *Black Spirits: A Festival of New Black Poets in America*. Edited by Woodie King, Jr. New York: Vintage, 1972.

Anderson, Sherwood. "Song of the Soul of Chicago." *Others: Magazine of the New Verse* 4 (June 1917): 3–4.

——. *Southern Odyssey: Selected Writings*. Edited by Welford Dunaway Taylor and Charles E. Modlin. Athens: University of Georgia Press, 1997.

Anthony, David H. "Max Yergan in South Africa: From Evangelical Pan-Africanist to Revolutionary Socialist." *African Studies Review* 34 (September 1991): 27–55.

Arberry, A. J. *Arabic Poetry: A Primer for Students*. Cambridge: Cambridge University Press, 1965.

Asante, Molefi Kete. *The Afrocentric Idea*. Philadelphia: Temple University Press, 1987.

Athanases, Steven A. "When Print Alone Fails Poetry: Performance as a Contingency of Literary Value." *Text and Performance Quarterly* 11 (April 1991): 116–127.

Attorney General A. Mitchell Palmer on Charges Made Against the Department of

Justice by Louis F. Post and others. Hearings. Committee on Rules, House of Representatives. 66th Cong., 2d sess. 2 vols. Washington, D.C.: Government Printing Office, 1920.

Aubert, Alvin. *Against the Blues.* Detroit: Broadside Press, 1972.

———. *Feeling Through.* Greenfield Center, N.Y.: Greenfield Review Press, 1975.

———. *Harlem Wrestler and Other Poems.* East Lansing: Michigan State University Press, 1995.

———. *If Winter Come: Collected Poems, 1967–1992.* Pittsburgh: Carnegie Mellon University Press, 1994.

———. "On Seeing the U. N. Building, New York." *Phylon: The Atlanta University Review* 17 (1956): 146.

Azikiwe, Nnamdi. *Liberia in World Politics.* 1934. Westport, Conn.: Negro Universities Press, 1970.

———. *My Odyssey: An Autobiography.* New York: Praeger, 1970.

Bacote, Clarence A. *The Story of Atlanta University: A Century of Service.* Atlanta: Atlanta University, 1969.

Badaracco, Claire. "Writers and Their Public Appeal: Harriet Monroe's Publicity Techniques." *American Literary Realism* 23 (Winter 1991): 35–51.

Badger, Reid. *A Life in Ragtime: A Biography of James Reese Europe.* New York: Oxford University Press, 1995.

Baker, Houston A., Jr. *Modernism and the Harlem Renaissance.* Chicago: University of Chicago Press, 1987.

Baksa, Robert. *Three Portraits: Composition for Low Male Voice to Prose Poems of Fenton Johnson.* Bryn Mawr, Pa.: Composers Library Editions, 1996.

Baldwin, James. *Nobody Knows My Name.* New York: Vintage International, 1993.

Baraka, Amiri [LeRoi Jones]. *The Autobiography of LeRoi Jones/Amiri Baraka.* New York: Freundlich Books, 1974.

———. "The Black Arts Movement." Speech delivered at the National Black Arts Festival, Atlanta, Ga., August 1994.

———. *Black Magic Poetry, 1961–1967.* Indianapolis: Bobbs-Merrill, 1969.

———. *Black Music.* New York: William Morrow, 1967.

———. "Black Nationalism vs. Pimp Art." *Rhythm* 1 (Summer 1970): 10–12.

———. *Blues People: Negro Music in White America.* New York: William Morrow, 1963.

———. *Hard Facts.* Newark: Congress of Afrikan People, 1975.

———. *Home: Social Essays.* New York: William Morrow, 1966.

———. "How You Sound?" 1959. In *The LeRoi Jones/Amiri Baraka Reader.* Edited by William J. Harris. New York: Thunder's Mouth Press, 1991.

———. "Hymn for Lanie Poo." 1961. In *The LeRoi Jones/Amiri Baraka Reader.* Edited by William J. Harris. New York: Thunder's Mouth Press, 1991.

———. "I from Six Persons." 1973. *Selected Plays and Prose of Amiri Baraka/LeRoi Jones.* New York: William Morrow, 1979.

——. *The LeRoi Jones/Amiri Baraka Reader.* Edited by William J. Harris. New York: Thunder's Mouth Press, 1991.

——. *The Moderns: An Anthology of New Writing in America.* New York: Corinth Books, 1963.

——. "The Nation Is Like Ourselves." 1970. In *Postmodern American Poetry.* Edited by Paul Hoover. New York: W. W. Norton, 1994.

——. *The Role of the Writer in Establishing a Unified Writers Organization.* Keynote address delivered at the National Black Writers Conference, Brooklyn, N.Y., March 1996. Newark: Privately printed, 1996.

——. *Selected Poetry of Amiri Baraka/LeRoi Jones.* New York: William Morrow, 1979.

——. *The System of Dante's Hell.* New York: Grove Press, 1965.

——. *Tales.* New York: Grove Press, 1967.

——. *Transbluesency: Selected Poems (1961–1995).* Edited by Paul Vangelisti. New York: Marsilio Publishers, 1995.

Beard, Rick, and Leslie Cohen Berlowitz, eds. *Greenwich Village: Culture and Counterculture.* New Brunswick, N.J.: Rutgers University Prss, 1993.

Beatty, Paul. *Joker, Joker, Deuce.* New York: Penguin Books, 1994.

——. *The White Boy Shuffle.* Boston: Houghton Mifflin, 1996.

Bedient, Calvin. "The Solo Mysterioso Blues: An Interview with Harryette Mullen." *Callaloo* 19 (1996): 651–669.

Bell, Bernard W. *The Folk Roots of Contemporary Afro-American Poetry.* Broadside Critics Series, no. 3. Detroit: Broadside Press, 1974.

Bellamy, Joe David. *The New Fiction: Interviews with Innovative American Writers.* Urbana: University of Illinois Press, 1974.

Bellman, Beryl L. *The Language of Secrecy: Symbols and Metaphors in Poro Ritual.* New Brunswick, N.J.: Rutgers University Press, 1984.

Benét, Stephen Vincent. "Foreword." *For My People.* By Margaret Walker. New Haven: Yale University Press, 1942.

——. *Selected Letters of Stephen Vincent Benét.* Edited by Charles A. Fenton. New Haven: Yale University Press, 1960.

Benjamin, Playthell. "In Defense of Black Schools." *Emerge* 3 (October 1991): 54–56.

Benton, Thomas Hart. *An Artist in America.* 1951. 3d ed. Columbia: University of Missouri Press, 1968.

Bernal, Martin. *Black Athena.* New Brunswick, N.J.: Rutgers University Press, 1987.

Berry, Faith. *Langston Hughes: Before and Beyond Harlem.* New York: Wings Books, 1995.

Bérubé, Michael. "Avant-Gardes and De-Author-izations: Harlem Gallery and the Cultural Contradictions of Modernism." *Callaloo* 12 (Winter 1989): 192–215.

——. "Eliot's Postwar Influence: Melvin Tolson and Modernism in the Academy." Paper read at the annual meeting of the Modern Language Association, Chicago, Ill., 30 December 1990.

——. *Marginal Forces/Cultural Centers: Tolson, Pynchon, and the Politics of the Canon.* Ithaca: Cornell University Press, 1992.

Bibbs, Hart LeRoi. *Polyrhythms to Freedom.* New York: Privately printed, 1962.

Black, Allida M. *Casting Her Own Shadow: Eleanor Roosevelt and the Shaping of Postwar Liberalism.* New York: Columbia University Press, 1996.

Black Fire: An Anthology of Afro-American Writing. Edited by LeRoi Jones and Larry Neal. New York: William Morrow, 1968.

Blyden, Edward Wilmot. *Black Spokesman: Selected Published Writings of Edward Wilmot Blyden.* Edited by Hollis R. Lynch. New York: Humanities Press, 1971.

Bone, Robert A. "The Background of the Negro Renaissance." In *Black History: A Reappraisal.* Edited by Melvin Drimmer. Garden City, N.Y.: Anchor Books, 1968.

"Books of Literary Interest." *Stratford Journal* 1 (Autumn 1916): 86.

Bourne, Randolph. "A Vanishing World of Gentility." Review of *The Many Years,* by Brander Matthews. *Dial* 64 (14 March 1918): 234–235.

Boyd, Melba Joyce. *Discarded Legacy: Politics and Poetics in the Life of Frances E. W. Harper, 1825–1911.* Detroit: Wayne State University Press, 1994.

Braddy, Haldeen. *Pershing's Mission in Mexico.* El Paso: Texas Western Press, 1966.

Braithwaite, William Stanley. *The House of Falling Leaves.* 1908. Miami: Mnemosyne, 1969.

——. "Introduction." *Anthology of Magazine Verse for 1913.* Cambridge, Mass.: W.S.B., 1913.

——. "Introduction." *Anthology of Magazine Verse for 1958.* New York: Schulte Publishing, 1959.

——. "The Negro in American Literature." 1925. In *The New Negro.* Edited by Alain Locke. New York: Atheneum, 1975.

——. "Robert Frost, New American Poet." 1915. In *Interviews with Robert Frost.* Edited by Edward Connery Lathem. New York: Holt, Rinehart and Winston, 1966.

——. "Some Contemporary Poets of the Negro Race." 1919. In *The William Stanley Braithwaite Reader.* Edited by Philip Butcher. Ann Arbor: University of Michigan Press, 1972.

——. *Victory! Celebrated by Thirty-eight American Poets.* Boston: Small, Maynard, 1919.

——. *The William Stanley Braithwaite Reader.* Edited by Philip Butcher. Ann Arbor: University of Michigan Press, 1972.

Brawley, Benjamin. *Africa and the War.* New York: Duffield, 1918.

——. Letter to William Stanley Braithwaite. 16 November 1919. William Stanley Braithwaite Papers. Box 1. Folder 21. Schomburg Center for Research in Black Culture, New York Public Library, New York.

——. "The Negro Genius." 1915. In *Black Nationalism in America*. Edited by John H. Bracey, Jr., August Meier, and Elliott Rudwick. Indianapolis: Bobbs-Merrill, 1970.

——. *The Negro Genius*. New York: Dodd, Mead, 1937.

——. *The Negro in Literature and Art in the United States*. New York: Duffield, 1930.

Brooks, Gwendolyn. *Selected Poems*. 1963. New York: Harper Perennial, 1996.

——, ed. *A Broadside Treasury, 1965–1970*. Detroit: Broadside Press, 1971.

Brown, Sterling A. "Count Us In." 1944. In *A Son's Return: Selected Essays of Sterling A. Brown*. Edited by Mark Sanders. Boston: Northeastern University Press, 1996.

——. "A Romantic Defense." *Opportunity: Journal of Negro Life* 9 (April 1931): 118.

Brown, W. O. "The Nature of Race Consciousness." *Social Forces* 10 (October 1931): 90–97.

Bruce, Dickson D. *Black American Writing from the Nadir: The Evolution of a Literary Tradition*. Baton Rouge: Louisiana State University Press, 1989.

Burns, E. Bradford. *Kinship with the Land: Regionalist Thought in Iowa, 1894–1942*. Iowa City: University of Iowa Press, 1996.

Bryan, Violet Harrington. *The Myth of New Orleans in Literature: Dialogues of Race and Gender*. Knoxville: University of Tennessee Press, 1993.

Bynner, Witter. "Desert Harvest." *Southwest Review* 14 (July 1929): 493–494.

Bywaters, Jerry. "Contemporary American Artists." *Southwest Review* 23 (April 1938): 297–306.

Call and Response: The Riverside Anthology of the African American Literary Tradition. Edited by Patricia Liggins Hill and others. Boston: Houghton Mifflin, 1998.

Cantey, Inez V. "Jesse Binga." *Crisis* 34 (December 1927): 329, 350, 352.

"Carrizal." Editorial. *Crisis* 12 (August 1916): 165.

Champion Magazine. 1916–1918.

Chauncey, George. *Gay New York: Gender, Urban Culture, and the Making of the Gay Male World, 1890–1940*. New York: Basic Books, 1994.

Christian, Marcus B. "McDonogh Day in New Orleans." *Opportunity: Journal of Negro Life* 12 (June 1934): 171.

Clairmonte, Glenn. "The Cup-Bearer: William Stanley Braithwaite of Boston." *CLA Journal* 17 (September 1973): 101–108.

Clement, Rufus E. Letter to William Stanley Braithwaite. 17 September 1940. William Stanley Braithwaite Papers. Box 1. Folder 24. Schomburg Center for Research in Black Culture, New York Public Library.

Clements, William M. "The 'Offshoot' and the 'Root': Natalie Curtis and Black Expressive Culture in Africa and America." *Western Folklore* 54 (October 1995): 277–301.

Collins, Phillip. "Solid as a Rock: Past and Present Architectural History of the African American Museum of Dallas." *ArtLies* 22 (Spring 1999): 24–26.

Conkin, Paul K. *The Southern Agrarians*. Knoxville: University of Tennessee Press, 1998.

Corn, Wanda M. *Grant Wood: The Regionalist Vision*. New Haven: Yale University Press, 1983.

"Criticism in Black Art Explored." *Black Forum* 2 (November/December 1972): 1–3.

Croce, Benedetto. *Aesthetic as Science of Expression and General Linguistic*. Translated by Douglas Ainslie. 2d ed. London: Macmillan, 1922.

Cronyn, George W., ed. *American Indian Poetry: An Anthology of Songs and Chants*. 1918. New York: Liveright, 1962.

Crunden, Robert M. *American Salons: Encounters with European Modernism, 1885–1917*. New York: Oxford University Press, 1993.

Cruse, Harold. *The Crisis of the Negro Intellectual*. New York: William Morrow, 1967.

Cullen, Countee, ed. *Caroling Dusk: An Anthology of Verse by Black Poets of the Twenties*. 1927. New York: Citadel Press, 1993.

——. "Heritage." 1925. In *Trouble the Water: 250 Years of African American Poetry*. Edited by Jerry W. Ward, Jr. New York: Mentor Books, 1997.

——. "Yet Do I Marvel." 1925. In *Call and Response: The Riverside Anthology of the African American Literary Tradition*. Boston: Houghton Mifflin, 1998.

Daniel, Walter C. *Black Journals of the United States*. Westport, Conn.: Greenwood Press, 1982.

——. "*Challenge* Magazine: An Experiment That Failed." *CLA Journal* 19 (June 1976): 494–503.

Davidson, Donald. *Poems, 1922–1961*. Minneapolis: University of Minnesota Press, 1966.

——. "Sanctuary." 1938. In *The Fugitive Poets*. Edited by William Pratt. New York: E. P. Dutton, 1965.

——. "A Sociologist in Eden." *American Review* 8 (December 1936): 177–204.

——. *The Tall Men*. Boston: Houghton Mifflin, 1927.

Davies, Mary Carolyn. "Fifth Avenue and Grand Street." In *Victory! Celebrated by Thirty-eight American Poets*. Edited by William Stanley Braithwaite. Introduction by Theodore Roosevelt. Boston: Small, Maynard, 1919.

Davis, Arthur P. "Integration and Race Literature." *Phylon: The Atlanta University Review* 17 (1956): 141–146.

Davis, Frank Marshall. *Livin' the Blues: Memoirs of a Black Journalist and Poet*. Edited by John Edgar Tidwell. Madison: University of Wisconsin Press, 1992.

Delafosse, Maurice. *The Negroes of Africa: History and Culture*. Translated by F. Fligelman. Washington, D.C.: Associated Publishers, 1931.

Delehanty, Randolph. *Ultimate Guide to New Orleans*. San Francisco: Chronicle Books, 1998.

Dennis, James M. *Grant Wood: A Study in American Art and Culture.* New York: Viking Press, 1975.

Dent, Tom. *Blue Lights and River Songs.* Detroit: Lotus Press, 1982.

——. *Magnolia Street.* New Orleans: Privately printed, 1976.

——. *Ritual Murder.* 1976. In *Black Southern Voices: An Anthology of Fiction, Poetry, Drama, Nonfiction, and Critical Essays.* Edited by John Oliver Killens and Jerry W. Ward, Jr. New York: Meridian Books, 1992.

——. *Southern Journey: A Return to the Civil Rights Movement.* New York: William Morrow, 1997.

DeSantis, Christopher C., ed. *Langston Hughes and the Chicago Defender: Essays on Race, Politics, and Culture, 1942–62.* Urbana: University of Illinois Press, 1995.

Destinations. Essence Records LP 1001 (1964).

Deutsch, Babette. "The Poem." *Poetry: A Magazine of Verse* 76 (June 1950): 136–137.

Dorman, Robert L. *Revolt of the Provinces: The Regionalist Movement in America, 1920–1945.* Chapel Hill: University of North Carolina Press, 1993.

Doss, Erika. *Benton, Pollock, and the Politics of Modernism: From Regionalism to Abstract Expressionism.* Chicago: University of Chicago Press, 1991.

Drake, St. Clair, and Horace R. Cayton. *Black Metropolis: A Study of Negro Life in a Northern City.* 2 vols. 1945. New York: Harper and Row, 1962.

Du Bois, W. E. B. "Binga." *The Crisis* 37 (December 1930): 425–426.

——. *The Souls of Black Folk.* 1903. New York: Gramercy Books, 1994.

——. "World War and the Color Line." *Crisis* 9 (November 1914): 28–30.

Dunbar, Paul Laurence. *Complete Poems.* New York: Dodd, Mead, and Company, 1913.

——. *Majors and Minors: Poems.* Toledo, Ohio: Hadley and Hadley, 1896.

Earle, Ferdinand, ed. *The Lyric Year: One Hundred Poems.* 1912. Freeport, N.Y.: Books for Libraries Press, 1971.

Eastman, Max. *Love and Revolution: My Journey Through an Epoch.* New York: Random House, 1964.

Ellis, George W. *Negro Culture in West Africa.* 1914. New York: Johnson Reprint, 1970.

Ellis, Mark. "'Closing Ranks' and 'Seeking Honors': W. E. B. Du Bois in World War I." *Journal of American History* 79 (June 1992): 96–124.

——. "J. Edgar Hoover and the 'Red Summer' of 1919." *Journal of American Studies* 28 (April 1994): 39–59.

Ellis, Thomas Sayers. "Starchild." 1993. *Callaloo* 21 (Winter 1998): 72.

Ellis, Thomas Sayers, and Joseph Lease, eds. *On the Verge: Emerging Poets and Artists.* Boston: Agni Press, 1993.

Emanuel, James A. "Blackness Can: A Quest for Aesthetics." In *The Black Aesthetic.* Edited by Addison Gayle, Jr. Garden City, N.Y.: Anchor Books, 1971.

Fabre, Geneviève. *Drumbeats, Masks, and Metaphor: Contemporary Afro-American*

Theatre. Translated by Melvin Dixon. Cambridge, Mass.: Harvard University Press, 1983.

"Fantasies." *Crusader* 4 (April 1921): 11.

Farmer, James. *Lay Bare the Heart: An Autobiography of the Civil Rights Movement*. New York: Plume, 1986.

Farnsworth, Robert M. *Melvin B. Tolson, 1898–1966: Plain Talk and Poetic Prophecy*. Columbia: University of Missouri Press, 1984.

Faulkner, Peter. *Modernism*. London: Methuen, 1977.

Favorite Magazine. 1918–1921.

Fearing, Kenneth. "A Dollar's Worth of Blood, Please." *Poetry: A Magazine of Verse* 52 (July 1938): 175–176.

——. *New and Selected Poems*. Bloomington: Indiana University Press, 1956.

Ferris, William H. *The African Abroad; or, His Evolution in Western Civilization, Tracing His Development Under Caucasian Milieu*. 2 vols. 1913. New York: Johnson Reprint, 1968.

——. "Negro Composers and Negro Music—Is There Race in Music? Is There Race in Art?" 1922. In *African Fundamentalism: A Literary and Cultural Anthology of Garvey's Harlem Renaissance*. Edited by Tony Martin. Dover, Mass.: Majority Press, 1991.

Firestone, Evan R. "Incursions of Modern Art in the Regionalist Heartland." *Palimpsest* 72 (Fall 1991): 148–160.

Fisher, Miles Mark. *Negro Slave Songs in the United States*. 1953. New York: Citadel Press, 1963.

Fladeland, Betty. *Men and Brothers: Anglo-American Slavery Cooperation*. Urbana: University of Illinois Press, 1972.

Flasch, Joy. *Melvin B. Tolson*. New York: Twayne Publishers, 1972.

Fleming, Robert E. *James Weldon Johnson*. Boston: Twayne, 1987.

Foner, Philip S. *American Socialism and Black Americans: From the Age of Jackson to World War II*. Westport, Conn.: Greenwood Press, 1977.

Fox, Stephen R. *The Guardian of Boston: William Monroe Trotter*. New York: Atheneum, 1970.

Frazier, E. Franklin. *Black Bourgeoisie*. Glencoe, Ill.: Free Press, 1957.

Freud, Sigmund. *Civilization and Its Discontents*. 1930. In *Civilization, Society, and Religion*. Edited by Albert Dickson. Pelican Freud Library, vol. 12. New York: Penguin, 1985.

Frost, Robert. Letter to Louis Untermeyer. 1 January 1916. In *The Letters of Robert Frost to Louis Untermeyer*. New York: Holt, Rinehart and Winston, 1963.

Fuller, Charles. *A Soldier's Play*. New York: Samuel French, 1981.

Gabbin, Joanne V. "Margaret Walker: A Mirrored Pool of Brilliance." *Callaloo* 22 (Winter 1999): v–vii.

Gaines, Kevin K. *Uplifting the Race: Black Leadership, Politics, and Culture in the Twentieth Century*. Chapel Hill: University of North Carolina Press, 1996.

Garvey, Marcus, Jr. "The West Indian in the Mirror of Truth." *Champion Magazine* 1 (January 1917): 267–268.

Gates, Henry Louis, Jr. "The Church." *Come Sunday: Photographs by Thomas Roma.* New York: Museum of Modern Art, 1996.

Gayle, Addison, Jr., ed. *The Black Aesthetic.* Garden City, N.Y.: Anchor Books, 1971.

Gibson, Donald B. *The Politics of Literary Expression: A Study of Major Black Writers.* Westport, Conn.: Greenwood Press, 1981.

Gilroy, Paul. *Small Acts: Thoughts on the Politics of Black Culture.* New York: Serpent's Tail Press, 1993.

Gioia, Dana. "Can Poetry Matter?" *Atlantic* 267 (May 1991): 94–106.

Gish, Robert Franklin. *Beyond Bounds: Cross-Cultural Essays on Anglo, American Indian, and Chicano Literature.* Albuquerque: University of New Mexico Press, 1996.

Golden, Harry. *Carl Sandburg.* Greenwich, Conn.: Fawcett Crest, 1962.

Gray, Paul H. "Poet as Entertainer: Will Carleton, James Whitcomb Riley, and the Rise of the Poet-Performer Movement." *Literature in Performance* 5 (November 1984): 1–12.

Grégoire, Henri. *On the Cultural Achievements of Negroes.* 1808. Translated by Thomas Cassirer and Jean-François Brière. Amherst: University of Massachusetts Press, 1996.

Gregory, Elizabeth. *Quotation and Modern American Poetry: Imaginary Gardens with Real Toads.* Houston: Rice University Press, 1996.

Griffin, Farah, and Michael Magee. "A Conversation with Harryette Mullen, 1997." *Combo* 1 (Summer 1998): 36–51.

Gruen, John. *The New Bohemia.* Chicago: A Cappella Books, 1990.

Hamlin, D. A. "Moral Husbandry: The Nashville Agrarians, Wendell Berry, and the Hidden Wound of Race." *JASAT: Journal of the American Studies Association of Texas* 28 (October 1997): 55–78.

Handlin, Oscar. *Boston's Immigrants: A Study in Acculturation.* Rev. ed. New York: Atheneum, 1977.

Harmon, Judith E. B. "A New Negro: James Weldon Johnson Re-Viewed." *Griot* 12 (Fall 1993): 1–12.

Harris, Bill. *Yardbird Suite: Side One, 1920–1940.* East Lansing: Michigan State University Press, 1997.

Harris, William J. "Introduction." *The LeRoi Jones/Amiri Baraka Reader.* Edited by William J. Harris. New York: Thunder's Mouth Press, 1991.

———. *The Poetry and Poetics of Amiri Baraka: The Jazz Aesthetic.* Columbia: University of Missouri Press, 1985.

Harrison, Alferdteen. "Looking Back: A Conversation with Margaret Walker." *Margaret Walker's 'For My People': A Tribute.* Jackson: University Press of Mississippi, 1992.

Hayden, Robert E. *Heart-Shape in the Dust.* Detroit: Falcon Press, 1940.

Heard, Nathan. *Howard Street.* New York: New American Library, 1968.

Hemenway, Robert E. *Zora Neale Hurston: A Literary Biography.* Urbana: University of Illinois Press, 1980.

[Henderson, Alice Corbin]. "Poetry of the American Negro." Review of *Songs of the Soil,* by Fenton Johnson. *Poetry: A Magazine of Verse* 10 (June 1917): 158–160.

Henderson, David. *De Mayor of Harlem.* New York: E. P. Dutton, 1970.

——. *Felix of the Silent Forest.* New York: Poets Press, 1967.

——. *The Low East.* Richmond, Calif.: North Atlantic Books, 1980.

——. *Neo-California.* Berkeley: North Atlantic Books, 1998.

——. "Neon Diaspora." In *Black Fire: An Anthology of Afro-American Writing.* Edited by LeRoi Jones and Larry Neal. New York: William Morrow, 1968.

——. *'Scuse Me While I Kiss the Sky: The Life of Jimi Hendrix.* 1978. New York: Bantam Books, 1981.

Henderson, Stephen E. "Cliché, Monotony, and Touchstone: Folksong Composition and the New Black Poetry." In *Black Southern Voices.* Edited by John Oliver Killens and Jerry W. Ward, Jr. New York: Meridian Books, 1992.

——. *Understanding the New Black Poetry: Black Speech and Black Music as Poetic References.* New York: William Morrow, 1973.

——. "Worrying the Line: Notes on Black American Poetry." In *The Line in Postmodern Poetry.* Edited by Robert Frank and Henry Sayre. Urbana: University of Illinois Press, 1988.

Henning, Barbara. "An Interview with Harryette Mullen." *Poetry Project Newsletter* no. 162 (October–November 1996): 5–10.

Hernton, Calvin C. "'Blood of the Lamb' and 'A Fiery Baptism.'" In *Amistad* 1. Edited by John A. Williams and Charles F. Harris. New York: Vintage Books, 1970.

——. *Coming Together: Black Power, White Hatred, and Sexual Hang-Ups.* New York: Random House, 1971.

——. "Dynamite Growing Out of Their Skulls." In *Black Fire: An Anthology of Afro-American Writing.* Edited by LeRoi Jones and Larry Neal. New York: William Morrow, 1968.

——. "Jitterbugging in the Streets." In *Black Fire: An Anthology of Afro-American Writing.* Edited by LeRoi Jones and Larry Neal. New York: William Morrow, 1968.

——. *Medicine Man: Collected Poems.* New York: Reed, Cannon, and Johnson, 1976.

——. "Remigrant." *Phylon: The Atlanta University Review* 15 (1954): 89.

——. *The Sexual Mountain and Black Women Writers: Adventures in Sex, Literature, and Real Life.* New York: Anchor Books, 1990.

——. "The Underlying Strife." *Phylon: The Atlanta University Review* 16 (1955): 462.

——. *White Papers for White Americans.* Garden City, N.Y.: Doubleday, 1966.

Hernton, Calvin, and Joseph Berke. *The Cannabis Experience: An Interpretive Study of the Effects of Marijuana and Hashish.* London: Peter Owen, 1974.

Hill, Patricia Liggins, and others, eds. *Call and Response: The Riverside Anthology of the African American Literary Tradition.* Boston: Houghton Mifflin, 1998.

Hill, Robert A., ed. *The Marcus Garvey and Universal Negro Improvement Association Papers.* 3 vols. Berkeley: University of California Press, 1983.

Holmes, Oliver Wendell. "Dorothy Q." 1871. In *Harper American Literature.* Edited by Donald McQuade and others. 2 vols. New York: Harper and Row, 1987.

Howard, Helen Addison. *American Indian Poetry.* Boston: Twayne, 1979.

Hubbard, Dolan. *The Sermon and the African American Literary Imagination.* Columbia: University of Missouri Press, 1994.

Hughes, Langston. *Collected Poems.* Edited by Arnold Rampersad with David Roessel. New York: Alfred A. Knopf, 1994.

——. "The Negro Artist and the Racial Mountain." 1926. In *The Portable Harlem Renaissance Reader.* Edited by David Levering Lewis. New York: Viking, 1994.

Hughes, Langston, and Arna Bontemps, eds. *The Poetry of the Negro, 1746–1970.* Garden City, N.Y.: Doubleday, 1970.

Hunt, Erica. *Arcade.* Illustrated by Alison Saar. Berkeley: Kelsey Street Press, 1996.

——. "Notes for an Oppositional Poetics." In *The Politics of Poetic Form: Poetry and Public Policy.* Edited by Charles Bernstein. New York: Roof Books, 1990.

Hurston, Zora Neale. "Characteristics of Negro Expression." 1934. In *The Sanctified Church.* Edited by Toni Cade Bambara. Berkeley: Turtle Island, 1981.

Hurston, Zora Neale, and Langston Hughes. *Mule Bone.* 1930. New York: Harper Perennial, 1992.

Hutchinson, James P. "Fenton Johnson: Pilgrim of the Dusk." *Studies in Black Literature* 7 (Autumn 1976): 14–15.

I'll Take My Stand: The South and the Agrarian Tradition. By Twelve Southerners. New York: Harper, 1930.

"Interracial Activities of National Organizations." *Journal of Negro Education* 2 (1933): 235–251.

Investigation Activities of the Department of Justice. U.S. Senate. 66th Cong., lst sess. Senate Document 153, vol. 12. Washington, D.C.: Government Printing Office, 1919.

Investigation of Administration of Louis F. Post, Assistant Secretary of Labor, in the Matter of Deportation of Aliens. Hearings. Committee on Rules, House of Representatives. 66th Cong., 2d sess. Washington, D.C.: Government Printing Office, 1920.

James, C. L. R., and others. *Fighting Racism in World War II.* New York: Pathfinder Press, 1980.

James, George G. M. *Stolen Legacy.* 1954. Newport News: United Brothers Communications Systems, 1989.

James, Willis Laurence. "The Romance of the Negro Folk Cry in America." *Phylon: The Atlanta University Review* 16 (1955): 15–30.

Jarraway, David R. "Montage of an Otherness Deferred: Dreaming Subjectivity in Langston Hughes." *American Literature* 68 (December 1996): 819–847.

Johns, Orrick. "Second Avenue." In *The Lyric Year: One Hundred Poems.* Edited by Ferdinand Earle. 1912. Freeport, N.Y.: Books for Libraries Press, 1971.

———. *Time of Our Lives: The Story of My Father and Myself.* 1937. New York: Octagon Books, 1973.

Johnson, Abby Arthur, and Ronald Maberry Johnson. *Propaganda and Aesthetics: The Literary Politics of Afro-American Magazines in the Twentieth Century.* Amherst: University of Massachusetts Press, 1979.

Johnson, Bernice. "Langston Hughes Reads Before a Large Audience." *Houston Informer,* 16 April 1932, p. 1.

Johnson, Fenton. "The Artist." *Others: A Magazine of New Verse* 5 (April–May 1919): 20.

———. "The Call of the Patriot." *Crisis* 13 (February 1917): 169–173.

———. "The Champion Magazine." *Champion Magazine* 1 (September 1916): 5.

———. *A Little Dreaming.* 1913. College Park, Md.: McGrath Publishing, 1969.

———. "My Love." *Crisis* 8 (March 1913): 240.

———. "The Negro Since the Armistice." *Favorite Magazine* (January 1921).

———. "The New Day." In *Victory! Celebrated by Thirty-eight American Poets.* Edited by William Stanley Braithwaite. Introduction by Theodore Roosevelt. Boston: Small, Maynard, 1919.

———. "Review of 1916." *Champion Magazine* 1 (January 1917): 237.

———. "The Soldiers of the Dusk." 1915. In *Early Black American Poets.* Edited by William H. Robinson, Jr. Dubuque, Iowa: William C. Brown, 1971.

———. "Song of the Whirlwind." 1915. In *The Norton Anthology of African American Literature.* Edited by Henry Louis Gates, Jr., and Nellie Y. McKay. New York: W. W. Norton, 1997.

———. *Songs of the Soil.* New York: F.J., 1916.

———. "The Story of Myself." *Tales of Darkest America.* Chicago: Favorite Magazine, 1920.

———. "Sweet Love O' Dusk." *Crisis* 34 (October 1927): 265.

———. *Tales of Darkest America.* Chicago: Favorite Magazine, 1920.

———. "Tired." *Others: A Magazine of the New Verse* 5 (January 1919): 8.

———. "Tired." In *Others for 1919: An Anthology of the New Verse.* Edited by Alfred Kreymborg. New York: Nicholas L. Brown, 1920.

Johnson, James Weldon. *Along This Way.* New York: Viking Press, 1933.

———. *God's Trombones: Seven Sermons in Verse.* 1927. New York: Penguin Books, 1990.

———. "Some New Books of Poetry and Their Makers." 1918. In *Selected Writ-*

ings. Edited by Sondra Kathryn Wilson. 2 vols. New York: Oxford University Press, 1995.

——, ed. *The Book of American Negro Poetry*. Rev. ed. 1931. New York: Harcourt Brace Jovanovich, 1983.

"Jones Is Acquitted of Weapon Charge in Newark Retrial." *New York Times,* 3 July 1969, p. 18.

Jones, Lester M. "The Editorial Policy of the Negro Newspapers of 1917–18 as Compared with That of 1941–42." *Journal of Negro History* 29 (1944): 24–31.

Jones, Patricia Spears. *The Weather That Kills*. Minneapolis: Coffee House Press, 1995.

Jordan, Norman. "News from Cleveland." *Journal of Black Poetry* 1 (Spring 1969): 61–62.

Jordan, William. "'The Damnable Dilemma': African-American Accommodation and Protest in World War I." *Journal of American History* 81 (March 1995): 1562–1583.

Joyce, Joyce A. *Ijala: Sonia Sanchez and the African Poetic Tradition*. Chicago: Third World Press, 1996.

Kazin, Alfred. *On Native Grounds: An Interpretation of Modern American Prose Literature*. New York: Reynal and Hitchcock, 1942.

Kerlin, Robert T. *Negro Poets and Their Poems*. Washington, D.C.: Associated Publishers, 1923.

Killens, John Oliver. *And Then We Heard Thunder*. 1963. Washington, D.C.: Howard University Press, 1984.

King, Woodie, Jr., ed. *Black Spirits: A Festival of New Black Poets in America*. New York: Vintage Books, 1972.

——. *Black Theatre Present Condition*. New York: National Black Theatre Touring Circuit, 1981.

Kofsky, Frank. *Black Nationalism and the Revolution in Music*. New York: Pathfinder Press, 1970.

Kostalanetz, Richard, ed. *Dictionary of the Avant-Gardes*. Chicago: A Capella Books, 1993.

Kouwenhoven, John A. *The Arts in Modern American Civilization*. 1948. New York: W. W. Norton, 1967.

Kreymborg, Alfred. *Edna: The Girl of the Street*. New York: Guido Bruno, 1919.

——. "Improvisation." *Alfred Kreymborg*. Pamphlet Poets. New York: Simon and Schuster, 1928.

——. "Red Chant." *Crisis* 17 (November 1918): 31.

——. *Troubadour: An Autobiography*. New York: Boni and Liveright, 1925.

Langellier, Kristin M. "From Text to Social Context." *Literature in Performance* 6 (April 1986): 60–70.

"Langston Hughes." Editorial. *Houston Informer,* 16 April 1932, p. 2.

Lauter, Paul, and others, eds. *Heath Anthology of American Literature*. 2d ed. 2 vols. Lexington, Mass.: D. C. Heath, 1994.

Leckie, William H. *The Buffalo Soldiers: A Narrative of the Negro Cavalry in the West.* Norman: University of Oklahoma Press, 1967.

Levernier, James A. "Wheatley's 'On Being Brought from Africa to America.'" *Explicator* 40 (1981): 25–26.

levy, d. a. *Zen Concrete and Etc.* Edited by Ingrid Swanberg. Madison, Wisc.: Ghost Pony Press, 1991.

Levy, Eugene. *James Weldon Johnson: Black Leader, Black Voice.* Chicago: University of Chicago Press, 1973.

Lewis, David Levering. "Shortcuts to the Mainstream: Afro-American and Jewish Notables in the 1920s and 1930s." In *Jews in Black Perspectives: A Dialogue.* Edited by Joseph R. Washington, Jr. Rutherford, N.J.: Fairleigh Dickinson University Press, 1984.

———. *W. E. B. Du Bois: Biography of a Race, 1868–1919.* New York: Henry Holt, 1993.

Liebow, Elliot. *Talley's Corner: A Study of the Negro Streetcorner Man.* Boston: Little, Brown, 1967.

Locke, Alain. "The New Negro." In *The New Negro.* Edited by Alain Locke. 1925. New York: Atheneum, 1975.

———, ed. *The New Negro.* 1925. New York: Atheneum, 1992.

Logan, Rayford W. *The Betrayal of the Negro: From Rutherford B. Hayes to Woodrow Wilson.* 1965. New York: Da Capo Press, 1997.

Longfellow, Henry Wadsworth. "A Psalm of Life." In *American Poetry: The Nineteenth Century,* vol. 1. New York: American Library, 1993.

Lord, Albert B. *The Singer of Tales.* Harvard Studies in Comparative Literature, 24. Cambridge, Mass.: Harvard University Press, 1964.

Lowell, Amy. *Tendencies in Modern American Poetry.* New York: Macmillan, 1917.

Lowenthal, Max. *The Federal Bureau of Investigation.* New York: William Sloane Associates, 1950.

Lynch, Acklyn. *Nightmare Overhanging Darkly: Essays on Black Culture and Resistance.* Chicago: Third World Press, 1992.

Mackey, Nathaniel. *Strick: Song of the Andoumboulou 16–25.* Spoken Engine CD 90807-16252 (1995).

———. *Whatsaid Serif.* San Francisco: City Lights, 1998.

Maddox, Brenda. *D. H. Lawrence: The Story of a Marriage.* New York: Simon and Schuster, 1994.

Madhubuti, Haki R. [Don L. Lee]. "Black Writing." *Journal of Black Poetry* 1 (Fall–Winter 1971): 85–86.

Major, Clarence, ed. *The New Black Poetry.* New York: International Publishers, 1969.

Major, Gerri, and Doris E. Saunders. *Black Society.* Chicago: Johnson Publishing, 1976.

Mangione, Jerre. *The Dream and the Deal: The Federal Writers' Project, 1933–1943.* New York: Equinox Books, 1972.

Marable, Manning. *Black Leadership.* New York: Columbia University Press, 1998.

Markham, Edwin. "The Man with the Hoe." 1896. In *American Poetry: The Nineteenth Century.* Edited by John Hollander. 2 vols. New York: Library of America, 1993.

Matthews, Brander. *Gateways to Literature and Other Essays.* 1912. Freeport, N.Y.: Books for Libraries Press, 1971.

McDarrah, Fred W., ed. *Kerouac and Friends: A Beat Generation Album.* New York: William Morrow, 1985.

McDonough, Kaye. "Bob Kaufaman Reading at Vesuvio's, 1973." *Umbra 5: Latin/Soul Anthology* (1974): 78–79.

McKay, Claude. "In Bondage." 1920. In *The Passion of Claude McKay: Selected Poetry and Prose, 1912–1948.* Edited by Wayne F. Cooper. New York: Schocken Books, 1973.

McMurry, Linda O. *Recorder of the Black Experience: A Biography of Monroe Nathan Work.* Baton Rouge: Louisiana State University Press, 1985.

Mearns, Hughes. *Creative Youth.* Garden City, N.Y.: Doubleday, Page, 1927.

Millay, Edna St. Vincent. "Renascence." In *The Lyric Year: One Hundred Poems.* Edited by Ferdinand Earle. 1912. Freeport, N.Y.: Books for Libraries Press, 1971.

Monroe, Harriet. *A Poet's Life: Seventy Years in a Changing World.* New York: Macmillan, 1938.

[———]. "Sir Oracle." *Poetry: A Magazine of Verse* 9 (January 1917): 211–214.

———. "Tradition." *Poetry: A Magazine of Verse* 2 (May 1913): 67–68.

Monroe, Harriet, and Alice Corbin Henderson, eds. *The New Poetry: An Anthology.* New and enlarged ed. New York: Macmillan, 1924.

Moore, Harry T. "Enter Beatniks: The Bohème of 1960." *Garrets and Pretenders: A History of Bohemianism in America,* by Albert Parry. New York: Dover, 1960.

Mootry, Maria K. " 'Down the Whirlwind of Good Rage': An Introduction to Gwendolyn Brooks." In *A Life Distilled: Gwendolyn Brooks, Her Poetry and Fiction.* Edited by Maria K. Mootry and Gary Smith. Urbana: University of Illinois Press, 1987.

Moses, Wilson Jeremiah. *The Golden Age of Black Nationalism, 1850–1925.* New York: Oxford University Press, 1988.

Moss, Alfred A., Jr. *The American Negro Academy: Voice of the Talented Tenth.* Baton Rouge: Louisiana State University Press, 1981.

Mott, Frank Luther. "Literature with Roots." In *Out of the Midwest: A Collection of Present-Day Writing.* Edited by John T. Frederick. New York: Whittlesey House, 1944.

Mullen, Harryette. "Any Lit." *Black Renaissance/Renaissance Noir* 1 (Spring/Summer 1998): 48.

———. "Momma Sayings." 1981. In *Trouble the Water: 250 Years of African American Poetry.* Edited by Jerry W. Ward, Jr. New York: Mentor, 1997.

——. *Muse and Drudge*. Philadelphia: Singing Horse Press, 1995.

——. *S*PeRM**K*T*. Philadelphia: Singing Horse Press, 1992.

——. *Tree Tall Woman*. Galveston: Energy Earth, 1981.

——. *Trimmings*. New York: Tender Buttons Press, 1991.

Myers, D. G. *The Elephants Teach: Creative Writing Since 1880*. Englewood Cliffs, N.J.: Prentice-Hall, 1996.

Nadel, Ira B., ed. *The Letters of Ezra Pound to Alice Corbin Henderson*. Austin: University of Texas Press, 1993.

Napier, Winston. "Affirming Critical Conceptualism: Harlem Renaissance Aesthetics and the Formation of Alain Locke's Social Philosophy." *Massachusetts Review* 39 (Spring 1998): 93–112.

Neal, Larry. *Visions of a Liberated Future: Black Arts Movement Writings*. Edited by Michael Schwartz. New York: Thunder's Mouth Press, 1989.

Nelson, Cary. *Repression and Recovery: Modern American Poetry and the Politics of Cultural Memory, 1910–1945*. Madison: University of Wisconsin Press, 1989.

Nielsen, Aldon Lynn. *Black Chant: Languages of African-American Postmodernism*. Cambridge: Cambridge University Press, 1997.

——. *Reading Race: White American Poets and the Racial Discourse in the Twentieth Century*. Athens: University of Georgia Press, 1988.

Odum, Howard W. *Race and Rumors of Race: Challenge to American Crisis*. Chapel Hill: University of North Carolina Press, 1943.

O'Hara, Frank. "The Day Lady Died." 1959. In *Collected Poems*. Edited by Donald Allen. New York: Alfred A. Knopf, 1972.

Olender, Maurice. *The Languages of Paradise: Race, Religion, and Philology in the Nineteenth Century*. Cambridge, Mass.: Harvard University Press, 1992.

Olson, Charles. *Projective Verse*. 1950. New York: Totem Press, 1959.

O'Meally, Robert. *Lady Day: The Many Faces of Billie Holiday*. New York: Arcade, 1991.

O'Neill, William L. *The Last Romantic: A Life of Max Eastman*. New York: Oxford University Press, 1978.

"The Opportunity Dinner." *Opportunity: Journal of Negro Life* 3 (June 1925): 176–177.

Osborne, Eddie. "Miami's Theatre of Affro Arts." *Black Creation* 4 (Summer 1973): 38–39.

Others: A Magazine of the New Verse 4 (June 1917). New York: Kraus, 1967.

Ottley, Roi. *New World A-Coming: Inside Black America*. Boston: Houghton Mifflin, 1943.

Park, Robert Ezra. *Race and Culture*. Glencoe, Ill.: Free Press, 1950.

Parker, Clara M. "The New Poetry and the Conservative American Magazine." *Texas Review* 6 (October 1920): 44–66.

Parker, George Wells. "The African Origin of the Grecian Civilization." *Journal of Negro History* 2 (July 1917): 331–344.

——. *Children of the Sun.* 1918. Baltimore: Black Classic Press, 1981.

Pawa, J. M. "Black Radicals, White Spies: Harlem, 1919." *Negro History Bulletin* 35 (October 1972): 129–133.

Pearce, T. M. *Alice Corbin Henderson.* Southwest Writers Series, no. 21. Austin: Steck-Vaughn, 1969.

Penty, A. J. "The Restoration of Property." *American Review* 8 (February 1937): 457–496.

Perdomo, Willie. *Where a Nickel Costs a Dime.* New York: W. W. Norton, 1996.

Perelman, Bob. *The Marginalization of Poetry: Language Writing and Literary History.* Princeton: Princeton University Press, 1996.

——. *The Trouble with Genius: Reading Pound, Joyce, Stein, and Zukofsky.* Berkeley: University of California Press, 1994.

Pinson, Hermine. *Mama Yetta and Other Poems.* San Antonio: Wings Press, 1999.

"Poetic Justice." *Newsweek* 15 January 1968: 24.

Post, Louis F. *The Deportations Delirium of Nineteen-Twenty.* Chicago: Charles H. Kerr, 1923.

Poston, Robert L. "Dunbar, Braithwaite, McKay—An Analysis." 1925. In *African Fundamentalism: A Literary and Cultural Anthology of Garvey's Harlem Renaissance.* Edited by Tony Martin. Dover, Mass.: Majority Press, 1991.

Pound, Ezra. "Hugh Selwyn Mauberley." 1920. In *Selected Poems.* New York: New Directions, 1957.

Powell, Kevin. "Mental Terrorism." In *In the Tradition: An Anthology of Young Black Writers.* New York: Harlem River Press, 1992.

Powell, Kevin, and Ras Baraka, eds. *In the Tradition: An Anthology of Young Black Writers.* New York: Harlem River Press, 1992.

Powell, Richard J. *Black Art and Culture in the Twentieth Century.* New York: Thames and Hudson, 1997.

Pratt, William, ed. *The Fugitive Poets.* New York: E. P. Dutton, 1965.

Priddy, Bob. *Only the Rivers Are Peaceful: Thomas Hart Benton's Missouri Mural.* Independence, Mo.: Independence Press and Herald, 1989.

Pritchard, N. H. "Aswelay." 1963. In *Dices or Black Bones: Black Voices of the Seventies.* Edited by Adam David Miller. Boston: Houghton Mifflin, 1970.

——. *The Matrix: Poems, 1960–1970.* Garden City, N.Y.: Doubleday, 1970.

Ra, Jarbari Aziz. *The Vision.* Houston: Afronese Black Press, 1989.

Rampersad, Arnold. *The Life of Langston Hughes.* Vol. 2, 1941–1967. New York: Oxford University Press, 1988.

Randall, Dudley, ed. *The Black Poets.* New York: Bantam, 1971.

Ray, David, and Robert M. Farnsworth, eds. *Richard Wright: Impressions and Perspectives.* Ann Arbor: University of Michigan Press, 1973.

Redding, J. Saunders. "James Weldon Johnson and the Pastoral Tradition." 1973. In *A Scholar's Conscience: Selected Writings, 1942–1977.* Edited by Faith Berry. Lexington: University of Kentucky Press, 1992.

———. *To Make a Poet Black.* 1939. Ithaca: Cornell University Press, 1988.

Redmond, Eugene. *Drumvoices: The Mission of Afro-American Poetry.* Garden City, N.Y.: Anchor Press, 1976.

Reed, Christopher Robert. *The Chicago NAACP and the Rise of Black Professional Leadership, 1910–1966.* Bloomington: Indiana University Press, 1997.

Reed, Ishmael. *The Last Days of Louisiana Red.* Garden City, N.Y.: Doubleday, 1974.

———. *Mumbo Jumbo.* Garden City, N.Y.: Doubleday, 1972.

Reid, Mark A. *Redefining Black Film.* Berkeley: University of California Press, 1993.

Report of the National Advisory Commission on Civil Disorders. Introduction by Tom Wicker. New York: Bantam Books, 1968.

Review of *The Black Man's Part in the War* by Sir H. H. Johnston. *Journal of Negro History* 3 (July 1918): 331–332.

Revolutionary Radicalism. Report of the Joint Legislative Committee Investigating Seditious Activities, State of New York. 3 vols. Albany: J. B. Lyon Company, 1920.

Rexroth, Kenneth. *American Poetry in the Twentieth Century.* New York: Herder and Herder, 1971.

———. "Jazz and Poetry." 1958. In *Kerouac and Friends.* Edited by Fred W. McDarrah. New York: William Morrow, 1985.

Reynolds, Grant. "What the Negro Soldier Thinks." *Crisis* 51 (September 1944): 289–291, 299.

Rifkin, Jeremy. *The End of Work: The Decline of the Global Labor Force and the Dawn of the Post-Market Era.* New York: G. P. Putnam's Sons, 1995.

Riley, James Whitcomb. "The Days Gone By." In *American Poetry: The Nineteenth Century.* Edited by John Hollander, vol. 2. New York: Library of America, 1993.

———. "The Old Swimmin' Hole." 1883. In *American Poetry: The Nineteenth Century.* Edited by John Hollander, vol. 2. New York: Library of America, 1993.

Rittenhouse, Jessie B. "Contemporary Poetry." *Bookman* 46 (February 1918): 678–683.

———. *My House of Life: An Autobiography.* Boston: Houghton Mifflin, 1934.

Robbins, Richard. *Sidelines Activist: Charles S. Johnson and the Struggle for Civil Rights.* Jackson: University Press of Mississippi, 1996.

Rogers, J. A. *The Real Facts About Ethiopia.* 1936. Baltimore: Black Classic Press, 1982.

———. *Sex and Race.* 3 vols. 1941–1944. New York: Helga M. Rogers, 1970.

———. "Social Equality—What Is It?" *Favorite Magazine* (November–December 1920): 495, 519.

———. "William Monroe Trotter." *World's Great Men of Color.* 2 vols. 1947. New York: Collier Books, 1972.

Rogers, Kim Lacy. *Righteous Lives: Narratives of the New Orleans Civil Rights Movement.* New York: New York University Press, 1993.

Roskolenko, Harry. "On Kenneth Koch Again: A Rebuttal." *Poetry: A Magazine of Verse* 86 (June 1955): 177–178.

Rowell, Charles H. "An Interview with Margaret Walker: Poetry, History and Humanism." *Black World* 25 (December 1975): 4–17.

Rubeo, Ugo. "Voice as Lifesaver: Defining the Function of Orality in Etheridge Knight's Poetry." In *The Black Columbiad: Defining Moments in African American Literature and Culture.* Edited by Werner Sollors and Maria Diedrich. Cambridge, Mass.: Harvard University Press, 1994.

Russell, Ross. Review of Charles Mingus, *A Modern Jazz Symposium of Music and Poetry,* Bethlehem BCP 6026. *Jazz Review* 3 (February 1960): 31–32.

Salaam, Kalamu ya. *Hofi Ni Kwenu (My Fear Is For You).* New Orleans: Ahidiana, 1973.

——. *Ibura.* New Orleans: Ahidiana, 1976.

——. *My Story, My Song.* AFO Records CD 95-1128-2 (1996).

——. *What Is Life? Reclaiming the Black Blues Self.* Chicago: Third World Press, 1994.

Saltmarsh, John A. *Scott Nearing: An Intellectual Biography.* Philadelphia: Temple University Press, 1991.

Sampson, Henry T. *The Ghost Walks: A Chronological History of Blacks in Show Business, 1865–1910.* Metuchen, N.J.: Scarecrow Press, 1988.

Sanchez, Sonia. "A Ballad for Stirling Street." 1970. *A Broadside Treasury, 1965–1970.* Edited by Gwendolyn Brooks. Detroit: Broadside Press, 1971. 147.

——. *Does Your House Have Lions?* Boston: Beacon Press, 1997.

——. "Queens of the Universe." *Black Spirits: A Festival of New Black Poets in America.* Edited by Woodie King, Jr. New York: Vintage Books, 1972.

——. *We A BaddDDD People.* Detroit: Broadside Press, 1968.

Sandburg, Carl. Letter to Alice Corbin Henderson. 27 November 1917. *The Letters of Carl Sandburg.* Edited by Herbert Mitgang. New York: Harcourt, Brace and World, 1968.

——. "The Poor." 1916. In *The New Poetry: An Anthology.* Edited by Harriet Monroe and Alice Corbin Henderson. New York: Macmillan, 1917.

Sanders, Ed. *Tales of Beatnik Glory.* New York: Citadel Press, 1995.

[Schnittkind, Henry Thomas]. "The Aims of the Stratford Journal." *Stratford Journal* 1 (Autumn 1916): 3–7.

Semmes, Clovis E. "The Dialectics of Community Survival and the Community Artist: Phil Cohran and the Affro-Arts Theater." *Journal of Black Studies* 24 (June 1994): 447–461.

Shabazz, Amilcar. "Art Truths: Houston's Artistic Traditions and the Problem of Respectability." *Art Lies,* no. 15 (Summer 1997): 20–22.

Shelton, E. C. "The Negro: 'Those Are My Achievements.'" Cartoon. *Champion Magazine* 1 (December 1916): 168.

Sherman, Joan R., ed. *The Black Bard of North Carolina: George Moses Horton and His Poetry.* Chapel Hill: University of North Carolina Press, 1997.

Smith, Henry Nash. "'Culture.'" *Southwest Review* 13 (January 1928): 249–255.

Smitherman, Geneva. "The Black Idiom and the New Black Poetry." *Black Creation* 6 (1974–1975): 81–86.

Sollors, Werner. *Amiri Baraka/LeRoi Jones: The Quest for a "Populist Modernism."* New York: Columbia University Press, 1978.

Spears, Monroe K. *Dionysus and the City: Modernism in Twentieth-Century Poetry.* New York: Oxford University Press, 1970.

Spellman, A. B. *The Beautiful Days.* New York: Poets Press, 1965.

Spingarn, J. E. *Creative Criticism and Other Essays.* New York: Harcourt, Brace, 1931.

——. "The New Criticism." 1910. *Criticism in America: Its Function and Status.* New York: Harcourt, Brace, 1924.

Spivey, Donald. *The Politics of Miseducation: The Booker Washington Institute of Liberia, 1929–1984.* Lexington: University Press of Kentucky, 1986.

"Statement of the Ownership, Management, Circulation, Etc." *Stratford Journal* 1 (Autumn 1916): 86.

Stedman, Edmund Clarence, ed. *An American Anthology, 1787–1900.* Boston: Houghton Mifflin, 1900.

Stegner, Wallace. "The Trail of the Hawkeye: Literature Where the Tall Corn Grows." *Saturday Review of Literature* 18 (30 July 1938): 3–4, 16–17.

Stoddard, Lothrop. *Re-Forging America: The Story of Our Nationhood.* New York: Charles Scribner's Sons, 1927.

——. *The Rising Tide of Color Against White World-Supremacy.* New York: Charles Scribner's Sons, 1921.

Sundiata, Sekou. "Mandela in Harlem (June, 1991)." *Aloud: Voices from the Nuyorican Poets Cafe.* Edited by Miguel Algarín and Bob Holman. New York: Henry Holt, 1994.

Symons, Arthur. "In the Wood of Finvarra." 1900. *Poetry of the Victorian Period.* 3d ed. Edited by Jerome Hamilton Buckley and George Benjamin Woods. Glenview, Ill.: Scott, Foresman, 1965.

Talley, Thomas W. *The Negro Traditions.* Edited by Charles K. Wolfe and Laura C. Jarmon. Knoxville: University of Tennessee Press, 1993.

Tate, Allen. "Preface." In *Libretto for the Republic of Liberia.* By M. B. Tolson. New York: Twayne Publishers, 1953.

Tate, Claudia. "Introduction." In *Georgia Douglas Johnson: Selected Works.* New York: G. K. Hall, 1997.

Tate, Greg. *Flyboy in the Buttermilk: Essays on Contemporary America.* New York: Simon and Schuster, 1992.

Taylor, Clyde R. *The Mask of Art: Breaking the Aesthetic Contract—Film and Literature.* Bloomington: Indiana University Press, 1998.

Terkel, Studs. *"The Good War": An Oral History of World War II.* New York: Ballantine Books, 1984.

Thomas, Lorenzo. "Askia Muhammad Touré: Crying Out the Goodness." *Obsidian: Black Literature in Review* 1 (Spring 1975): 31–49.

Thomas, W. C. *I'm Into Something I Can't Turn Loose.* Jewel Records LPS 0050 (1970).

Thompson, Lawrance. *Robert Frost: The Years of Triumph, 1915–1938.* New York: Holt, Rinehart and Winston, 1970.

Thorpe, Earl E. *The Mind of the Negro: An Intellectual History of Afro-Americans.* Baton Rouge: Ortleib Press, 1961.

Tietjens, Eunice. *Profiles From China: Sketches in Verse of People and Things Seen in the Interior.* Chicago: Ralph Fletcher Seymour, 1917.

Tolson, Melvin B. *Caviar and Cabbage: Selected Columns by Melvin B. Tolson from the "Washington Tribune," 1937–1944.* Edited by Robert M. Farnsworth. Columbia: University of Missouri Press, 1982.

——. "Claude McKay's Art." *Poetry: A Magazine of Verse* 83 (February 1954): 287–290.

——. "Dark Symphony." *Atlantic Monthly* 168 (September 1941): 314–317.

——. *A Gallery of Harlem Portraits.* Edited by Robert M. Farnsworth. Columbia: University of Missouri Press, 1979.

——. *Libretto for the Republic of Liberia.* New York: Twayne Publishers, 1953. Reprinted in *Norton Anthology of African American Literature.* Edited by Henry Louis Gates, Jr., Nellie Y. McKay, and others. New York: W. W. Norton, 1997.

——. *Rendezvous with America.* New York: Dodd, Mead, 1944.

Touré, Askia Muhammad [Rolland Snellings]. "The Crisis in Black Culture." In *Black Arts: An Anthology of Black Creations.* Edited by Ahmed Alhamisi and Haroun Kofi Wangara. Detroit: Black Arts Publications, 1969.

——. "Dawnsong." In *Call and Response: The Riverside Anthology of the African American Literary Tradition.* Boston: Houghton Mifflin, 1998.

——. "Earth." In *Black Fire: An Anthology of Afro-American Writing.* Edited by LeRoi Jones and Larry Neal. New York: William Morrow, 1968.

——. *From the Pyramids to the Projects: Poems of Genocide and Resistance.* Trenton, N.J.: Africa World Press, 1990.

——. *JuJu: Magic Songs for the Black Nation.* Chicago: Third World Press, 1970.

——. "Malcolm X as International Spokesman." *Liberator* 6 (February 1966): 6.

——. "Mississippi Concerto." In *Black Fire: An Anthology of Afro-American Writing.* Edited by LeRoi Jones and Larry Neal. New York: William Morrow, 1968.

——. *Songhai!* New York: Songhai Press, 1972.

——. "Sunrise." In *Black Fire: An Anthology of Afro-American Writing.* Edited by LeRoi Jones and Larry Neal. New York: William Morrow, 1968.

Trilling, Diana. "The Other Night at Columbia: A Report from the Academy." 1959. In *Kerouac and Friends.* Edited by Fred W. McDarrah. New York: William Morrow, 1985.

Turner, W. Burghardt, and Joyce Moore Turner, eds. *Richard B. Moore, Caribbean Militant in Harlem: Collected Writings 1920–1972.* Bloomington: University of Indiana Press, 1988.

Untermeyer, Louis. *The New Era in American Poetry.* New York: Henry Holt, 1919.

Vanderwood, Paul J., and Frank N. Samponaro. *Border Fury: A Picture Postcard*

Record of Mexico's Revolution and U.S. War Preparedness, 1910–1917. Albuquerque: University of New Mexico Press, 1988.

Van Wienen, Mark W. *Partisans and Poets: The Political Work of American Poetry in the Great War.* New York: Cambridge University Press, 1997.

Wagner, Jean. *Black Poets of the United States: From Paul Laurence Dunbar to Langston Hughes.* Translated by Kenneth Douglas. Urbana: University of Illinois Press, 1973.

Walker, Alice. "In These Dissenting Times." *Revolutionary Petunias and Other Poems.* New York: Harcourt, Brace Jovanovich, 1973.

———. *October Journey.* Detroit: Broadside Press, 1973.

Walker, David. *David Walker's Appeal.* 1830. Introduction by James Turner. Baltimore: Black Classic Press, 1993.

Walker, Margaret. "For My People." *Poetry: A Magazine of Verse* 51 (November 1937): 81–83.

———. *For My People.* New Haven: Yale University Press, 1942.

———. "Four Poems." *New Challenge* 2 (Fall 1937): 49–50.

———. "Harriet Tubman." *Phylon: The Atlanta University Review* 5 (1944): 326–330.

———. *How I Wrote "Jubilee" and Other Essays on Life and Literature.* Edited by Maryemma Graham. New York: Feminist Press, 1990.

———. "I Want to Write." 1934. In *On Being Female, Black, and Free: Essays, 1932–1992.* Edited by Maryemma Graham. Knoxville: University of Tennessee Press, 1997.

———. *On Being Female, Black, and Free: Essays, 1932–1992.* Edited by Maryemma Graham. Knoxville: University of Tennessee Press, 1997.

———. "Richard Wright." In *Richard Wright: Impressions and Perspectives.* Edited by David Ray and Robert M. Farnsworth. Ann Arbor: University of Michigan Press, 1973.

———. *Richard Wright: Daemonic Genius.* New York: Warner Books, 1988.

———. "Sorrow Home." *Opportunity: Journal of Negro Life* 16 (May 1938): 139.

———. "The Spirituals." *Opportunity: Journal of Negro Life* 16 (August 1938): 237.

———. "The Struggle Staggers Us." *Poetry: A Magazine of Verse* 52 (July 1938): 198.

———. *This Is My Century: New and Collected Poems.* Athens: University of Georgia Press, 1989.

Walker, Margaret, and Nikki Giovanni. *A Poetic Equation.* Washington, D.C.: Howard University Press, 1974.

Ward, Jerry W., Jr. "Literacy and Criticism: The Example of Carolyn Rodgers." *DrumVoices Revue* 4 (Fall/Spring 1994/95): 62–65.

———. "Southern Black Aesthetics: The Case of Nkombo Magazine." *Mississippi Quarterly* 44 (Spring 1991): 143–150.

———. "A Writer for Her People: An Interview with Dr. Margaret Walker Alexander." *Mississippi Quarterly* 41 (Fall 1988): 515–527.

———, ed. *Trouble the Water: 250 Years of African American Poetry.* New York: Mentor, 1997.

Wattles, Willard. "On Reading the Braithwaite Anthology for 1916." *Poetry: A Magazine of Verse* 10 (April 1917): 52–54.

Watts, Steven. "Walt Disney: Art and Politics in the American Century." *Journal of American History* 82 (June 1995): 84–110.

Weiss, Nancy J. "The Negro and the New Freedom." *The Segregation Era, 1863–1954.* Edited by Allen Weinstein and Frank Otto Gatell. New York: Oxford University Press, 1970.

Wells, Ida B. *Crusade For Justice: The Autobiography of Ida B. Wells.* Edited by Alfreda M. Duster. Chicago: University of Chicago Press, 1970.

West, Cornel. "The Dilemma of the Black Intellectual." *Cultural Critique* 1 (Fall 1985): 109–124.

West, Hoyt. "Last Frontier? Yes, of White American-Born." *West Texas Today* 18 (September 1937): 15, 24–25.

Whitehead, Don. *The FBI Story.* New York: Random House, 1956.

Widdemer, Margaret. *Golden Friends I Had.* Garden City, N.Y.: Doubleday, 1964.

———. *Jessie Rittenhouse: A Centenary Memoir-Anthology.* South Brunswick: Poetry Society of America, 1969.

Wilbers, Stephen. *The Iowa Writers' Workshop: Origins, Emergence, and Growth.* Iowa City: University of Iowa Press, 1980.

Williams, Ellen. *Harriet Monroe and the Poetry Renaissance: The First Ten Years of "Poetry," 1912–22.* Urbana: University of Illinois Press, 1977.

Williams, Kenny J. "An Invisible Partnership and an Unlikely Relationship: William Stanley Braithwaite and Harriet Monroe." *Callaloo* 10 (Summer 1987): 516–550.

Williams, Mance. *Black Theatre in the 1970s and 80s.* New York: Greenwood Press, 1985.

Williams, William Carlos. "A Twentieth-Century American." Review of works by H. H. Lewis. *Poetry: A Magazine of Verse* 47 (January 1936): 227–229.

Work, Monroe N. "The Passing Tradition and the African Civilization." *Journal of Negro History* 1 (January 1916): 34–41.

Wright, Richard. *Black Boy.* 1945. New York: Harper Perennial, 1966.

———. "Blue Print for Negro Writing." 1937. In *Richard Wright Reader.* Edited by Ellen Wright and Michel Fabre. New York: Harper and Row, 1978.

———. "Early Days in Chicago." In *Cross Section 1945: A Collection of New American Writing.* Edited by Edwin Seaver. New York: Book Find Club, 1945.

———. "The Literature of the Negro in the United States." 1957. In *White Man, Listen!* By Richard Wright. Garden City, N.Y.: Anchor Books, 1964.

Wright, Richard. *White Man, Listen!* 1957. New York: Harper Perennial, 1995.

Yerby, Frank. "Health Card." 1944. In *The Best Short Stories by Negro Writers.* Edited by Langston Hughes. Boston: Little, Brown, 1967.

Young, Kevin. "Everywhere Is Out of Town." In *On the Verge: Emerging Poets and Artists.* Edited by Thomas Sayers and Joseph Lease. Boston: Agni Press, 1993.

———. "Jack Johnson." *Callaloo* 21 (Winter 1998): 31–42.

Zu-Bolton, Ahmos. *Ain't No Spring Chicken: Selected Poems.* New Orleans: Voice Foundation, 1998.

———. *A Niggered Amen.* San Luis Obispo, Calif.: Solo Press, 1975.

Zurier, Rebecca. *Art for the Masses: A Radical Magazine and Its Graphics, 1911–1917.* Philadelphia: Temple University Press, 1988.

Index

About the Author

Lorenzo Thomas was born in Panama and received his B.A. from Queens College (City University of New York). He is Professor of English at the University of Houston–Downtown and the editor of *Sing the Sun Up: Creative Writing Ideas from African American Literature* (1998).